ETHICS AND STATECRAFT

ETHICS AND STATECRAFT

The Moral Dimension of International Affairs
SECOND EDITION

Edited by Cathal J. Nolan

Foreword by Joel H. Rosenthal

Humanistic Perspectives on International Relations

Westport, Connecticut
London

Library of Congress Cataloging-in-Publication Data

Ethics and statecraft : the moral dimension of international affairs / edited by Cathal J.
Nolan ; foreword by Joel H. Rosenthal.—2nd ed.
    p.   cm.—(Humanistic perspectives on international relations, ISSN 1535–0363)
    Includes bibliographical references and index.
    ISBN 0–313–31493–4 (alk. paper)—ISBN 0–275–98305–6 (pbk. : alk. paper)
    1. International relations—Moral and ethical aspects. I. Nolan, Cathal J. II. Series.
JZ1306E876   2004
172′.4—dc22   2003070690

British Library Cataloguing in Publication Data is available.

Library of Congress Catalog Card Number: 2003070690
ISBN: 0–313–31493–4
    0–275–98305–6 (pbk.)
ISSN: 1535–0363

First published in 2004

Praeger Publishers, 88 Post Road West, Westport, CT 06881
An imprint of Greenwood Publishing Group, Inc.
www.praeger.com

Printed in the United States of America

The paper used in this book complies with the
Permanent Paper Standard issued by the National
Information Standards Organization (Z39.48–1984).

10 9 8 7 6 5 4 3 2 1

In memory of Edith Torrance Duff

Contents

Acknowledgments

The editor is thankful to the following for their contributions, direct and indirect, large and small, especially for encouragement to press on with what they regarded as a worthwhile and interesting project: Edward M. Bennett, Washington State University; Kal Holsti and Mark Zacher, University of British Columbia; Linda B. Miller, Wellesley College, and Delmar Smyth, York University; The editorial and production staff at Praeger provided their now familiar high standard of advice and assistance.

The idea for this book predated the idea for a conference on its major themes by almost one year, and the writing was already underway. Yet the final versions presented to the editor by the contributors are clearly the better for having been put through a mill of criticism by scholars representing the fields of history, moral philosophy and political science, who gathered in Vancouver, British Columbia, in October 1993. The editor thus wishes to extend special thanks to Robert J. Myers, past President, Joel H. Rosenthal, current President, and Matthew E. Mattern, Program Assistant, of the Carnegie Council on Ethics and International Affairs. The Council provided generous financial and other support that enabled the contributors and interested persons to gather in Vancouver, for what all involved have since described as a most memorable, helpful, and satisfying conference. Uncommon thanks are also due to Brian Job, Director of the Institute of International Relations, University of British Columbia (which cosponsored and hosted the conference), and to Terry Kersch who worked tirelessly on behalf of the Institute and helped bring the gathering to pass.

Series Foreword

Cathal J. Nolan

International relations is a thoroughly humanistic subject. All its actors are human beings, or they are institutions and organizations built and controlled by human intention and maintained by daily decision making. Individual states, which emerged as the most powerful and decisive actors on the world stage over the past 350 years, are not reified constructs with an independent will or social reality beyond human ken or volition. Properly regarded, they are wholly human constructs. All states are designed for, and are bent to, the realization of goals and aspirations of human communities. That is true whether those ambitions are good or evil, spiritual or material, personal or dynastic, or represent ethnic, national, or emerging cosmopolitan identities. So, too, is the international society of states a human construct, replete with its tangled labyrinth of international organizations, an expansive system of international law which creates binding obligations across frontiers, ancient norms of diplomacy and ritualized protocol, webs of economic, social, and cultural interaction, and a venerable penchant for disorder, discord, and war.

Immanuel Kant observed with acute accuracy, "Out of the crooked timbre of Humanity, no straight thing was ever made." The endless drama of human affairs thus gives rise to motley events, decisions, and complex causal chains. At the international level, too, we encounter the foibles of human beings as individuals and in the aggregate, and come upon a mix of the rational and irrational in human motivation. All that makes formal "modeling" of international politics a virtual impossibility—a fact which is itself a source of deep frustration to idealistic reformers and social scientists alike. On the other hand, precisely because international relations is so deeply humanistic a subject, it is a rich realm for the exercise of broad political and moral judgment. It is a natural arena for serious ethical reflection by and about those who frame foreign policies and practice statecraft. It is proper for scholars and informed citizens to praise or censure leadership decisions and actions. In short, as in all realms of human endeavor, moral judgment is not only implicit in every decision or action (or inaction) taken in international relations, it is a core duty of leadership, an apt function of scholarship, and a basic requirement for any educated citizenry.

These facts are clear, and even self-evident. At its classical best, political science understood them and therefore drew its questions from the conversation across time of the great political thinkers, as well as from current policy debates, to examine both in a rich discourse which was historically and philosophically aware, even as it was rigorous and well-grounded empirically. In contrast, much contemporary political science purports to describe and explain international relations through elaboration of objective "laws" of politics or economics, which entirely overlook its humanistic character. At its modern and postmodern worst, the discipline is prone to mere methodological preoccupations, striking elaborate poses about arcane topics, and impenetrable prose. For instance, positivism's search for a "rational choice" model of human conduct assumes that individuals are "rational actors" who purposively seek to maximize their interests. In seeking a universal, deductive theory (broadly modeled on academic economics, where similar methodologies are employed with little explanatory success), too many political scientists eschew historical or philosophically informed case study in favor of a crude reduction of all politics to formal models. These usually engage extreme simplifications, couched in an obscurantist terminology, which model what was already known or is obvious, or they are so generalized that they account for nothing specific. Over that thin substance is then spread a thick veneer of false rigor, packaged in mathematical formulas which are, and are intended to be, intimidating to the uninitiated. Left out is the fact that most things of lasting importance in human affairs may be explained, not by "rational choices," but by ideology and ignorance, blundering and stupidity, courage and self-sacrifice, enlightened vision, fanaticism, or blind chance (what Machiavelli called *fortuna*).

Alternately, the "critical theory" school in political science rejects any epistemology holding that reality exists separately from the academic observer and is therefore objectively knowable to any real degree. All knowledge about international relations instead merely reflects the biases and power interests of the observer (the usual suspects are racial, class, or economic elites). Scholars are warned against the attempt to achieve objective knowledge of the reality of international relations, which traditionally was the moral and intellectual *raison d'être* of their profession. Rather than seek to impartially map out, explore, and explain the international society of states and its complex subsystems and mores—a feat said to be impossible—scholars are to directly engage and change the world (even though that, too, ought to be impossible, if they are unable to understand it in the first place). Too often, this leads to polemical studies which purport to unmask elites whose pervasive and corrupt power is said to sustain and operate a fatally unjust international system. There is much intolerance and angry posturing here as well, in calls for "exposure" of fellow-traveling academic approaches identified as legitimizing and reinforcing irredeemably illicit power structures. In sum, in its epistemological assertion that all knowledge is radically subjective or merely political, critical theory denies the possibility of objective knowledge or the value of other scholarly traditions.

This series does not support the contention that all significant political action is reducible to rational choice, or that it is impossible to acquire objective knowledge about world affairs. Instead, it promotes a classical, humanistic approach to international relations scholarship. It is dedicated to reviving and furthering the contribution to understanding made by classical studies—by knowledge of history, diplomacy, international law, and philosophy—but it is agnostic regarding the narrow ideology or specific policy conclusions of any given work. It supports scholarly inquiry that is grounded in the historical antecedents of contemporary controversies, and well versed in the great traditions of philosophical inquiry and discourse. The series recognizes that, at its most incisive, international relations is a field of inquiry which cannot be fully understood outside its historical context. The keenest insights into the meaning of economic, legal, cultural, and political facts and issues in contemporary world affairs are always rooted in appreciation that international society is a historical phenomenon, not a theoretical abstraction or a radical departure from prior experience. Hence, the series welcomes interdisciplinary scholarship dealing with the evolution of the governing ideas, norms, and practices of international society. It encourages a dialectic rooted in abiding intellectual, ethical, and practical interests which for centuries have concerned and engaged intelligent men and women as they tried to reconcile the historical emergence of modern states with wider or older notions of political community.

This series is especially interested in scholarly research on the varied effects of differences in power—whether economic, political, or military—on relations among nations and states. The causes of war and the supports of peace, both in general and concerning specific conflicts, remain a core interest of all serious inquiry into international relations. Similarly, there is an enduring need for studies of the core requirements of international order and security, and of international political economy, whether regionally or globally. Also welcome is scholarship that is concerned with the development of international society, both in the formal relations maintained by states and in broader demands for political, economic, social, and cultural justice on the subnational and even individual level. Finally, the series promotes scholarly investigation of the history and changing character and status of international law, into international organization, and any and all other means of decentralized governance which the states have invented to moderate their conflicts and introduce a measure of restraint and equity to the affairs of international society.

Foreword: Biography, Ethics, and Statecraft

Joel H. Rosenthal

One of the first things one notices in the field of ethics and international affairs is the "level of analysis" problem. Shall we look at the *international system* as our target of analysis, the *nation state*, or the *individual statesman*? Naturally, all must be considered together, although it is reasonable to single out any one for alternative analysis. One way to deal with this problem is by using the conventions of history and biography. This approach allows for giving due weight to all three levels, while placing an emphasis on the individual and the role of conscience. There are few more compelling sources for the study of ethics and international affairs than the true stories and historical experiences of statesmen who made hard choices in reconciling principle and power. In the tradition of Aristotle and Plutarch, we can learn from example and from biography: one cannot deny the moral power of good stories.

The challenge for us is to make some sense of these stories, perhaps to extract some generalizations that may allow us to get beyond individual examples as a string of anecdotes. There is of course a legitimate question as to how theoretically rigorous one can be in this area: the theme of moral statesmanship is by its very nature not conducive to "scientific" study that would please natural scientists and social science quantifiers. Yet as this volume demonstrates, this theme is nevertheless thematically cogent and worthy of systematic study.

One of the objectives of this volume is to bridge the gap between the literature of moral judgment on specific events (e.g. the Holocaust, the Vietnam War), and the literature that assesses individual leaders. The literature of events enjoys the benefit of credible normative criteria such as human rights standards or the application of just war theory. But as Brian Job of the University of British Columbia has noted, "the quality of debate often breaks down when individual leaders are examined. Decisions are either explained away as a result of someone's idiosyncratic or pathological nature, or are portrayed as if the individual in office had no individual input in determining the course of events (i.e., he/she was 'the product of his/her time and culture')." Fortunately we are not in completely uncharted territory in dealing with this problem.

One look at the great literature of Western civilization reveals the central place of the perennial themes of free will vs. chance, character vs. fate, and the individual vs. destiny; they are the animus of Tolstoy's *War and Peace*, Melville's *Moby Dick*, and Machiavelli's *The Prince*, among many others. Many pages have been devoted to the theme of how the great individual such as Napoleon, Ahab, or the prince moves within history. The individual sometimes seems to be at the mercy of overwhelming historical forces, while at other times it appears as though one great man can move history by a singular force of will. Tolstoy outlines the problem of biography and history in his infamous and ponderous "Second Epilogue" on the subject of "what forces move history?"

In 1789 a ferment arises in Paris, it grows, spreads, and is expressed by a movement of peoples from west to east. Several times it moves eastward and collides with a counter-movement from the east westward. In 1812 it reaches its extreme limit, Moscow, and then, with remarkable symmetry, a counter-movement occurs from east to west, attracting to it, as the first movement had done, the nations of middle Europe. The counter-movement reaches the starting point of the first movement in the west—Paris—and subsides.

During that twenty-year period an immense number of fields were left untilled, houses were burned, trade changed its direction, millions of men migrated, were impoverished, or were enriched, and millions of Christian men professing the law of love of their fellows slew one another.

What does this all mean? Why did it happen? What made those people burn houses and slay their fellow men? What were the causes of those events? What force made those men act so?[1]

In the course of his 1,000-plus page narrative and discursive conclusion, Tolstoy makes it plain that modern history must consider a variety of irreducible factors.

Given this perspective, how then can we possibly theorize about these matters of free will, contingency, historical force, and moral choice? There are at least five points that emerge in a review of the literature in this field that may serve to organize discussion and study: 1) the construction of narratives; 2) the distinction between perfectionist and nonperfectionist ethics; 3) the theme of necessity and choice; 4) the issue of individual versus collective morality; and 5) the role and resonance of international moral norms.

In a recent article entitled "The Cold War's End Dramatizes the Failure of Political Theory," John L. Gaddis observes that the modern theoretical approaches to the study of international relations have failed on their own ambitious terms: they have failed to increase the reliability of prediction, and they have failed to remove uncertainty from political action. Because of the nature of international relations, variables cannot be reduced or isolated for close study—the conditions required of a controlled experiment cannot be achieved. In something of a prescriptive conclusion Gaddis writes, "in practice we tend to fall back upon the only simulative technique that successfully illustrates the general and the specific, the regular and the irregular, the predictable and the unpredictable. We construct narratives."[2]

The narratives examined here—consisting primarily of the biographies and specific experiences of statesmen—are an integral part of how we might improve our understanding of ethics and international affairs. These narratives reveal the timeless philosophical quandaries all humans face, yet they account for history and context: they consider ethics in terms of both principle and practice. As William Kilpatrick, a professor of education at Boston University, writes: "the connection between narrative and morality is an essential one, not merely a useful one. The Ph.D. needs the story 'part' just as much as [anyone]. In other words, story and moral may be less separable than we have come to think. The question is not whether the moral principle needs to be sweetened with the sugar of the story, but whether moral principles make any sense outside the human context of stories."[3] There is a natural instinct for those of us interested in ethics and international affairs to get down to cases, to merge theory and practice through example.

This focus on narratives, as well as ethics and decision-making, enables us to get to the root of ethics, which is human agency—or real people acting in history. Despite their focus on the international system, the conditions of anarchy and the primacy of power and interests, realists such as Hans J. Morgenthau and Kenneth W. Thompson conclude: "Ethical rules have their seat in the conscience of individual men. Government by clearly identifiable men who can be held personally responsible for their actions is therefore the precondition for the existence of an effective system of international ethics."[4]

This assertion leads to a second theme in discussing statecraft, and that is the issue of perfectionism vs. nonperfectionism. Max Weber calls this the distinction between the "ethics of ultimate ends," and the "ethics of responsibility."[5] Without delving too deeply into this distinction here, most people are willing to cede some ground to Weber and the realists on this point, and most understand statecraft to be concerned with moral choice that frequently if not regularly requires the balancing of competing moral claims, and the choosing of the lesser of two evils. Decision-making always involves reconciling the desirable with the possible: the political arena is not the realm for the blind pursuit of moral imperatives without regard for consequences. For this reason, saints, by their very nature, do not make good politicians, and politicians are generally not suited for sainthood. One will find very few pure Kantians among statesmen anywhere— that is, statesmen who strictly adhere to principles over consequences, and the virtues of reason over the lessons of experience.

This gets to the heart of the matter concerning statecraft, and a third theme— the problem of necessity and choice. The frequent justification given by statesmen for their actions is, "I had no choice but to do x." As Arnold Wolfers puts it in his essay on "Statesmanship and Moral Choice":

Machiavelli and Machiavellianism have stood for a doctrine that places princes and sovereign states under the rule not of ordinary morality, but of the "reason of state," considered an amoral principle peculiar to the realm of politics. German writers have been particularly insistent that ethical standards that apply to private individuals cannot measure the behavior of states which are said to be guided by necessity.

Wolfers goes on to note that in general, "the English speaking world . . . has been unwilling to admit any peculiar ethics of state behavior."[6]

This generalization aside, Wolfers is correct in conveying the basic tension between an almost nihilistic Machiavellian realism that posits all action in terms of national interests and maximizing power, and a more nuanced view that seeks to reconcile morality and power, and does not see power accumulation and balance of power as exclusive moral ends in themselves. "In every case," writes Wolfers, "the interpretation of what constitutes a vital national interest and how much value should be attached to it is a moral question. It cannot be answered by reference to alleged amoral necessities inherent in international politics; it rests on value judgments." This is where the character of the individual states-man comes into play.

If nothing else, it is imperative for us to expand the inquiry into the "choice" part of the dialectic between necessity and choice. While the enmity of the international system may not give the statesman the complete freedom that he would ideally like, he is rarely boxed in to such an extent that all of his choices are gone. Is it possible that in many instances where statesmen justify their actions in terms of being boxed in to the point of "no choice," that the box is of their own making?

A fourth theme is the one suggested by the title of Reinhold Niebuhr's well-known book of 1932, *Moral Man and Immoral Society* (a book, one should note, that was about socialism and domestic politics, not international affairs). Niebuhr makes much of the distinction between the moral behavior of individuals and the moral behavior of social groups. The question, easily extrapolated from this argument, is: how can one live a moral life (and make moral choices) in the context of an immoral or amoral world; and for our purposes, how can a statesman pursue a moral foreign policy in the context of nationalism, self-interest, and international anarchy? It is a theme that has had considerable resonance over the years, often referred to in debates over individual and collective morality.

The essential point of this debate concerns social dynamics. How much weight, if any, do we want to give to Niebuhr's observation that "group relations can never be as ethical as those which characterize individual relations"? Niebuhr observes that "one of the tragedies of the human spirit [is] its inability to conform its collective life to individual ideals. As individuals, men believe that they ought to serve each other and establish justice between each other. As racial, economic and national groups they take for themselves whatever their power can command."[7] The statesman, of course, stands at the apex (or vortex, depending on how you look at it) of this dilemma—he or she is an individual, with a conscience of his or her own, acting on behalf of a social group.

In discussions of this sort, the Italian Cavour's aphorism: "What rogues we would be if we did for ourselves what we do for our country" immediately springs to mind. But as Greg Russell points out in his study of Hans Morgenthau and political realism, upon further reflection, the choice is not so stark: "What changes for the nature and role of moral judgment on either [the individual or collective] level is not the action itself, but the social environment within which . . . norms must function" (in our case, this environmental imperative refers to the security-power dilemma—the consistent drive for power as a measure of insuring national security).[8] As for Niebuhr, David Little's analysis is apt: "The interesting question is not whether there is an irreconcilable conflict between individual and collective morality as Niebuhr says there is. . . . The interesting question concerns the shades of difference between what is morally expected of individuals in comparison with nations and other groups, and that requires more careful analysis than Niebuhr gave the matter."[9]

A fifth and final point relates to the standards or yardsticks by which statesmen themselves make judgments, and by which we ourselves might make judgments. Obviously, much is left to conscience and how an individual perceives his or her options, circumstances, and duties. Yet part of how statesmen (and we as individuals) perceive "right" and "wrong" depends on how we understand the "rules of the game" in international affairs. What role do international moral norms play in shaping the words and deeds of policy-makers? One of the objectives of this volume is to describe this interaction, and in this way, describe the connection between normative and empirical concerns.

By international moral norms, we mean the prescriptive principles of desirable behavior to which most nations can and do agree. These norms embody the ideals and principles by which a community—even a world community—defines itself. The evolution of international moral norms (and their effect on statecraft) tells us much about world history and our current situation. Much of this story is told in Dorothy V. Jones's book *Code of Peace: Ethics and Security in the World of Warlord States*, where she outlines the origins and evolution of principles such as the sovereign equality of states, the presumption of nonintervention, the recognition of human rights, and the principle of self-determination have not been created in a vacuum.[10] As Jones illustrates, these principles have arisen from the hard-won lessons of war and peace throughout world history, and especially in the twentieth century. They have shaped the beliefs and actions of statesmen, and in turn, they have been shaped and reshaped by them.

This volume gives due consideration to the aforementioned three levels of analysis, as well as the five points outlined above. At the very least, it provides a

modicum of discipline and organization that enables us to extract some generalized wisdom from case studies such as the ones that are explored. In this way,
this book opens an important pathway to the study of ethics and international
affairs and is a genuine contribution to this burgeoning field.

NOTES

1. Leo Tolstoy, *War and Peace* (Chicago: Encyclopedia Britannica/Great Books Edition, 1952), pp. 675–76.

2. John Lewis Gaddis, "The Cold War's End Dramatizes the Failure of Political
Theory," *The Chronicle of Higher Education* 38 (July 26, 1992), p. A44.

3. William Kilpatrick, "The Moral Power of Good Stories," *American Educator* 17
(Summer 1993), pp. 24–30.

4. Kenneth W. Thompson, *Political Realism and the Crisis of World Politics* (Washington, DC: University Press of America, 1982), p. 157.

5. See Max Weber, "Politics as a Vocation," in Hans Gerth and C. Wright Mills,
eds., *From Max Weber: Essays in Sociology* (New York: Oxford University Press, 1946).

6. Arnold Wolfers, *Discord and Collaboration: Essays on International Politics*
(Baltimore: Johns Hopkins University Press, 1962), pp. 47–65.

7. Reinhold Niebuhr, *Moral Man and Immoral Society* (New York: Charles Scribner's Sons, 1932).

8. Greg Russell, *Hans J. Morgenthau and the Ethics of American Statecraft* (Baton
Rouge: Louisiana State University Press, 1990), p. 156.

9. David Little, "The Recovery of Liberalism: *Moral Man and Immoral Society* Sixty
Years Later," *Ethics & International Affairs* 7 (1993), p. 198.

10. Dorothy V. Jones, *Code of Peace: Ethics and Security in the World of Warlord
States* (Chicago: University of Chicago Press, 1991).

Preface to the Second Edition

Cathal J. Nolan

The editor and contributors to the first edition of *Ethics and Statecraft* were pleased with the positive reception it received and the wide readership it garnered. Academic reviewers praised the book for its clarity of presentation, the soundness of its scholarship, and an appropriate focus on individual human agency as the fulcrum of ethical concern in foreign policy strategies and decision making. It is also notable that, in an era where far too much political science is marred by scientistic pretension and obscurantist writing, the book saw wide university adoptions not just at the graduate level but also for introductory politics and social science courses. This confirmed the editor's and contributors' original judgment that the study of important debates of abiding moral significance, clearly presented, both deserves and retains the attention of modern college students. Professors at several institutions of higher learning who used the book in class reported that it helped awaken students to their own place in the ongoing drama of human history, world politics, and moral debate. Similarly, the response of the educated reading public confirmed that good political history about important ideas and decisions, which is also written well, consistently attracts intelligent men and women who are concerned with the moral significance of great events of the past, as well as their own times.

Changes have been made in the second edition which improve the logic of presentation and enhance the general usefulness of the book. The chapters by Anthony Lentin on Lloyd George and John Lewis Gaddis on the Cold War, which appeared in the first edition, are gone. Although studying Lloyd George can be highly instructive, it was judged that recounting his amusingly rascally nature does not illuminate moral issues in world politics beyond what is discussed in other cases elsewhere in the book. Instead, an entirely original chapter has been added by William N. Tilchin on Theodore Roosevelt. Why TR? Because despite never leading his nation in war, he was a singular statesman whose foreign policy principles and axioms were successful not only in their own day but much later. After several decades of neglect, much of TR's strategic thinking was revived and reinjected into American statecraft. Moreover, this happened not just simultaneously with the emergence of the United States as the predominant power of the present age, but *because* TR's sense of the obligations of power best suited the country's extraordinary strengths, lasting political values, and grave responsibilities. Tilchin carefully walks us through the complex statecraft of Theodore Roosevelt, making a powerful case that he consistently displayed the necessary strength of will, an ability to reason about long-term diplomatic and strategic consequences, and other traits of character necessary to proper and morally informed decision making. Furthermore, America's twenty-sixth president displayed a degree of perspicacity that transcended both his era and the more parochial interests of his nation. This is best appreciated in light of the fact that the disaster of military isolationism and political appeasement in the 1930s and the myth and confidence-shattering experience of World War II were suffered through before the lessons of TR's method of foreign policy were revived as foundation stones of American statecraft. These lessons were "formidable and credible deterrent power, broadly conceived U.S. interests, and Anglo-American solidarity and preeminence." Tilchin makes a powerful case that TR's statecraft was not merely well attuned to the problems of his own time, but that it teaches timeless lessons about the appropriate and successful use of great national power to national and international moral ends.

Similarly, it was decided that an overview of the enormity of the Cold War in just one chapter offered readers less insight into the role of moral reasoning in statecraft than a close study of one of the major, hot contests of that era: the war in Indochina. That conflict raised important questions that abide still in the decision-making halls of Washington and arguably apply to all democracies as they are called upon by elements of their own citizenry, and by the international community of states, to intervene in behalf of humanitarian or other just causes. Are democracies ever obliged to intervene or fight to preserve the national liberties of other peoples? And, even if that premise is accepted as a convincing moral perquisite, may it be trumped by prudential concern about likely excessive moral costs and unintended policy consequences? David Armstrong explores the tortuous moral meaning of the Vietnam War in an essay of exceptional sophistication, erudition, and subtlety. He surveys the competing moral lessons that have been drawn from the Vietnam conflict, "ranging from the need for a new American isolationism to the requirement for American interventions to employ overwhelming force." What emerges from his analysis is the conclusion that neither interventionist nor noninterventionist policies hold a monopoly on morality or on the lessons of Vietnam. But he is emphatic that, however difficult and morally clouded their task might be, key decision-makers cannot escape moral as well as practical responsibility for the outcome of their decisions. He suggests that a central lesson of Vietnam arises from study of the intentions and character of top decision-makers, and he calls for a return to understanding of the classic virtues of statesmanship—"wisdom, insight, prudence, common sense, pragmatism, tolerance, willingness to compromise where necessary, a knowledge of history . . . and an ability to see things from other perspectives." Such an approach, he suggests, rather than blind following of "implacable moral or ideological certainties," offers a better chance for a world of "common decency, common humanity, and a preference for peace over war."

To better fit these new essays into the book, the original framework has been significantly changed. Now, the organization of the volume better situates chapters that play to one another on one of three grand themes: the moral obligations and pitfalls of peacemaking, the ethics and statecraft of war, and the ethics and statecraft of major international reform ("transformation"). In addition, original chapters by Cathal Nolan on FDR and World War II, Carl Hodge on Konrad Adenauer and the rehabilitation of postwar Germany, and Paul Marantz on Eduard Shevardnadze and the decline and fall of the Soviet Union have been revised and updated.

CHAPTER 1

Introduction

Cathal J. Nolan

> Those who would treat politics and morality apart will never understand the one or the other.
> —John, Viscount Morley of Blackburn, *Rousseau* (1876)

An animating concern, and part of the underlying logic, of the scholarly enterprise leading to this book is to rekindle academic inquiry at the intersection of political analysis, diplomatic history, and philosophical investigation. That is why mostly senior diplomatic historians and philosophically-minded political scientists were asked to contribute to this collective study. Their essays are of high quality, confirming that there is a bright future for interdisciplinary and normative inquiry in this field: among students and scholars there exists an untapped reserve of interest in reviving a philosophically and historically informed understanding of world politics.

Another concern of this text is to call attention to the ethically ambiguous role of decision-makers acting under the constraints and imperatives of real world situations that impose real consequences, rather than to dwell on abstract moral propositions or the construction of theoretical models. The explicit purpose of this volume is to show that the individual leader is a major conduit by which ethical considerations enter into the decision-making process of states, and thereby affect the course and nature of international politics. This text thus offers an unusual concentration on historical/political biography, suggesting that it is a necessary part of any consideration of the ethics of statecraft. This approach cuts to the heart of the question of the place of ethics in international affairs—the contention that the foundation of ethics is human agency, which is always acted out in a context of ambiguity, competing moral claims, and unforeseen consequences.

The subjects of this text were selected based on their involvement with a range of hard moral issues that are central to the conduct of statecraft, with representative examples of leaders in peacetime, wartime, and times of sweeping political change. There are no clear cut cases here, and solutions to ethical dilemmas are not obvious. Contributors do not engage in airy academic scribblings about "contending moral paradigms," and other such fashionable clichés. Instead, they express empathy with the difficulties, as well as opportunities, that changing circumstances and public responsibility present to the ethical practice of statecraft. This volume sets out questions of international ethics as they are encountered by decision-makers in real life: as dirty, gray, uncertain choices, which once made are likely to be forever unsatisfactory to the moral purist or political ideologue. As a result, the chapters present moral issues in foreign policy for what they really are: great and difficult dilemmas—not hurdles on the path to political sainthood—faced by flesh and blood human beings who must act with limited knowledge and under enormous pressures of time and political constraint, who yet remain responsible for consequences of huge import. Cases from the highly important Anglo/American legacy in international affairs are included, along with cases from other national traditions. Some chapters present a striking counterpoint to the liberal-internationalist concerns and assumptions that dominate recent English-language writing on ethics and world affairs. Readers will therefore encounter a different (and often misunderstood) moral tradition, one attached to political realism. Encapsulated in the ideas of prudence and virtue, this tradition upholds a set of qualities that inform independent moral judgment and are rooted in caution, consideration of opposing interests, deliberation, forethought, foresight, preparedness, wariness, and—if and whenever possible—candor with adversaries as well as allies.

Contributors were asked to look—straight in the eye—at real life moral dilemmas faced by prominent national leaders, about whom we know a fair deal but who operated under conditions of restricted knowledge and limited power to effect change. The global stature and wide influence of these leaders rendered their actions (or inactions) of considerable moral and political gravity. Their central participation in decision-making, and the pivotal nature of the events with which each was involved, make them stand out as appropriate choices for sober reflection. These are not the small-fry of history and politics. To the contrary, we all live within the consequences—moral, political and otherwise—of their actions and decisions. Otto von Bismarck dominated not only his nation but his era, elevating Germany through war to the pinnacle of the European state system, from where he also presided over the "Eastern Question" and oversaw the final partition of Africa. Theodore Roosevelt and Woodrow Wilson continue to cast remarkable shadows over the twentieth century, in particular its grand experiments with international organization, collective security, and decentralized international governance. As the twentieth century closed, both Wilson and TR far surpassed in lasting significance their contemporary and fellow visionary, Vladimir I. Lenin. Franklin Roosevelt and Winston Churchill led two great democracies in the biggest war either nation ever faced, and each had to address ethical problems of extraordinary complexity and consequence. Their moral accomplishments are dealt with here without mawkishness, just as their uneasy compromises, deceits, and flaws are discussed without the majestic condemnation born of hindsight that the living frequently dispense regarding the dead. And so with the other leaders: Dag Hammarskjöld, Konrad Adenauer, and Eduard Shevardnadze were also statesmen of major significance, whose complex choices and actions are subjected to sustained moral reflection. The volume also contains two important thematic essays. One discusses the situational nature of ethical questions and the role of virtue at the international level, and the other explores the moral dilemmas raised by U.S. involvement in the Vietnam War.

The Carnegie Council on Ethics and International Affairs made a generous offer to sponsor a conference on biography, ethics, and statecraft, using the existing structure and essays in the book, already under commission, as the framework. Council sponsorship enabled most contributors to meet under the auspices of the Institute of International Relations, University of British Columbia, in Vancouver in October 1993. Papers were delivered before an invited, international gathering of interested scholars, government officials and Council officers. Debate was lively, as presentations were subjected to close scrutiny by assembled historians, moral philosophers, political scientists, and political theorists, with each bringing to bear the varied methodologies and insights of their disciplines. Although unanimity on specific or final moral judgments sometimes eluded the gathering—as perhaps it should on such profound issues as war, peace, and political transformation—an important consensus developed on the set of questions necessary to think systematically about issues of ethics and statecraft. The conference thus highlighted a number of core themes that appear in nearly all the essays, as diverse as their subjects are. It was generally agreed that these themes emerged out of the essential practice of statecraft, as reflected in the case studies. It also was made clear that the ethical dimension of world affairs cannot be properly or fully understood without explicitly stating and directly addressing the questions that are raised at the level of individual decision-makers.

Of what did this consensus consist? First, it was accepted that analysts must assess the extent to which ethical concerns can be considered separate from diplomatic practice. They must ask: to what degree do these concerns arise from the nature of foreign policy and specific situations encountered in the real world by national leaders, rather than descend out of an Olympian cloud of abstract reasoning or absolute principle? This was seen as the critical issue by most participants. Moreover, it spoke directly to the second but related question: what criteria should be used to judge the ethical content of actual decisions? Many argued forcefully for historical and situational empathy and discrimination. Others asked if this was enough, suggesting that formal moral theory still has a role to play in assisting leaders to make difficult choices, and analysts to assess the choices actually made. Moral theory might provide an "Archimedean point" for articulating first principles for deducing ethical action and making judgments. Or it might at least help to articulate a moral sense, and enable consideration of the inevitable trade-offs and contradictions of difficult problems. In this context, all participants praised the case study approach for allowing close examination of a leader's motives and means, as well as the consequences of his or her actions and decisions. Examining actual decisions made by men and women on the great moral questions in world affairs highlights the extant role of volition in foreign policy, no matter how otherwise constrained a policy context might be. These studies thus help account for the three components critical to any application of moral reasoning to problems of statecraft: What were the motives of the decision-makers involved? Did they have reasonable, alternative means at their disposal that might have allowed them to effect different choices than the ones they actually made? And what were the real, as well as perceived and potential, consequences of the choices they faced?

A final element of the consensus was that analysts of ethics and international affairs must address the issue of what qualities are truly desirable in men and women involved in public affairs, without assuming that private virtue guarantees moral success on the international plane. It was generally accepted that the realm of statecraft often raises different moral questions and may call for qualities other than those celebrated in the private domain. Put another way, the common assumption that good public policy will necessarily flow from having people of private virtue in positions of authority seems erroneous. The record suggests that the road to foreign policy (and even moral) disaster may well be paved with the good intentions of decent people. Thus, while it is a *necessary* beginning, it is not a *sufficient* basis for judgment to ask whether leaders remained true to their internal or declared principles once great power was theirs. We should ask as well if they adhered to, and sought to advance, the normative conventions of international society and international law, or of some developed moral theory that reached beyond their personal outlook. And we must be prepared to accept that peculiar circumstances may permit leaders to depart, with absolution, from some moral conventions if their decisions serve competing ethical purposes and needs. Similarly, leaders who achieve admirable moral ends while also conducting an instrumental foreign policy may do so in spite of a gravely flawed private character. They may even be successful (morally speaking, not just politically) because of behavior that would be widely excoriated if it aimed solely at private ends. Gentlefolk are quite properly found ethically wanting if they read each others' mail; they ought not in general to lie either, or use force to impose their will on others. Yet, under certain circumstances, governments and national leaders are likely to have a moral *obligation* to use such means in the service of higher public goods. Bluntly stated, private sinners may well make excellent national leaders—and remarkably often, as matters turn out. Equally, under specific conditions private vices may actually take form as public virtues. This is one of several paradoxes concerning the ethics of statecraft to emerge from comparison of the case studies in this volume.

In "The Situational Ethics of Statecraft," political scientist Robert H. Jackson argues that international ethics is inescapably an applied ethics, as well as inherently "a subject of history and politics." For Jackson, the ethics of statecraft are indigenous to its practice rather than imported from some distant, abstract realm. As a result, his aim is not to develop a grand theory, but to provide a working framework for bringing ethical questions into contact with real situations. In addition to exposing the realm of human agency in international affairs, this approach leads to a necessary appreciation that national leaders actually exercise little control over the large events of world history and politics, which should, in turn, lead to a moderation of history's judgment of those leaders. To do less than recognize this is to ignore a vital, and sometimes determining, component of leadership. He thus lays out what should be a central burden of all concerned with moral reasoning and politics, and gives voice to a question that is implicit in other chapters in this volume: given the limits imposed by the real world, what are the necessary dimensions of a morally responsible statecraft? Put another way, what qualities should we look for when assessing the actions and decisions of national leaders, or when choosing them?

In the process of laying out the basis for moral judgment, Jackson lends justification to the logic that governed the design of this book. Because empathy with real world problems and limitations faced by leaders is the key to a proper moral understanding, he insists, it is necessary to take a historical approach to problems of ethics and statecraft. Indeed, historical and situational empathy is a strong moral duty of academics ("the ethics of scholarship"). It may even be the only proper basis for their assumption of a right to judgment of other men and women who, unlike historians or professors of politics, make decisions that actually have consequences in the public world. His closing appeal is for adoption of a moral standard that looks to the best foreign policy choices that circumstances permit, rather than to an absolutist or perfectionist ethics. How can a leader achieve this standard? By returning to cultivation of the classical idea of "the virtues," or those "mental dispositions and disciplines" that permit one to discharge moral duties despite "the risks involved and thus the temptation to do otherwise." Jackson's closing remarks point us to an ethics of imperfection— of imperfect knowledge, empathy, and judgment. His call for a situational understanding of international ethics becomes the moral equivalent of Bismarck's definition of politics as the "art of the possible."

In "Realism and Idealism in Historical Perspective," historian Otto Pflanze seeks to demonstrate that no "realist" has ever been so pure a practitioner of *Realpolitik* as to be utterly unconcerned with ethical and ideological concerns, just as no "idealist" statesman has been totally unconcerned with power. He begins with a sketch of the history of European diplomacy, pausing to consider the contributions of Niccolò Machiavelli, Cardinal Richelieu, Frederick the

Great, Immanuel Kant, and the *leitmotif* of the "classical school," the idea of *raison d'état*. Pflanze presents these thinkers and ideas as part of a centuries-long struggle between universal monarchy and the balance of power. This trend culminated in the Napoleonic challenge to the balance of power, the great settlement of the Congress of Vienna, and the relative stability provided by a ruling European aristocracy whose power had not yet been undermined by the industrial revolution. Yet, Pflanze notes, the Napoleonic revolution changed much. The congress system and Concert of Europe had to create and then sustain an artificial balance of power, where in the eighteenth century it was assumed that balance was a natural political mechanism.

He next asks if the thought and practice of Bismarck rank him as the most gifted practitioner of the classical school of diplomacy, untouched by the age of ideology and nationalism in which he lived, or whether he was more modern than his usual image suggests. It is noted that Bismarck's religious convictions, born of a late conversion to pietism, merely reinforced a sense of obligation to follow the dictates of reason and conscience. The question of nationalism is more important, raising the possibility of a lurking—if parochial—idealism. But Pflanze points out that for Bismarck the Prussian state preceded the German nation, which greatly separated him from the radical nationalists of his own day, and the Nazis and others who came after them. Pflanze portrays Bismarck as a moderating influence on Prussia's generals and nationalists, even during the wars of Prussian expansion and German unification (Denmark, 1864; Austria, 1866; France, 1870–1871). He emphasizes the positive moral accomplishment of Bismarck's later support for a continental equilibrium that helped keep the peace for several decades. He also points out the "Iron Chancellor's" refusal to countenance a war to preempt the revival of French power after 1871. Pflanze concludes that such studied moderation places Bismarck firmly within the classical school and allows us to judge him a situational ethicist, albeit one who—like the classical school of European diplomacy itself—joined idealism and realism in a nervous and tentative embrace.

In "Franklin D. Roosevelt and Defensible Deceit in World War II," by Cathal J. Nolan, the argument is presented that lying is, at times, a requisite of diplomacy even for a democracy. Provocatively, Nolan contends that there are occasions when a national leader is not only justified in lying to the public, but may be morally obligated to do so. He details the calculated deceits that Roosevelt purveyed and cultivated to get America into World War II, to sustain the war effort, and to commit the United States to postwar activism. The question is then posed: Were the facts of FDR's moral dilemma as he faced the threat from Nazi Germany of sufficient salience that circumstances make his deceptions defensible? Issue is taken with those who would have us believe that lying by elected leaders is the worst betrayal that can befall a democracy. Nolan insists that, on those rare occasions where the nation is genuinely facing grave danger, deceit by a national leader in order to move opinion and policy where it otherwise might not go, but needs to go, is entirely defensible. He presents a counterfactual scenario suggestive of the practical and moral consequences had isolationists kept the United States both unprepared and unwilling to fight the Axis powers, and thereby permitted Nazi Germany to win World War II. He maintains that, unlike Lyndon Johnson's delusional perception of the stakes in Vietnam, "aggressive, expansionist Germany under the control of Adolf Hitler and the Nazis *in fact* posed a potentially mortal danger to the United States." This makes all the difference in judgment of the decision to deceive. Yet FDR is also criticized for lying too easily, overmuch and pettily, while overcoming opposition to Lend-Lease to Moscow and in needless smears against the loyalty of entire ethnic groups. Nolan affirms Roosevelt as a morally conscious leader, praising him for "shouldering . . . personal responsibility for morally ambiguous solutions to the problems of statecraft." FDR may have been morally flawed, but he also was a statesman who enjoyed nearly absolute power without succumbing to absolute corruption.

Where Nolan maintains that we must recognize that small transgressions are permissible under the special moral dispensation of wartime, Stephen A. Garrett's "Political Leadership and 'Dirty Hands' " is a ringing rejection of the assertion that it is permissible to perform heinous acts simply because one is opposing an enemy that is greatly evil. This is the problem of "dirty hands," a term serving as shorthand for the degree to which political authority, when wielded by otherwise decent persons, may be required to perform or to tolerate actions that would be seen as evil if they took place in the private sphere. Garrett notes two justifications commonly offered for having dirty hands (for upholding the moral exceptionalism of leaders) in wartime: that they represent collective rather than individual moral obligations, and that conducting a war is an inherently more brutal enterprise than looking after one's private affairs. He does not dismiss these claims for special moral exemption cavalierly. But his essential argument is that the legitimate gap between the private and public moral realms can be so overstated as to falsely imply a complete lack of connection between them. He lays out a series of tests by which the problem of dirty hands may be judged: the intuitive values of leaders themselves; consequentialism, or the search for realistic alternatives and weighing of likely outcomes; and universalization, or the principle of the categorical imperative, that requires that actions undertaken reflect sensitivity to the interests of all affected parties.

The case he uses to illustrate his argument is Winston Churchill's involvement in the bombing of German cities during World War II, a policy which resulted in over 500,000 civilian deaths. Garrett demonstrates that Churchill and Bomber Command took the deliberate decision to devastate Germany's cities in part owing to technical factors relating to night time bombing, and partly in order to keep down British casualties by deflecting Allied pressure for an early invasion of the continent. But he also shows the decision sprang most directly from a deliberate calculation that city bombing might fatally undermine German civilian morale, and thus hasten the end of the war. Applying his tests, he finds Churchill unnecessarily callous toward German civilians; inconsistent in appraising alternative outcomes; and aware of, but not in the end swayed by, a categorical moral obligation to spare enemy civilians to the highest degree feasible with successful prosecution of the war. Churchill, found wanting to some degree on all three tests, is therefore judged to be guilty of deep hypocrisy, and is held culpable in German civilian deaths; yet he is not condemned for any essential wickedness. Admitting to admiration of his subject's other accomplishments and traits, Garrett nonetheless concludes that the policy of city bombing left "a permanent blot on [Churchill's] moral escutcheon."

Arthur S. Link challenges cruder realist views in "The Higher Realism of Woodrow Wilson." This important piece, first published in 1962, is reprinted here with a postscript looking back on a half-century of debate about the meaning of Wilson's life and works. Link notes that during the Cold War, among academic realists and Europeans, the view persisted of Wilson as "essentially a destructive force in modern history because he was visionary, unrealistic, provincial, and ignorant of European problems, zealous and messianic in conceit." But who was more realistic? Was it those European leaders who thought they could impose lasting solutions over the resistance of a great nation like Germany? Or Wilson, who stood above the fever and hysteria of war even while conducting it, and then offered a peace plan that might have endured because it recognized the inevitability of reconciliation once the carnage was over and the passions it brought had subsided? While conceding that Wilson was, at his core, a Christian idealist rather than an instrumental strategist, Link takes strong issue with the overall image presented by realist critics. He argues that Wilson was a realist of a different sort, portraying him as a leader of enormous vision who pursued "a higher realism" in all his politics, including at the Paris Peace Conference. Wilson's vision has proven more perceptive and more realistic over the longer term than the severe demands for a narrow and punitive peace of Georges Clemenceau. But Wilson was also an idealist, in the sense of subordinating immediate or material goals to superior moral purposes. That fed his belief in a national mission—his vision of America as leader of a community of nations organized around peaceful and principled pursuits, rather than just another imperial power playing the old game of balance and aggrandizement. He did not, as some critics have charged, misunderstand the classical system of international politics. In fact, he was quite capable of playing the old game by the old rules, as he demonstrated in Mexico. But in the end he rejected *Realpolitik* prescriptions as unrealistic over the long term. Furthermore, he never succumbed to "that greatest twentieth century delusion, that it is necessary to win wars even at the risk of losing everything for which they are fought." With understandable satisfaction, Link quotes an early critic, George F. Kennan, who has since come to see Wilson as "ahead of any other statesman of his time." Link concludes that Wilson's principles have lasting importance for the post–Cold War era.

In "The World Outlook of Dag Hammarskjöld," Dorothy V. Jones assesses the pursuit of an ethical statecraft given the constraints and limitations of the office of UN Secretary General. She argues that Hammarskjöld's view of the United Nations was a dynamic one, in which the role of international organization and international law was that of global standard setter. Among Hammarskjöld's major contributions to ethics and statecraft was his sense that political goals must be pursued with full consciousness of the time frame needed to accomplish them. This "temporal perspective" became a major influence on the means he chose in pursuit of any given goal. Hammarskjöld enjoyed a unique position, in that he could take a wider view of ethical obligations than a national leader acting under the pressures of domestic politics and the moral claims of the concepts of the nation and the national interest. This tendency was reinforced by his insistence on taking the long view, which led him always to actions that he thought might help push back a receding wall that hid a future of increased interstate cooperation. His was an evolutionary approach to UN problems, looking past the coexistence of nations in his own day toward real cooperation in some distant future. Jones illustrates this with Hammarskjöld's role in the Lebanon crisis of 1958. She contends that Lebanon showed that Hammarskjöld was aware of and accepted an existing, rule-based system of international ethics—that encoded in the UN Charter and other multilateral treaties. He worked within this legal and normative system, as it applied in the real world, to contain contemporary conflicts without foreclosing possibilities for enhanced international cooperation. He thereby "made the interpretive vacuum into a space for maneuver, and he constantly enlarged that space, all the while referring back to the Charter as authorization for his actions." If these efforts made member states uncomfortable with the more assertive role Hammarskjöld gave the office of Secretary General, that too was part of the evolutionary process that he foresaw leading one day to expanded international order and justice.

Carl C. Hodge explores a central paradox of postwar German history: Konrad Adenauer's perception that "arming Germany's second democracy was critical to its survival" and to its "claim to a place among civilized states," despite his lifelong opposition to what the militarists had done in and to Germany. The chapter is fundamentally sympathetic. Hodge views Adenauer's achievements as "in some respects more impressive and possibly more durable than those of the Iron Chancellor." Animated by a Weberian "ethic of responsibility," Adenauer assumed a mandate to personally interpret the best interests of the German nation and then force the country in that direction. He thus set out to do no less than change the whole course of German history. With few assets, foreign or domestic, he was forced to rely on political instinct and a strong sense of which roads in Germany's past had led to its ruin in 1945. He dismissed the *Realpolitik* maxim that there could be no permanent friendships among nations, but only a fleeting coincidence of interests. The Kaiserine and Nazi idea that Germany could be at the same time powerful and isolated, thought Adenauer, was a great illusion that had led the nation to utter disaster. He proposed instead to link Germany with a wider political and economic community. Utilizing Arthur Link's terminology, Hodge assesses this decision as constituting a "higher

realism" about Germany's national interest, represented most clearly by Adenauer's determination to join Germany to the Western alliance. This end could
be advanced so far by economic cooperation; but it could be cemented perma-
nently only by German rearmament within a context of alliance commitments
to European peace and security. Along this road lay more rapid recovery, but
also the chance to make a clean break with Germany's "discredited tradition"
of military independence and diplomatic duplicity. Noting and admiring Adenauer's capacity for finesse and opportunism at the tactical level, Hodge relates
the complex maneuvers undertaken to persuade allies and the German public to
accept this basic realignment. In a few short years this wily Chancellor secured
his own political mastery of Germany, provided a firm defense of its population
within the Western alliance system, and redeemed its sovereignty and commitment to democracy. Hodge judges him to have done so out of a sincere commitment to democracy and security in all of Europe, and shrewd recognition
that the means linking these two moral ends was rapid rearmament, of the very
nation whose armies had just a few years before destroyed Europe's cities and
slaughtered its peoples on a colossal scale.

In "Eduard Shevardnadze and the End of the Soviet System," Paul Marantz
points out that Shevardnadze rose to the top of a political system most noted
for producing "opportunists, careerists, or worse." Yet, he retained a personal
moral code that importantly influenced his politics as he came to play a critical
role in the transformation of the Soviet Union from totalitarian superpower to
broken empire, and then to incipient democracy in Russia. "Everything is rotten," he once told his close friend Mikhail Gorbachev, "it has to be changed."
For Shevardnadze, insists Marantz, this "new thinking" was not merely another
shift in the party line, to be mouthed in public for the sake of career advancement. He seems to have believed it, as evidenced by the fact that three themes
from his thinking entered into his policy-making. First, Shevardnadze saw an
urgent need for the Soviet Union to end its self-imposed isolation from the wider
international community, and show instead a new trustworthiness. Rather than
the two ineluctably antagonistic worlds depicted in Marxist and Soviet dogma,
he recognized the existence of a single world community of civilized states. He
chafed at the Soviet Union's self-destructive refusal to join in the full benefits
of this community in the areas of international law and commerce, and longed
for the real security he thought was to be had by ending the Cold War confrontation with the West. This fed his second concern, a desire to end the arms
race that had so damaged Soviet interests by causing neighbors to grow fearful
of Soviet intentions, and which had drained the economy and impoverished the
population. But Shevardnadze's most important contribution probably came in
his third area of concern, his opposition to the excessive secrecy of the Soviet
policy process, which he worked to end for both principled and pragmatic reasons. In all this Shevardnadze was "a fervent Westernizer." But was he really
motivated by a moral vision, or was he just responding—like some other Soviet
leaders—to changing circumstances? Marantz concludes that Shevardnadze's

values appeared to be both sincerely held and important to the transformation of Soviet society. After all, the opening of the Soviet system at the time and in the way it actually opened and changed was not inevitable, much as the idea of inevitability may appeal to those whose imagination cannot rise above hindsight. Moreover, the policies Shevardnadze supported "went right to the heart of the problem" of declining Soviet power and prestige. But Marantz closes with a caveat: without full access to archives and other primary sources we cannot say with certainty whether Shevardnadze acted from conviction, or rather was merely adept at packaging needed changes in the language of moral purpose.

A lake of ink has been spilled concerning the differences between "realists," in the academic sense, and "idealists." In the 1920s and 1930s a raft of self-declared realist scholars and commentators vehemently rejected what they saw as the excessive legalism and moralism underlying the Versailles settlement. Wilson's foreign policy came in for special condemnation, for its putative ignorance of the realities of the balance of power and the role of force in world affairs, and for what was seen as a foolhardy effort to displace these hard realities with mere moral constructs. Conventional academic wisdom soon had it that world politics was inescapably a stage where players engaged in a raw contest for power. In this nearly unmitigated realm of Darwinian struggle, nations could expect to cling to existence only by embracing *Realpolitik*, or even *Machtpolitik*, assumptions and prescriptions. Several generations of political science students were taught that the fundamental, underlying reality of world affairs is a Hobbesian anarchy wherein the "condition of Man . . . is a war of everyone against everyone."[1] Evidence of interstate concern for a political order cognizant of questions of justice was dismissed, as a facade concealing harder antagonisms. This veneer had to be stripped away, coarser realists said, to reveal the unchanging reality of coercion through the naked exercise of power, unrestrained except by countervailing power and an equilibrium of brutality and fear. This vulgar worldview was served up both as a depiction of reality and as a quasi-philosophical justification for a smug amoralism about foreign policy. Those fond of the pedigree (though not necessarily the content) of the classics then quoted, to justify their amoralism, Thucydides' famous statement of moral and political pessimism: "know that in human reckoning the question of justice only enters where there is equal power to enforce it, and that the powerful exact what they can and the weak grant what they must."[2] Yet the most profound realist writers were always aware of the moral realm, and qualified hard portrayals of world politics at its worst by pointing as well to large-scale social and normative features of the states system, such as international law and organization.[3] They were joined by others, working overtly within a normative framework, who suggested that in the modern era there was at least as much caricature as fact in coarse, amoral images of international affairs.[4]

In short, differences between realists and idealists are not the truly unbridgeable academic divide. It is instead the gulf between humanistic and scientistic (not scientific) approaches to social science that cannot be spanned. The rise

within the social sciences of a crude, yet pervasive, positivism has been profoundly damaging to normative understanding of the meaning of world affairs.
This scientistic prejudice of much contemporary political science threatens to
suffocate the essential humanism that suffused classical political and social science inquiry, including classical realism.[5] Politics is a plain, blunt subject demanding plain, blunt words. Yet too much modern political science writing is
tedious and pretentious, and suffused with arcane methodologies that obscure
the truly important intellectual, practical, and moral purposes of political study.
This results from an extreme narrowness of philosophical vision—or even consciousness—of many of its practitioners, who explicitly and proudly reject any
concern for the normative dimension of world affairs. Among positivists, the
classical notion that philosophical inquiry is a key pathway to understanding
social and political matters is seen as quaint at best, and at worst as threatening
the ongoing project of compiling a "science of politics." Such disregard of the
normative realm is further aggravated by an attendant affliction of ahistoricism,
in which the very nature of history and the craft of historians are miscast. The
former is viewed as a rudimentary compilation of data, while the latter are seen
as data collectors, without much to offer by way of analysis or theory. Only
gestation of historical data under the more rigorous, quantitative methods used
by doctors of politics, it is suggested, can lead to the birth of a "theoretical"
and "scientific" understanding of public events. Above all, any effort to use
moral reasoning to uncover the meaning of political actions is dismissed as
methodologically archaic, as it is supposedly irretrievably subjective and non-
scientific. In addition to their inherent humor, these are profoundly flawed and
damaging (to the truth) conceits; for in neglecting the normative realm positivists
necessarily fail to understand the essential nature of power politics as well.

The contributors to this book include some who might be described as realists,
and others who may be read as idealists. But it is much more important that for
all—as for most people on a near-instinctual basis—it is entirely natural to
explore the ethical dimensions of statecraft, and to consider matters of political
power and interest as imbued with normative content. A shared premise—one
that positivists utterly fail to grasp—is that no adequate understanding of international relations is possible in the absence of normative inquiry. There is also
recognition that moral norms as governing ideas already significantly shape international relations and the context of statecraft in the real world.[6] Thus, a key
purpose this volume serves is to begin to close the artificial chasm that has
opened between realist and idealist scholarly communities, that hitherto have
used different analytical languages and arrived at dissimilar conclusions about
the essential nature of world politics, but are not as far apart in their normative
concerns as is often thought. In this regard, it bears repeating that the most
profound realist thinkers have always clearly understood and noted the importance of normative concerns in international relations, just as shrewder idealists
have not been unaware of the role of power and the interplay of interest in the
affairs of states.[7]

In addition, there is a shared cognizance among the contributors of the special problems of morality and foreign policy decision making. In particular, there is a common appreciation of three considerations: 1) the centrality to normative analysis of historical and situational context; 2) the need to focus not just on the motivations of key decision-makers, but also on the means available to them; and 3) the requirement to assess potential as well as actual consequences of moral choices. Because of this understanding of the complexity of the ethics of statecraft, the contributors to this volume are not unduly shocked by political expedience any more than they are overly impressed by mere moralizing rhetoric. National leaders are neither utterly condemned for their less savory actions, nor raised up in hagiography for their fine words and unsupported declarations of good intentions or noble aims. Instead, they are treated with temperate judgment, derived from the historical, psychological and situational empathy each author brings to bear. The innate human tendency to harshness of judgment of past actions is thereby mitigated by consideration of the extraordinary circumstances and pressures with which these individuals contended, and the sharp limits on their knowledge of others' intentions, and of real outcomes. The result is a set of portraits of key leaders struggling with great moral issues in critical political settings. Many are sympathetic, yet—in the spirit of Oliver Cromwell's famous command to his court painter—they still depict their subjects truly, with "roughnesses, pimples, warts and everything."

NOTES

1. Thomas Hobbes, *Leviathan*, Part I, Chapter IV (1651). That is not to deny that realists had valid targets in that era, and since. It is certainly true that much writing by "world federalists," some normatively inclined international lawyers, and others, has deserved the characterization of naïveté and excessive abstraction cast upon it by realists.

2. Thucydides, "Melian Dialogue," *History of the Peloponesian Wars* (New York: Washington Square Press, 1963), p. 181.

3. For example, see Hedley Bull's influential and important treatise, *The Anarchical Society* (London: Macmillan, 1977); and Hans J. Morgenthau, *Politics Among Nations: The Struggle for Power and Peace*, 6th ed. (New York: Alfred A. Knopf, 1985).

4. See the important corrective to neo-realism's overstatement of the idea and the reality of international anarchy represented by Terry Nardin and David R. Mapel, eds., *Traditions of International Ethics*, Cambridge Studies in International Relations #17 (Cambridge: Cambridge University Press, 1992).

5. This contrast emerges clearly in any comparison of the flexible insights of humanistic, "realist" writers such as Hedley Bull or Martin Wight, with the arid models of the state system offered up by a positivist "neo-realist" like Kenneth Waltz.

6. Among recent works on these themes the most ambitious in its normative conclusions is Dorothy V. Jones, *Code of Peace: Ethics and Security in the World of the Warlord States* (Chicago: University of Chicago Press, 1991). Also see Louis Henkin, et al. *Right vs. Might: International Law and the Use of Force* (New York: Council on Foreign Relations, 1991); and idem, *How Nations Behave: Law and Foreign Policy* (New

York: Council on Foreign Relations, 1968; 1979). A more skeptical, though still sympathetic, view of the evolution of international norms is Cathal J. Nolan, "The United States, Moral Norms and Governing Ideas in World Politics," *Ethics and International Affairs*, Vol. 7 (1993), pp. 223–39; and idem, *Principled Diplomacy: Security and Rights in U.S. Foreign Policy* (Westport, CT: Greenwood, 1993), passim.

7. For instance, see Morgenthau's discussion of the moral basis of the balance of power in *Politics Among Nations*, pp. 233–40. An important study of moral content in modern realist thought is Joel H. Rosenthal, *Righteous Realists: Political Realism, Responsible Power, and American Culture in the Nuclear Age* (Baton Rouge: Louisiana State University Press, 1991).

I

THE SETTING

CHAPTER 2

The Situational Ethics of Statecraft

Robert H. Jackson

ETHICS AND SKEPTICS

Anyone who writes on the ethics of statecraft immediately meets with skepticism on the part of those international relations scholars who see only a contradiction in that expression. For them the conduct of foreign or military policy is governed by self-interest and expediency and not by morality; it is an instrumental and not a normative subject: power politics. A study that is undertaken without skepticism about the ethical limits of international relations should raise doubt: foreign policy is shot through with instrumental practices. Yet such skepticism would be more solidly based and thus more realistic if the ethics of statecraft were understood not as an absolute morality divorced from possibility and necessity but, rather, as a situational ethics in which both circumstances and judgment have an extremely important place. The main thrust of my argument is not to respond directly to such skepticism—that would require a far lengthier chapter. My aim is more limited: to outline the normative criteria involved in the ethics of statecraft. Suppose that a state leader wanted to act responsibly in foreign or military policy: what normative considerations would he or she have to take into account?

Ethics is usually considered to be a philosophical subject—moral philosophy—to which there are various well-known approaches: the virtues, natural law, rights-based theories, utilitarianism, and communitarianism, among others. This chapter makes no attempt to canvass these approaches—except for a brief

Some arguments in this chapter originated in conversations with Terry Kersch. I also wish to acknowledge the financial support of the Social Sciences and Humanities Research Council of Canada.

discussion of the political virtues. The ethics of statecraft is an applied ethics: the normative criteria that apply to state leaders in their conduct of foreign policy.[1] It is an intermediate subject located between the general preoccupations of moral philosophers and the specific concerns of policy analysts and current affairs commentators.

The task of applied ethics is not to spell out a general theory of international ethics; nor is it to provide informed commentary on international events. The task is to bring ethical questions into contact with real situations, for it is with that that state leaders must deal. Statesmen and stateswomen must do that to justify their actions to others and to themselves, which is an inescapable requirement of being in their position; scholars must do it to understand statesmen's actions and locate statecraft on the map of human conduct. In that sense the ethics of statecraft is a subject of history and political science.

DIMENSIONS OF RESPONSIBLE STATECRAFT

The ethics of statecraft is fundamentally about hard choices confronted by statesmen and stateswomen who are obliged to operate in a world over which they exercise limited control at the best of times. But it is a world in which they are still responsible for whatever they do or fail to do. Faced with the fratricide in Bosnia what should the President of the United States or the leaders of the European Union do?[2] There is no easy or simple answer. The question arises for those particular leaders, more than others, because they are in a better position to do something, and even if they decide to do nothing they are affecting the situation by their inaction. They cannot escape from that responsibility.

Hard choices are decisions that cannot be avoided, and involve not merely economic or political costs but also moral liabilities. One is reminded here of Charles de Gaulle's definition of a state leader "as somebody who takes risks, including moral risks."[3] De Gaulle may have been thinking of his own role in organizing the Free French forces in opposition to the Vichy collaborationist government in France during the Second World War, an act which risked dividing the French nation. A recent example of what de Gaulle surely had in mind is the 1993 decision of Israeli Prime Minister Yitzhak Rabin and PLO leader Yassir Arafat to take, after decades of bitter and bloody conflict, the very high risk of signing an accord and trusting the other to embark in good faith on a course of reconciliation between the Israeli and Palestinian peoples. Both leaders made this decision despite the real risk of a loss of support in their own political constituencies and, indeed, a fatal division of them. This extraordinary event cannot begin to be captured by a purely instrumental method of analysis, such as regarding it merely as a high stakes game of poker.[4]

We arrive at a fundamental problem of normative international relations theory which goes right back to its beginnings: what moral qualities should a state leader possess? Most students of international ethics probably recognize that this ancient question is at the heart of their subject. To understand the ethics of statecraft it is necessary to imagine what it must be like to be in the shoes of statesmen and stateswomen at the time choices are made. To do that is to adopt what is essentially an historical approach.[5] Only in that way can we realistically hope to comprehend the normative pressures on state leaders and thereby do justice to their choices. This requires not only knowledge of their circumstances but also empathy with them. Since scholars usually cannot be present when decisions are made, arguably the next best thing is to study past or recent decisions with reference to the historical or contemporary evidence.

One of the foregoing approaches is particularly relevant to the evaluation of the normative predicaments in which state leaders often find themselves: the virtues, and specifically civic or political virtue.[6] When we judge the conduct of state leaders with reference to the virtues, we are not judging it by a rule or a consequence. Instead, we are judging it in relation to what could reasonably be expected of a person of sound mind and good character in the circumstances. For example, we expect leaders to base their policies on correct information and to conduct them with due care and attention to the situation at hand: in short, we expect them to use prudential ethics. This assumes that leaders are responsible agents. In a famous essay Max Weber identified politics in its deepest meaning with a demanding "ethic of responsibility": a struggle that involved "relentlessness in viewing the realities of life, and the ability to face such realities and to measure up to them . . . [the politician] then acts by following an ethic of responsibility and somewhere he reaches the point where he says: 'Here I stand; I can do no other.' "[7] Even if this sounds overly dramatic and seems to echo the voice of Martin Luther, it would still be hard to find a better portrayal of the distinctive virtues involved in statecraft, which is by any standard a tough game.[8]

Perhaps a few caveats are necessary to avoid any misunderstanding about the purpose of this chapter. The applied ethics of statecraft, as I conceive of it, is not about giving advice to national leaders concerning the right thing to do in the circumstances. Academics usually do not have sufficient detailed knowledge of the situation to give sound practical advice—certainly I possess no such information. Nor is it about judging the actions of leaders after the event, knowing how it turned out: that privileged information is unavailable at the time decisions must be made, which is part of the moral risk involved. The academic equivalent of "Monday morning quarterbacking" is a poor foundation for international ethics. The job of the political scientist is to make sense of statecraft as a form of human conduct: to chart the special normative territory in which national leaders are obliged to operate when conducting foreign policy. This involves trying to capture in theoretical rather than practical terms what it must be like to carry on responsibly in a world of considerable normative complexity, ambiguity and uncertainty.

The ethics of statecraft, as Weber I think rightly claims, is fundamentally an ethics of responsibility: it concerns the distinctive responsibilities of persons who occupy high offices of state.[9] By "responsibilities" I mean the legal and moral duties of state leaders in exercising the powers of their offices in the conduct of foreign policy: that is, the public decisions and actions for which they are answerable. State leaders are commonly assumed to have such responsibilities, and in democracies they are routinely and vigorously criticized whenever they fail to live up to them. Politics and even international politics is never represented in popular discourse as a purely instrumental activity divorced from normative concerns. On the contrary, such concerns are a conspicuous feature of political life. Never-ending media reports routinely track the important public decisions and actions of national leaders on a daily basis, and political commentaries subject them to continuous and often strenuous appraisal which inevitably invokes standards of conduct that such leaders are expected to observe. Responding to the public's moral concerns, which fluctuate in reaction to the latest television images from around the world, is a trying responsibility of state leaders in a democracy.

The distinctive responsibilities of state leaders, for Max Weber, derive from their control of the state's monopoly of legitimate force: with power comes responsibility. Since national leaders have access to greater power and certainly greater armed force than anyone else, they also carry heavier responsibilities, arguably the heaviest responsibilities of anyone. However, even if it is clear that in managing such power the responsibilities of statesmen and stateswomen at the present time begin at home, it is not obvious where they end. Are they confined within the boundaries of their own countries or do they extend to other countries and other people beyond those boundaries? Are sovereign states freestanding moral and legal communities—what classical theorists refer to as "perfect associations"—or are they part of a more extensive community of states or community of humankind? When national leaders embark on war are they responsible only to their own people, or to other people as well, such as their adversaries or third parties affected by their military actions?

There are basically two conflicting approaches to these questions which disclose a rift valley that runs through the ethics of statecraft. I can only summarize them in passing. The first approach is usually referred to as realism: the doctrine that state leaders are accountable only to their own people, whose rights they must respect, interests they must defend, and welfare they must promote.[10] International relations is an instrumental realm in which statecraft is dictated by considerations and calculations of national self-interest. For classical realists there is little or no room within a national leader's responsibilities for concerns about the rights, legitimate interests, and welfare of foreign countries and populations; how one deals with them is always a question of one's own national interest.

The second approach, which embodies two distinct doctrines, does provide for such responsibilities. One branch, what I shall refer to as legalism, assumes the existence of a society of states.[11] Legalism is particularly apt for grasping the responsibilities of state leaders to one another and to the state system as a whole. Legalism obviously does not reject the sovereign state; it only rejects the claim that sovereignty signifies only independence and internal authority without any external rights and duties. It emphasizes, to the contrary, that sovereignty is a shared international institution and not merely a differentiating marker of separate states: for example, international boundaries are a joint institution which always define the limits of the territorial jurisdiction of more than one state. Sovereignty is expressed not only by the right to legislate within a state jurisdiction, but also by the right to sign treaties, to lawfully make war, to conduct diplomatic relations, and to engage in other legal and legitimate transactions with other sovereign states.

Another branch, what I shall refer to as humanism, assumes the existence of a community of humankind.[12] This is a universal or cosmopolitan ethics in which respect for human beings everywhere is an overriding normative consideration in foreign policy. If this approach is taken to its logical conclusion, states lose their normative autonomy and are reduced to being merely instrumentalities for protecting human rights and providing for human welfare: political machinery devoid of normative value. An exclusively humanist world would be a world without any other fundamental communities, including nation-states—a visionary state of affairs that was considered to be far-fetched even by Immanuel Kant, arguably the greatest humanist theorist of modern times.[13] Yet even though sovereign states remain profoundly important, universal human rights are nowadays enshrined in international law, promoted by diplomacy, and voiced by public opinion, and at least to that extent humanism captures a distinct reality of contemporary world politics.

There is an academic tendency, among international relations scholars at the present time, to take a realist or legalist or humanist or some other exclusive approach to the ethics of statecraft. That may very well be necessary to come up with a coherent philosophy of international ethics; different theories of international relations may also be usefully pigeonholed on that basis. But it is gravely misleading to adopt any such one-dimensional approach to the applied ethics of statecraft: state leaders necessarily find themselves in a pluralist world in which they are pushed and pulled in different directions by diverging and even conflicting normative considerations. In their conduct of foreign policy they must operate at the intersections of different norms. In so doing they cannot be fully responsible agents if they base their decisions on realist or legalist or humanist considerations (or any other norms) to the exclusion of all the rest; they must pay respect to each one at the appropriate time and place. It is the task of scholars who are interested in the moral conduct of national leaders to capture that contradictory normative reality which, to my mind, should be the main focus of applied ethical studies in international relations.

THE NORMS OF WAR

The foregoing doctrines are easy enough to outline in abstract terms as normative principles of modern statecraft. The real challenge is to explore and hopefully fathom the significance and efficacy of these different and sometimes conflicting norms in concrete international practice. Because all of these norms are nowadays more than merely academic, this is an intelligible, if neglected, political science research project. These norms are historic actualities, normative considerations that leaders are expected to observe when engaging in foreign policy. I am not saying that they are always respected; I am only saying that they exist as operative international standards which can be invoked when judging the conduct of state leaders.

This historical actuality is evident in the laws of war, which are generally acknowledged standards of conduct even though they continue to be violated—sometimes with impunity, as in the Iraqi invasion of Kuwait or the fratricidal war in Bosnia. But we can intelligibly condemn the belligerents in those conflicts only because there are well-founded norms for making such judgments. The laws of war contain prohibitions against—among other things—armed invasion and occupation of foreign territory without cause, and against the intentional military targeting of civilians. The underlying assumption of such norms is roughly as follows: state leaders and soldiers make choices even when at war; in making those choices they know what is justified conduct and what is not; they can be expected to do the right thing; and they know that if they fail to do it they can be condemned and—if possible—punished. That punishment admittedly is very difficult to carry out in practice—but this points to the structural problem of law enforcement in international affairs, which is more difficult to dispense than in most domestic political systems.

Today aggression is the capital crime of international relations and self-defense is the cardinal justification for waging war. A war of aggression and a war of self-defense are military actions which unavoidably entail norms: the violation of a rule and the invocation of a rule. Norms can be invoked either to condemn or to justify military actions, as they were in the case of Iraq's invasion and occupation of Kuwait on August 2, 1990. The UN Security Council, in a succession of major resolutions, the first of which (Resolution 660) was adopted without a dissenting vote on the day of the invasion, characterized the action as "a breach of international peace and security," demanded "that Iraq withdraw immediately and unconditionally all its forces," and went on to justify its own actions against Iraq entirely by reference to international law and specifically Chapter VII of the UN Charter. Not only those many states that condemned the action but also those few that excused it always made reference to what were claimed to be the pertinent and valid international norms which governed such actions.[14] No public authority of which I am aware merely said "Iraq really landed a knockout blow against Kuwait!" or more anxiously, "How does this affect our interests and what, if anything, should we do about it?" and left it at that. Hedley Bull once characterized war as "an inherently normative phenomenon."[15] That is certainly how the Gulf War was portrayed in governmental and popular discourse at the time.

The language of war is of course profoundly instrumental, for it involves expedient human efforts to attack others with armed force or to defend against such attacks. But war is also a normative activity in very significant part— unavoidably so because of the human suffering it causes. And necessarily so, for if armed conflict were merely an instrumental transaction between belliger- ents we could not coherently condemn inhumane acts of war, such as the inten- tional targeting of civilians in the siege of Sarajevo and other Bosnian cities and towns. All we could intelligibly comment on would be the cleverness or foolishness of such actions, the misfortune of noncombatants caught in the con- flict, and any other instrumental consequences that figured in the combat or flowed from it. Yet public commentary on the Bosnian war was not confined to this purely instrumental vocabulary; it was overtly and thoroughly normative from the beginning. Unless we consider that commentary to be meaningless we are obliged to assume that there are norms involved in war.

The complete disregard of those norms, indeed the contempt in which they were held by virtually all the belligerents, is the source of the dismay and revulsion that most observers felt about the conflicts in the former Yugoslavia. There is no other way to make sense of such reactions except to regard them as irrational or phony—which is the assessment one would have to make if one adhered to the conviction that war is a purely instrumental activity. The refer- ence against which public reactions to the bombardment of Sarajevo are com- pletely intelligible is the standard of military conduct embodied in the Geneva Conventions which forbids the intentional targeting of civilians. I do not believe that anyone who is familiar with particular armed conflicts, such as the Gulf War or the war in Bosnia, can reasonably deny that they always provoke a normative response. Such responses presuppose what have traditionally been referred to as "civilized" standards of conduct.

What can still be doubted, however, is the efficacy of those standards: un- fortunately they are all too often observed only in the breach. Or they are en- forced inconsistently or unequally, thus implying a double standard. The skeptic would perhaps point to the recent wars in the Gulf and Bosnia to clinch the argument: why were aggression and human rights violations punished by force in the former case but not in the latter? I would argue that these cases really underline the morally vexing character of the ethics of statecraft and the nec- essarily central place in it of circumstance and judgment. The ethics of statecraft is fundamentally a situational ethics, and these two cases are significantly dif- ferent.

THE SITUATIONAL ETHICS OF STATECRAFT

Scholars can second-guess the normative choices of state leaders at the time, or judge them after the event knowing how they turned out. But that is not the same as having to make the choices themselves. Probably the best scholars can do in that regard is try to grasp the situations of the people involved: to imagine what it must be like to be in the shoes of a president or a prime minister at the time that decisions were confronted and taken. In doing this we are doing justice to the people we are studying. That might be a preliminary definition of the ethics of scholarship. About the last thing scholars should do is look down upon national leaders from some Olympian height of abstract moral philosophy. For by overlooking the specific circumstances that affect leaders' decisions, in all likelihood scholars will only end up misconstruing those decisions and perhaps deriding them as well. But neither should scholars engage in what Herbert Butterfield once referred to as "official history": the tendency to glorify the decisions and actions of those in power.[16] That debases scholarship by transforming it into hagiography. Max Weber's famous lecture on "Politics as a Vocation" is a good antidote for both of these academic disorders.[17]

The key to understanding the applied ethics of statecraft is the correct appreciation of circumstances. Circumstances are by definition confining considerations, rather than enabling or accommodating ones, that limit what one is able to do. They are actualities which must be taken into account in making or carrying out a decision—if one hopes to be successful. In conventional legal thought, responsibility is always affected by circumstances, and circumstances are usually a mitigating factor in determining responsibility. Thus, not only would it be foolish to ignore the circumstances, it would be irresponsible. By overlooking the specific circumstances in which state leaders find themselves, in all likelihood scholars will only end up misconstruing leaders' decisions and perhaps misrepresenting them as well. Circumstances are not fixed, but shift and change so that at one time or place an opportunity for action might arise which might not exist at another. Here is the voice of Edmund Burke who was far closer to the centers of power than most academics:

A statesman differs from a professor in a university; the latter has only the general view of society; the former, the statesman, has a number of circumstances to combine with those general ideas, and to take into his consideration. Circumstances are infinite, and infinitely combined; they are variable and transient. . . . A statesman, never losing sight of principles, is to be guided by circumstances; and, judging contrary to the exigencies of the moment, he may ruin his country forever.[18]

Important decisions involving foreign policy are always affected by the circumstances in which they are made. Consider, for example, President Harry Truman's fateful decision in August 1945 to drop nuclear bombs on Hiroshima and Nagasaki. Many have subsequently condemned that decision as immoral— usually on the humanist grounds that it deliberately targeted civilians. But any moral appraisal would only be convincing if it took into account Truman's responsibilities in the circumstances at the time—which was the climax of a world war in which the United States was a victim of Japanese aggression at Pearl Harbor and had for several years fought a series of fierce island-hopping campaigns, at great sacrifice in American lives, to drive Japanese forces back across the Pacific. We would have to consider the choice Truman faced at that time: whether to use the bomb and hopefully bring the war to a speedy and favorable conclusion by killing or maiming an unknown but probably very large number of Japanese civilians, or to order an invasion of Japan which would almost certainly result in additional heavy losses to American troops and probably even higher casualties to Japanese civilians. We should also remember that he had only two nuclear bombs at his disposal and there was no guarantee that they would explode.

Truman's moral responsibility, as seen from the perspective of situational ethics, was to determine which military measures would bring victory and the prospect of future world peace with the least additional suffering. If his decision stands condemned it must not have been the best choice in the circumstances— perhaps that would have been a harmless demonstration of one bomb in the hope of provoking Japanese leaders to capitulate. Even if that stratagem failed, none of the bomb's strategic advantages would have been lost and the one bomb remaining could still be deployed in the hope of ending the war then and there. But the Japanese leaders would now bear the responsibility. Of course there may be other circumstances which affected Truman's decision, and this brief discussion assumes that both bombs would explode. The point is simply that his decision cannot be adequately understood or appraised without taking the circumstances into account.

In approaching and making decisions, national leaders could perhaps fail to recognize their circumstances or could misunderstand them; or they could ignore them even if they were aware of them. But they could not escape from them because a circumstance is, by definition, a surrounding and impinging state of affairs that we cannot control and bend to our will, but something in which we are entangled nonetheless. Since circumstances are always particular, by definition, there can be no fixed and permanent ethical precepts governing such decisions. For if decision-makers are reasonable and informed of the situation in which they find themselves, their decisions must change as circumstances change. There can only be the requirement that due account be taken of all the relevant circumstances before making a decision. That would be a requirement of responsible statecraft. Thus, for example, it might be possible and desirable to conduct armed humanitarian intervention in some countries, but not in others, owing to differences in circumstances: a responsible leader might authorize armed humanitarianism in postwar Iraq but refuse to take the same action in Bosnia on the prudential grounds that the latter case involved unacceptable risks to the personnel of the intervening power.[19]

Since the decisions and actions of state leaders are always made in concrete circumstances of time and of place, scholars who seek to understand the ethics of statecraft are obliged to adopt some version of situational ethics. This is not the ethics of the ideal choice or the best choice or even the optimal or most profitable or least costly choice. Rather, it is the ethics of the best choice under the circumstances, or perhaps the least bad choice if, in the circumstances prevailing at the time, all choices are lamentable to some degree—perhaps the situation of Truman in 1945. That, recalling Weber, is the decision that we feel bound to make, however reluctantly, after canvassing the options available, taking into account as best we can their foreseeable consequences, taking stock of the responsibilities of our office as we understand them, and being honest with ourselves and forthright with others.[20] Arguably the best a responsible leader could hope from such a decision is not that its consequences will prove his or her sagacity; it is that he or she will be able to live in clear conscience with the consequences, whatever they turn out to be. Arnold Wolfers identifies "the best moral choice that circumstances permit" as the distinctive ethics of statecraft: "nonperfectionist ethics."[21] That is as good a definition of the subject as I have been able to find.

Wolfer's concept of nonperfectionist ethics supplies a strategic vista for studying normative choices in international relations, but it perhaps still understates a crucial element: the actors and their conduct. For once we bring circumstances into the picture we must also bring actors equally into that picture: we are only interested in circumstances for the light they shed on human conduct. What can we reasonably expect of statesmen and stateswomen in the circumstances of foreign affairs in which they find themselves? We can only answer this question if we have some realistic and reasonable way of judging their conduct.

As indicated, I am convinced that the best way is by returning to the classical idea of the virtues. By the "virtues" I refer to the mental dispositions and disciplines that are required to make the best choice that circumstances permit, or the least bad choice if all choices are adverse to some degree, which is not uncommon in international relations. To act virtuously in the circumstances is to stick to one's post and discharge one's duty despite the difficulties and risks involved and, thus, despite the temptation to do otherwise. One definition of political virtue is the ability to steady down, to ignore the surrounding clamor, to forbear from acting according to impulse or passion or temptation, and to carefully determine the best available course of action. And, having done that, to act or refuse to act, as the case may be.

This involves "character": the strength of will, reasoning power, and other mental dispositions and disciplines to do what is morally required in the circumstances. One might be tempted to say that President John F. Kennedy demonstrated character in facing down the Soviets during the Cuban Missile Crisis in 1962, but one might equally argue that in backing down and doing what obviously was the right thing at the time, it was perhaps the Soviet leader, Nikita Khrushchev, who was in the more difficult situation and demonstrated the greater character—not overlooking for a moment that he was responsible for the crisis in the first place. The Cuban Missile Crisis could, of course, be read instrumentally as a high stakes poker game: but that reading would completely fail to capture the huge moral risks and awesome burden of responsibility of the key players involved.

In referring to character I am not here talking about "personality": that is a behavioral propensity and subjective identity of particular individuals, and not a conduct requirement of anyone in the same circumstances. Whatever may be the personality of a particular leader we must expect the same standard of conduct, the same display of character, in the same situation. Otherwise we are adrift in an ocean of relativism. Character is not personality; the second is a psychological category, but the first is a moral category. When we study somebody's character we are not merely studying his or her propensities to act; we are studying his or her disposition and discipline in behaving (or endeavoring to behave) in accordance with standards of conduct: to do the right thing in the circumstances. The ethics of statecraft is not about describing or explaining the personal behavior of particular state leaders; it is about construing their public actions with reference to the standards of conduct which apply to them. A personality is something we all have, but character is something we do not always demonstrate. Character is a moral faculty which stems from the ever present possibility of human shortcomings and failings.

Just as the ethics of statecraft is a special branch of applied ethics, so also are the political virtues a specialized area of the virtues which spring from the unique position and predicaments of national leaders. Because presidents, prime ministers and other high public officials hold the fate of so many people in their hands and at the same time have at their disposal greater destructive power than anyone else, a necessary political virtue is undoubtedly prudence, which has been called "the center of gravity" around which the entire scheme turns.[22] Both Aristotle and Aquinas placed prudence at the center of political ethics. Burke regarded prudence as a general virtue but in politics as "the first of virtues."[23] It is important to emphasize that I am not here referring to instrumental or self-regarding prudence—where leaders are expediently thinking only of themselves or their regimes. Rather, I refer to normative or other-regarding prudence—where the other is anyone whose rights, interests and welfare depend upon the decisions and actions of leaders.[24] Prudence in this meaning is clearly a moral concept and not an instrumental one.

Prudence is disclosed by forethought and deliberation before an important decision or action is taken: careful preparation and attention to the situation in its concreteness, and insight into its dangers and potentialities. Thus lack of foresight, miscalculation, and recklessness are among the greatest political vices because they needlessly put at risk others who rely or depend upon us. Saddam Hussein was justifiably condemned for subjecting his soldiers and the civilian population of Iraq to unnecessary peril and suffering in not backing down when the UN Security Council (Resolution 678) presented him with "one final opportunity" to vacate Kuwait, or face war with the Coalition powers. The moral grounds for such condemnation are the dictates of prudence in statecraft. Prudential ethics dictate wariness, precaution and preparation before any momentous actions are taken from which it is difficult to turn back. State leaders cannot throw caution to the wind, according to Burke, even or perhaps especially at moments of great general enthusiasm for action: "to dare to be fearful, when all about you are full of presumption and confidence, and when those who are bold at the hazard of others would push your caution and disaffection, is to show a mind prepared for its trial."[25]

Although prudence is at the center of international ethics, it is by no means the sole political virtue. If prudence is singled out to the exclusion of other virtues, as realist theorists are prone to do, the hard choices which characterize the ethics of statecraft are obscured. There is a constellation of political virtues which throw light on the conduct of state leaders in different circumstances. One could readily identify honor, good faith, loyalty, resolve, courage, vision, compassion, and justice as having important places in that constellation. We do not expect leaders only to be prudent; we also expect them to be honorable, courageous, compassionate, and just.[26] The importance of any virtue would depend, in part, on the situation being confronted. Winston Churchill used the following as a motto for his history of the Second World War: "In war: resolution; in defeat: defiance; in victory: magnanimity; in peace: goodwill."[27] The people who are needed as leaders during times of war obviously are not the same as those required during times of peace because the circumstances are different, indeed very different. One could say the same about the virtues in war: if we are not prepared to struggle long and hard, our chances of succeeding or even surviving obviously will be reduced and will in all likelihood be put in jeopardy. But the point is not to enumerate the political virtues or to investigate how they are acquired or exercised—that would call for another chapter. The point is merely to emphasize that when we begin to view statecraft from the angle of situational ethics we are led to this approach.

We expect statesmen and stateswomen to know not only when it is necessary to be cautious and when to be bold, but also when it is necessary to be compassionate and the appropriate time and occasion to demonstrate other virtues. How they know this is of course a matter of good character and sound mind but, beyond that, it is fundamentally a matter of their experience in exercising the powers of the state. From experience comes judgment, which involves knowing how to decide such things, knowing what is the right thing to do under the circumstances—undoubtedly the most important practical moral faculty of statecraft.

Any light that the scholar can throw on the subject of judgment is of course always limited, because judgment in any role is a faculty which derives very largely from experience in that position. Although we can profit from the experience of others there is a definite limit to the extrapolations we can make from such vicarious learning. Experience ultimately is personal: something which somebody acquires from practice, but not something which somebody else can fully possess without having a comparable experience. The chef can write a cookbook which attempts to distill his or her experience of cooking, but somebody else cannot become a chef merely by reading that book because the book is necessarily only an abridgement of the chef's concrete knowledge, a large portion of which must remain inarticulate.[28] We can derive insights about statecraft from the memoirs of Churchill or de Gaulle, but we cannot become

great state leaders ourselves simply by reading about their trials and achievements. Here we come up against the limits of scholarship in seeking to understand statecraft.

Scholars can still grasp the central place of judgment in international ethics.
We can be aware of the normative considerations and constraints that were
involved in the particular case and the circumstances in which the decision was
made. Admittedly that is not the same as being able to determine the right course
of action in theory or in advance. A political philosopher might say that it is all
very well to appreciate that ethical decisions in international relations are normatively complicated and often involve choosing between rival normative considerations. But how does one choose? What is the basis of choice? The
philosopher is looking for some overruling consideration: perhaps the principle
of fairness, perhaps the principle of utility, perhaps reciprocity, or perhaps dis-
tributive justice. That is what a coherent moral philosophy requires. But it is
not what an applied ethics can require because, in practice, it is impossible to
answer such questions in the abstract or in advance: one can only answer them
in the actual event. That is a fundamental difference between moral philosophy
and applied ethics: the latter is always an empirical inquiry.

CONCLUSION

The foregoing discussion underlines an important and perhaps even a defining
characteristic of the ethics of statecraft: it resembles politics in some fundamental respects. Indeed, it is I think best understood as the morality of international
politics. The best choice in the circumstances is the moral equivalent of the art
of the possible: the ethics of imperfection.[29] I have also suggested that we inhabit
a political world that is characterized by normative pluralism, which means that
statesmen and stateswomen inevitably face difficult choices because they stand
at the intersections of competing, diverging and—in some cases—even conflicting norms. That pluralism is the basic normative characteristic of international
relations.

But how could there be international ethics in such a pluralistic world—i.e.,
international standards of conduct? I believe the answer is associated with the
moral outlook of liberalism. In that regard, the ethics of statecraft is closely
related to the liberal virtues, of which the ability to deal responsibly with diversity is perhaps the foremost virtue. That discipline has been captured very
nicely by Stephen Macedo: "The liberal ideal will not appeal to those who seek
a final, definitive answer to the great question of how to live. . . . Liberalism
imposes burdens of choice on individuals in a pluralistic milieu without the
assurance of complete and final right answers to the question of how to live."[30]
What is true of a liberal society is, if anything, even truer of international relations, which is the ultimately pluralistic world. Because of the diversity of
human values around the world there can be no definitive answers about how
to live in such a normative sphere. There can only be a general recognition of

such diversity and respect for it. The virtuous national leader is anyone who, in having to act internationally, always resolutely strives to observe that fundamental rule. If we had to locate the heart of international ethics perhaps this is where we would find it.

NOTES

1. It also applies to domestic policy, but that raises a different set of normative questions.

2. The full name is, of course, Bosnia-Hercegovina.

3. Quoted by Stanley Hoffmann, *Duties Beyond Borders* (Syracuse, NY: Syracuse University Press, 1981), p. 18.

4. The analogy of statecraft with a poker game is misleading insofar as poker is governed by noninstrumental rules which must be observed by everyone, without exception, for the game to be played at all, as well as by instrumental stratagems which constitute winning play. See the discussion in Chapter 2. For an elaboration of this fundamental distinction see M. Oakeshott, "The Rule of Law," *On History and Other Essays* (Oxford: Blackwell, 1983), pp. 119–65.

5. In adopting this perspective I have been strongly influenced by R.G. Collingwood, *The Idea of History* (New York: Oxford University Press, 1956), Part V.

6. For a recent analysis of statecraft in these terms see Cornelia Navari, "English Machiavellism" (Unpublished paper presented at the Seminar on International Political Theory at the London School of Economics and Political Science, 10 December, 1993).

7. Max Weber, "Politics as a Vocation," in H.H. Gerth and C. Wright Mills, eds., *From Max Weber: Essays in Sociology* (New York: Oxford University Press, 1958), pp. 120–28.

8. Max Weber was a Lutheran.

9. For an important recent study see Daniel Warner, *An Ethic of Responsibility in International Relations* (Boulder: Lynn Reiner, 1991).

10. I refer here only to classical realism, which is a normative theory of international relations; I do not refer to contemporary neorealism, which tries to avoid ethical questions.

11. Martin Wight uses the term "rationalism" to refer to the same idea. See G. Wight and B. Porter, eds., *International Theory: The Three Traditions* (London: Leicester University Press, 1991). Max Weber uses the term "legality" to describe the political state in which the ethic of responsibility prevails. See *From Max Weber*, pp. 79ff.

12. Martin Wight uses "revolutionism" to capture this idea. Many scholars, following Kant, prefer "cosmopolitanism." See his "Idea for a Universal History with a Cosmopolitan Purpose," in Hans Reiss, ed., *Kant's Political Writings* (Cambridge: Cambridge University Press, 1977), pp. 41–53.

13. See "Perpetual Peace: A Philosophical Sketch," reprinted in Reiss, *Kant's Political Writings*, pp. 93–130.

14. See the numerous examples recorded in M. Weller, ed., *Iraq and Kuwait: The Hostilities and Their Aftermath* (Cambridge: Grotius Publications, 1993).

15. Hedley Bull, "Recovering the Just War for Political Theory," *World Politics*, Vol. 31 (1979).

16. Herbert Butterfield, "Official History: Its Pitfalls and Criteria," *History and Human Relations* (London: Collins, 1951), pp. 182–224.

17. "Politics as a Vocation," in Gerth and Mills, eds., *From Max Weber: Essays in Sociology*, pp. 77–128.

18. Quoted by Albert R. Coll, "Normative Prudence as a Tradition of Statecraft," *Ethics and International Affairs*, Vol. 5 (1991), p. 45.

19. I have discussed this case, and other cases, at greater length in "Armed Humanitarianism," *International Journal*, Vol. XLVIII (Autumn 1993), pp. 579–606.

20. This standard has also been identified by Michael Oakeshott as the most appropriate one for appraising human conduct in politics. See *Rationalism in Politics and Other Essays* (New and Expanded Edition) (Indianapolis: Liberty Press, 1991).

21. Arnold Wolfers, "Statesmanship and Moral Choice," in *Discord and Collaboration* (Baltimore: Johns Hopkins University Press, 1965), p. 51. Stanley Hoffmann adopts a similar approach in *Duties Beyond Borders*.

22. Ronald Beiner, "The Moral Vocabulary of Liberalism," in J.W. Chapman and W.A. Galston (eds.), *Virtue: Nomos XXXIV* (New York: New York University Press, 1992), p. 153.

23. Quoted by L.I. Bredvold and R.G. Ross, eds., *The Philosophy of Edmund Burke* (Ann Arbor: University of Michigan Press, 1967), p. 38.

24. See Coll, "Normative Prudence as a Tradition of Statecraft."

25. Quoted by Bredvold and Ross, *The Philosophy of Edmund Burke*, p. 38.

26. For a probing discussion of the role of "honor" see Geoffrey Best, *Honour Among Men and Nations* (Toronto: University of Toronto Press, 1982).

27. Winston S. Churchill, *The Second World War: Triumph and Tragedy* (Boston: Houghton Mifflin, 1953), p. vii.

28. This distinction between the possession of political experience and the academic recognition of its significance is a huge and complicated subject into which I cannot digress. For an extended discussion see Oakeshott, *Rationalism in Politics and Other Essays*.

29. The leading commentator on human imperfection in politics is Burke. See, especially, "Letters on a Regicide Peace," in F.W. Raffety, ed., *The Works of Edmund Burke*, Vol. VI (London: Oxford University Press, 1928).

30. See Stephen Macedo, *Liberal Virtues* (Oxford: Clarendon Press, 1991), Ch. 7.

II

WAR

"Bodyguard of Lies": Franklin D. Roosevelt and Defensible Deceit in World War II

Cathal J. Nolan

Truly, to tell lies is not honorable. But when the truth entails tremendous ruin, to speak dishonorably is pardonable.
—Sophocles, *Cruesa* (fragment)

Truth . . . never comes into the world but like a bastard.
—John Milton (1643)

In war, the truth must be protected by a bodyguard of lies.
—Winston Churchill (attributed)

This chapter sets out to accomplish a difficult task: to defend lying, on occasion, by a democratic government. This proposition is unpleasant, which is why I have stated it so baldly; to do less would be to dissemble, and thereby defeat the purpose of the exercise. Most of us feel, I assume, a certain political—if not natural—squeamishness at any suggestion that lying in public affairs is defensible, especially in a democracy. Beyond that shared disquiet I suspect that this proposal is more difficult for Americans to accept than it is for some other, perhaps more cynical (or is it just more tory?), peoples. That is so not only because of a rooted, democratic political culture, but due to the experiences of the Vietnam War and Watergate. Those events left an often painfully naïve generation seared with cynicism, by the supposed "revelation" that presidents lie. A growing sense of the dangers of presidential deceit was reinforced for

I am grateful to Professor Emeritus Edward M. Bennett, of Washington State University, for his insightful comments on an earlier draft of this chapter.

many in the 1980s, by what were widely seen among foreign policy analysts as exaggerated reasons for intervention in the Caribbean and in Central America, and by the Iran-Contra affair. Other generations under other circumstances have been more tolerant of deceit, most notably during wartime. Prior to Vietnam the argument was more acceptable among policy elites that lying to the public by high officials was excusable, if vital national interests were at stake that plain folks—either through prejudice or lack of knowledge—did not apprehend. Since the end of the Vietnam War something of a consensus has developed that lying by public officials was a proximate if not a primary reason for the escalation of immersion in that disastrous conflict, and hence that lying is itself a threat to the national interest. That thesis has considerable merit, certainly regarding Vietnam and probably generally as well. And yet, does it hold true for all cases? If moralistic overreaction would deny legitimacy to any other instance of deliberate deceit, might this not result even in dangers to the public good? Aware of the opposition this notion is likely to engender, I nonetheless suggest that moral absolutism condemning all lying in public affairs is an emotionally gratifying position, but hardly an intellectually satisfying one.

The practices of deceit dealt with here are not the usual stuff of warmaking, about the moral legitimacy of which there should be little disagreement. Assuming that a cause is genuinely just, the propriety of lying to the enemy is a moral given because of the obvious need to conceal one's capabilities for reasons of defense. Passive deception of an enemy in wartime is an integral component of virtually every military plan. Terms such as "camouflage," "feint," or "stratagem" are particular references to the overall need to confuse and deceive an enemy, so that one can better kill its troops, incapacitate its armies and destroy its ability to resist. Disinformation and propaganda go further: they are forward measures to deceive the enemy. But they may also cross a line into active deceit of one's own population, in order to sustain national morale. Surely in these areas at least we ought to abstain from a position of moral absolutism, that holds it improper to ever lie to one's own people, even when the nation is at war. In warfare there are usually much higher moral goods at stake, such as the preservation of life (primarily on one's own side, of course), and more important, of national values and perhaps national identity.

But let me push the argument further, to suggest that the special conditions of wartime statecraft mean that leaders may actually be morally obligated to lie. Most clearly, they must deceive their own people about troop movements, ship sailings, productivity figures, and strategic plans. This type of lying to one's own simply reinforces the deceptions one is attempting to foist upon the enemy. Moreover, releasing misleading or false information, maintaining extreme secrecy, and other such wartime deceits are generally accepted by the vast majority of citizens. "Loose lips sink ships" was the way a famous World War II slogan had it, a caution that was as often as not roughly enforced on the factory floor or along the waterfront by workers themselves. It is not these mundane wartime lies—if I may be permitted that phrase—with which I am concerned (they do not, in fact, unduly concern me on any level). Rather, I am interested in the grand, strategic lies in which statesmen take recourse in the face of public resistance to their policies. Specifically, I wish to consider the calculated deceits that Franklin Roosevelt purveyed and cultivated to get America into World War II, to sustain its war effort, and then to commit it to postwar activism. What were the uncomfortable facts of his moral dilemma? Were his deceptions defensible? If so, what were the benefits and losses the nation incurred? In what ways did he deceive the American public? To what extent were his lies pardonable by circumstance? And what price, if any, was paid for them later?

My argument is simple: even between democratic leaders and the peoples they lead, deceit may be defensible when the nation is *in extremis*. Indeed, in times of great crisis and danger, such as faced the United States and civilization itself before and during World War II, lying to the public in order to get it to move to a position from which it would otherwise have fled may well have been the most morally defensible course of action. In short, what some others have rejected as Roosevelt's moral duplicity I will argue amounted to moral leadership in a wider sense. After all, his prewar manipulation of public opinion was essential to a statecraft that pursued immediate defense against a manifest danger, as well as longer term, enlightened self-interest. But I am not in the business of hagiography, and I will consider as well the eventual foreign policy costs of this lying. For expedient deception, even of political allies, was a practice that with Roosevelt became habitual. His reliance on personal charm to advance political goals, and his reputation for Tammany Hall scheming, are both well-known. With a political twist, he appears to have believed with Terence that "obsequiousness begets friends; truth hatred." Roosevelt was a man to whom dissembling came easily, and who did not like to tell disagreeable truths boldly. He thus continued to lie about his broad foreign policy goals to enemies and allies alike well after Pearl Harbor. Furthermore, to support his wartime and postwar plans he deliberately deceived the American public about the internal character of the Soviet Union, a maneuver that proved quite harmful in the end.

LIES AND THE NAZI THREAT

Professor Sissela Bok has written a wide-ranging and widely read treatise on lying.[1] She refers to Roosevelt's statecraft only once, mainly for purposes of comparison to Lyndon Johnson's conduct of the war in Vietnam. Yet what she has to say should, by contrast, help illustrate some of the points I wish to make. She agrees that the case of a public unwilling to face up to the imminent danger from Nazi Germany before World War II is:

a difficult one, and one on which reasonable persons might not be able to agree. The threat was unprecedented; the need for preparations and for support for allies great; yet the difficulties of alerting the American public seemed insuperable.

She asks "would this crisis, then, justify proceeding through deceit?" Her answer is a curiously theoretical and emotive one, given what we actually know about World War II:

> To consent to such a deception would, I believe, be to take a frightening step. Do we want to live in a society where public officials can resort to deceit and manipulation whenever they decide that an exceptional crisis has arisen? Would we not, on balance, prefer to run the risk of failing to rise to a crisis honestly explained to us, from which the government might have saved us through manipulation?... Only those deceptive practices which can be openly debated and consented to in advance are *justifiable* in a democracy.

She concludes that the deceit practiced by Roosevelt was probably inexcusable, and certainly unjustifiable; that the price paid in terms of broken domestic trust was too high; and—rather predictably—that the secrecy and deceit of the Vietnam War and the Nixon administration "grew at least in part because of existing precedents," by which she means Roosevelt.[2]

There is more than a little sophistry in that argument. Leave aside that advance consent by a democratic public to its own deception is a *non sequitur*. It is more telling that Professor Bok has removed the debate from the realm of facts and real world consequences to that of merely emotionally gratifying preferences. Of course the adult citizen in a democracy prefers being consulted to being duped. But that merely side-steps the larger moral issue of whether it is pardonable for leaders to dupe citizens anyway, if the security, core values, and independent life of a free nation are at stake, as they arguably were after 1938. More important, it is ethically glib to rank the threat from Nazi Germany in World War II with later misperceptions of the degree of threat to the national interest from the local communisms of Indochina. The hazard to the United States from Nazi Germany was of the first order, surpassed as a national danger in American history only by the disaster of the Civil War. Roosevelt did not merely "perceive" or "decide" that Nazi Germany was a fundamental threat to America's interest in an open and expansive world order, and ultimately to the survival of its liberal values at home as well. Aggressive, expansionist Germany under the control of Adolf Hitler and the Nazis *in fact* posed a potentially mortal danger to the United States. One may justly criticize several subsequent presidents for screening their decisions and actions from public scrutiny by facile comparison to the dilemma faced by Roosevelt, and for using rationalizations about mortal threats to the national interest when they knew that the existence of such threats was patently untrue. It is no doubt correct to hold that misinformation and misdirection of the public is neither politically necessary nor morally justifiable to support a mere brush fire war against some regional threat from a nation one-tenth one's own size and power, and when one's own citizens are in no way directly threatened. But that is a far cry from trying to prepare a nation, beguiled by isolationism and in full, wounded retreat from an earlier holocaust in Europe, to face an almost certain and ferocious onslaught against its physical security and national belief system by a Great Power like Nazi Germany. Yet that was the vital task which faced Roosevelt, and it is against that real world background that he must be judged.

It is therefore startling and more than a little disturbing that Professor Bok asks us to forego any consideration of the consequences of losing World War II—to put it most plainly—apparently solely to preserve our collective innocence from public lies. I submit that such arguments about abstract, public well-being are utterly inadequate as a guide to moral judgment of public officials or public affairs when the nation is truly *in extremis*. How can we accurately or fairly address the moral significance of Roosevelt's deceitful actions without some corresponding effort to assess the likely consequences of inaction? In this case, of all cases, the consequences of failure to use nearly any and all efforts to resist the Nazi evil would have been truly horrific. There is every reason to believe that had U.S. industrial might not been matched to Soviet manpower and Britain's strategic location (as a giant airfield and invasion platform off the coast of Europe), the Axis powers could well have triumphed. Had events gone just marginally differently than they actually did, the result would have been Germany's hegemony and a corresponding nazification of Europe, the Middle East, much of Africa, and possibly India, too. It is not trite to remind ourselves of the implications for the United States had American inaction permitted Germany to win World War II on such terms, for such considerations played themselves out in the minds of policy-makers of the day. Indeed, it is not only worthwhile to spell out the broad consequences of that nightmarish outcome, it is essential to any fair assessment of the moral probity of Roosevelt's choices and actions.

At the least, a German victory would have meant: the utter destruction of European Jewry, as well as mass executions of Gypsies, homosexuals, "mental defectives," and others not to the taste of the Nazi elite; the reenslavement of Slavic peoples, and probably the enslavement of Africans as well; extinction of the liberal idea in Europe; subjugation of dozens of nations, which must have led to endemic, violent resistance in following years; global dominance by the fascist powers, not just militarily but in terms of trade, international organization and the setting of international legal and moral norms; and an ineluctable pressure upon the United States to form a "Fortress Western Hemisphere" security zone, replete with construction of a severe "national security state" and deteriorating respect for national independence and domestic liberties in the Americas. Furthermore, Germany left to harvest the fruits of its victories in Europe, Russia, the Middle East, and Africa would soon have acquired nuclear weapons, a prospect truly horrifying when it is coupled with the fact that German scientists and engineers already enjoyed a five- to ten-year head start on missile and jet technology. In short, had Roosevelt failed to prepare the United States to enter decisively into World War II, Nazi Germany was likely to have won that war on terms that amounted to global dominance. The world must then have descended into a Cold War of a wholly different order. In this alternate Cold War, the United States would have been desperately—and possibly fatally—disadvantaged by not controlling western Europe or Japan. It would have faced, alone, an adversary far more adventurist, expansionist, and belligerent than the Soviet Union ever proved to be; and one in control of a greater industrial, resource, and technological base than even that of the United States. Those are the most "frightening," to use Professor Bok's word, and pertinent moral facts about this case; not whether Americans should have to live with the realization that victory came about in part because their leaders lied in order to prepare the nation to fight, and to supply its allies.

I do not think the scenario I have given for American inaction and German victory is far-fetched. Of vastly greater importance, neither did Franklin Roosevelt. He understood the consequences of Nazi victory, even without an American defeat, in comparable terms to those just listed (with the exception that he lacked full knowledge of the coming Holocaust against the Jews). He did not believe with the isolationists that America could remain secure, or ultimately survive as a liberal power in a fascist, lawless world.[3] Earlier and perhaps more deeply than some other Western leaders, he found Nazism utterly repugnant. He saw it as entirely antithetical to his personal, Christian values and liberal-capitalist ideology. Once he also became convinced that Nazi Germany presented a fundamental threat to the nation, his diplomacy aimed consistently at encouraging an encircling alliance of antifascist powers. He wanted to bring together the Western democracies, the Little Entente,[4] and the Soviet Union in an anti-German and antifascist front. However, he was constrained by domestic opposition to seek to keep the United States from formal membership in any alliance, or overt commitment to collective defense. The compromise he settled on was to make actual, through rearmament, some of the latent military power of the United States, for purposes of deterrence. While some might see that primary reliance on other states opposing Hitler as weak at best and cynical at worst, it is more accurate to say that Roosevelt's determination to see Nazism off the world stage was genuine, but that he remained hamstrung by the strength of isolationist opinion.[5]

On the other hand, it took him a number of years to develop an assertive diplomacy toward Germany. During his first term, as the crises in Europe and Asia built, he was more concerned about reforms at home than threats from abroad. In 1934 he used the lure of trade to correct an atrophied U.S. policy toward the Soviet Union by granting recognition. In part he hoped to engage the Soviets in his desired defensive front against Germany, just as Stalin hoped to engage the United States against Japan, but Roosevelt did not follow the opening with any sustained effort. Through most of the 1930s the United States offered Moscow, as it also offered London and Paris, little more than diplomatic encouragement.[6] FDR spoke of a "moral embargo" on arms sales, and of a "quarantine" of aggressors and the contagion of war. He also hinted to the Western democracies and the Soviet Union of his support for collective security, although the United States remained outside the League of Nations, and Congress refused to permit adherence even to the World Court. When tested by the outbreak of the Spanish Civil War, Roosevelt so feared a backlash from American Catholics in the 1936 election that he refused to lend any support to the Republican government in Madrid (which was strongly opposed by Catholics). Although strict neutrality permitted him to aid the Republican government as the legitimate government of Spain, he chose not to do so. That was a policy he came to regret even as he continued to speak publicly in defense of the arms embargo Congress imposed on both sides. Instead of attempting to educate public opinion to the national interest in supporting Madrid, he decided to avoid a domestic fight he felt certain he would lose. He then worked to counteract the embargo covertly, by sending limited aid to the Republicans, shipped through France during 1938 and 1939.[7]

Following the Munich Conference of September 29–30, 1938, Roosevelt broke with British and French appeasement—a policy he had never fully endorsed in any case. But he still had to concern himself with the appearances of neutrality, even as he became more assertive about defense preparedness and formulating a forward policy to deter and, ultimately, to defeat Hitler. He used executive authority whenever possible to bypass Congress and begin rearmament, not just for reasons of defense but in the hope of bolstering Britain and France and thereby deterring Germany. He hoped to have the democratic nations of Europe do the job themselves, but thought it might stiffen their spines to believe they would have U.S. backing in the event of war. He therefore sent instructions to William Bullitt, then Ambassador to France, to tell the French government that "if a war should break out we will certainly not take part in the beginning, but we will end it."[8] This message was sent with the clear knowledge that U.S. opinion at that point would not support even significant aid to Britain or France, let alone entry into combat. In addition to generating false hopes in Europe of American engagement, the man who had firmly stated that the only thing Americans had "to fear is fear itself," turned at home to generating false fears of an imminent German invasion of the hemisphere. Prior to the outbreak of war in Europe he repeatedly warned of German plans to invade Latin America, although he knew that the short-term threat was virtually nonexistent.[9] Nor did he hesitate to cast wide aspersions of treasonable disloyalty on the part of the German, Italian, and Japanese populations of Latin countries and the United States itself, hinting suggestively to favored journalists that he had information these people were organizing as Fifth Columnists for the fascist states (which a small minority of them were). He undertook this rather scurrilous deceit, too, in order to shatter the complacency of a nation still deluding itself that its prosperity and internal affairs were independent of European or Asian security, and the global balance of power.[10]

Roosevelt's scare tactics brought American public opinion slowly to the realization that at least hemispheric defense was prudent. This enabled him to gain approval from Congress for a huge increase in military spending, portrayed as entirely defensive in nature and as directed toward hemispheric defense. On the surface, it still looked like Roosevelt was prepared to lead only where public opinion was already inclined to follow. In fact, he had begun to manipulate public opinion on a grand scale, and always in the direction of increasing preparation for a direct clash with Germany. While he said in public that American rearmament was solely defensive, the very scale of that rearmament gave the lie to his statements. He admitted in private, and German intelligence concurred, that America was rearming not just to secure the Americas, but toward the day it could provide the Western democracies and their allies with an overwhelming military superiority over the fascist states. Beginning in 1938, U.S. war production was put on a path toward the point where it would be able to both supply Britain and France and build up a huge American army and a dominant navy. Professor Robert Herzstein puts the case succinctly: "The fact is Roosevelt wished to create a long term threat *to* Germany, and that required a major military buildup. In order to obtain the rearmament appropriations he needed, [he] conjured up a short term threat *from* Germany."[11]

Roosevelt wanted to form an anti-fascist coalition to deter German aggression, or at least confine the conflict should deterrence fail. However, intense domestic opposition to membership in any alliance or collective security system meant that he had to preserve the appearance and formal strictures of isolationism, while simultaneously encouraging other states to band together to oppose Germany. It was not a winning hand, but it was the only one the public and Congress would deal him. To strengthen it he called upon his fabled charm, his considerable guile, and a talent for easy deceit. Was he wrong to do so? Could he have achieved the same ends, of rearmament and strengthened deterrence, by appealing to the higher reason and better natures of average Americans? The record strongly suggests that any direct statement of the threat and appeal to the national interest in stopping Germany would have been disbelieved, and have failed. The evidence further suggests that such an approach actually would have deepened the public's impulse to plunge its head into the isolationist sands, so as not to face the prospect of involvement in the carnage that lay ahead.[12] Thus, when Roosevelt first asked for revision of the Neutrality Laws and repeal of the arms embargo those laws imposed, he was rebuffed by Congress and public opinion alike. Despite these setbacks, even before the Polish crisis of 1939 he was determined to use U.S. force against Germany if deterrence failed—not right away, and not if Britain and France could do the job alone, but ultimately. He believed that the last resort would not arrive for several more years, due to the twinned strength of the Royal Navy and the French Army (then the largest and still considered the finest in the world). He hoped Allied resistance would give him time enough to turn the tide of domestic opinion firmly his way, and more important, build U.S. military strength for the coming "rendezvous with destiny."[13]

Roosevelt thus continued to lend merely verbal support to Britain and France in their pale efforts to limit the European conflict short of war, and distantly to court the Soviets as well. As late as midsummer 1939 he still hoped that promises of American support might do some good, and that deterrence might yet suffice to deal with Hitler. Of course, it did not. With the outbreak of war, the debate in the United States shifted to competing interpretations of neutral rights, and the degree to which support should be given to the Western Allies. Thus, in November, 1939, an arms embargo provision in the 1935 Neutrality Act was repealed. While still far short of adopting a full rearmament posture, this at least represented movement in the direction of national preparedness for war. Roosevelt used the crisis to further accelerate rearmament (which was gaining popularity anyway for the return to prosperity it caused), and to call for conscription and the unprecedented creation of a million-man, peacetime army. Throughout 1940 he walked a tightrope between launching additional preparedness measures and rising suspicions that he was planning to enter the war on Britain's side. He repeatedly denied the charge, although by then he was determined to do just that. In the 1940 campaign he was forced by the good showing of a surprisingly adept opponent, Wendell Willkie, to pledge that "your boys are not going to be sent into any foreign wars."[14] That especially mollified traditionally Democratic voters in German, Irish and Italian-American communities, which contained the highest percentage of isolationist if not actually pro-Axis members. His promise was altogether expedient and political, though not entirely disingenuous: Roosevelt did intend to keep the country at peace if he could; he just had severe doubts that this was possible any longer, or that peace was still in the best interest of the nation. Besides, in his own mind and in confidential talks with foreign leaders, he made the distinction that he did not consider the war in Europe as truly "foreign," because it touched upon so many vital U.S. interests. However, Roosevelt believed that if he told the American people the whole truth all at once, instead of leading them gradually to the understanding that they were seriously threatened, he would be defeated in the next election and those who followed would be less inclined to prepare the nation to face the threat— or worse, might not even believe it existed and might prepare for it not at all.

Prior to 1940, Roosevelt refused to formally guarantee U.S. support for any anti-German policy that might entail the immediate risk of war, while privately giving repeated assurances to the Allies that the United States would join them in the longer-term. It was not until after the German *Blitzkrieg* had overrun Poland, Norway, Denmark, the Low Countries, and France, and chased the British Expeditionary Force back across the Channel, that the grip of isolationism on U.S. policy was loosened. Even then, isolationists in Congress still insisted on a "cash-and-carry" policy: belligerents were required to pay in advance and themselves carry away munitions and other goods, in the forlorn hope that a repeat of the U-boat crisis of 1915–1917 could be avoided and neutrality upheld. But facts, as John Adams once remarked, are decidedly "uncomfortable things." By midsummer 1940, Hitler's legions occupied nearly all Europe, a fact that was enough to discomfit all but the most irreconcilable isolationists. With Germany threatening to seize the French Mediterranean fleet and French bases in

West Africa, and the British stretched beyond their naval means in the Atlantic, Mediterranean, and Pacific, the threat to the Western Hemisphere was a clear and present danger.[15] America's historic isolation and security, enjoyed by grace of the Royal Navy since the end of the Napoleonic Wars, was gone. Moreover, its principal allies in the last war with Germany—Britain, France, and Russia— were, respectively, barely in the fight, defeated, or still in cahoots with Hitler. Yet at any point between Munich and the 1940 election, had Roosevelt told the American public that he intended to fight Germany if Nazism could not be defeated in any other way, he probably would not have survived politically. This was, therefore, no time to be overly concerned about honesty in government, or even about constitutional niceties.

Although reelection gave him greater security, from the election to Pearl Harbor speaking entirely forthrightly about foreign policy still would have un- dermined Roosevelt's political base to the point of defeating that policy—he was, after all, preparing to take the country into a war while proclaiming the very opposite.[16] Nonetheless, following the fall of France in June, 1940, and despite the defeatist cables he received from Ambassador to London Joseph Kennedy, FDR became driven by an overwhelming sense of the need for urgent action to support Britain. His crafty solution to the public relations problem was to depict every step he took toward greater engagement in the conflict with the Axis as motivated by peaceful intentions, constituting a move *away* from war. For example, in August 1940, he responded to desperate pleas from Britain by approving the "destroyers-for-bases" deal in which fifty old destroyers were swapped for 99-year leases on seven British island possessions in the Western Hemisphere. Three days later he flatly denied that the grant of destroyers to bolster Britain's convoy defenses was his central aim, which it was. Instead, he emphasized that he had strengthened America's own coastal and hemispheric defenses by acquiring outlying naval bases. He did not add that this would further project American naval power into the Atlantic, where it might be—and later was—deployed to supplement Royal Navy and Royal Canadian Navy ac- tion against the German U-boat threat.[17] That was a highly effective lie and major deceit by omission, which placed his critics in the position of seeming to oppose even direct defense of the United States. Omitted from discussion was his long-term, strategic—some would also say imperial—intention to have the United States displace Britain as the dominant naval power. Nor did he suggest that the new bases were to be used by the U.S. Navy to enforce a "Hemispheric Security Zone," intended to relieve the British of part of their convoy duties and which thereby promised soon to bring U.S. warships into direct conflict with German U-boats.[18]

If Roosevelt expressed his fears in private to only a select few, he spoke in real confidence of his long-range plans to only three highly trusted men: Henry Stimson, Harry Hopkins, and Sumner Welles.[19] Given this discipline, the ad- ministration proved adept at damage limitation when called out about one of its many deceits. For example, the Germans published certain captured Polish doc-

uments that showed Roosevelt had, in 1939, vehemently encouraged the Poles
to resist further appeasement, and had helped persuade the British and French
to honor their guarantees to Poland. This made Roosevelt look as though he
favored war, not peace. He responded with a favored, and once again effective,
deceptive technique: a disclaimer, designed for domestic consumption but made
by a foreign head of state or government, of what both Roosevelt and the foreign
statesman knew to be the truth. In this case, he sent Sumner Welles to Paris to
visit Eduard Daladier. The French Premier agreed to release a letter stating that
during the 1939 crisis Roosevelt and Bullitt had always made it clear to him
that the United States would not enter the war.[20] The documents (which were
real enough) were made to appear tainted by their passage through Nazi hands,
and with Daladier's partial truth about the Bullitt mission in circulation, this
worked to avert a crisis of confidence in the integrity of Roosevelt's assurances.
As a result, the majority of Americans continued to believe that their president
was working to keep them out of the war at all costs, when he was actually
doing everything he could to ensure that they eventually entered it.

By mid-1940, Roosevelt's fears about German hegemony had proved presci-
ent, but so too had U.S. rearmament been underway for several years. Because
of his foresight, ostensibly neutral America was already building a head of
economic steam toward a full war economy; that would stand the Allied cause
in good stead once full U.S. engagement in the war came about. Moreover, his
disingenuous public relations campaign was working, and began to provide him
at last with broadened foreign policy options. Public opinion toward Germany
was increasingly hostile, and hardening fast. It still favored any policy portrayed
as reducing the chance of U.S. entry into the war, but Roosevelt had reason to
believe the time had come to take additional, forward steps against Germany.[21]
U.S. policy began to display an openly anti-German character. By the spring of
1941 Roosevelt felt free to offer Britain virtually all aid short of war. He authorized huge arms sales and approached the military about a plan to share
equally with Britain all U.S. war production. All that remained was to devise a
means by which Britain could defer payment for all the munitions and equip-
ment American factories and shipyards were turning out, for London had liquidated its overseas holdings and drained its treasury. The solution was
Lend-Lease.

Lend-Lease was a brilliant expedient, one that Churchill ranked (with accuracy) among history's "most unsordid acts."[22] It also was a means for effecting
an Anglo/American alliance in all but name, and thus dramatically increased the
likelihood that the United States would be drawn into the European war: Why
should Hitler any longer seek to appease Roosevelt (as he had been doing since
1939, for instance by restraining his U-boat captains in the North Atlantic) when
American goods and loans were already flowing to the United Kingdom, and
American escort ships were engaging U-boats from the Gulf of Mexico to Ice-
land? Yet Roosevelt successfully sold Lend-Lease to the American public as a
policy that would keep the United States *out* of the Anglo/German war. Any

contrary suggestion by his critics and political enemies, that he was considering "sending armies to Europe," Roosevelt said, was "deliberate untruth."[23] Once again, he got away with it. The American public was eager for the relative prosperity of an economy placed on a wartime footing although it was still peacetime, and it was warming to the idea that as long as the British were going to do the actual fighting that stopped Hitler, the United States should supply the tools—as Churchill later put it, speaking disingenuously himself. That logic applied with even greater force to the vast manpower reserves of Soviet Russia, which Hitler's armies attacked in June 1941. Roosevelt's decision was therefore immediate and clear: with the enthusiastic support of Churchill, he offered Lend-Lease to Stalin. However, to gain Congressional approval he would have to maneuver against opposition from American conservatives and Catholics. In August he took the remarkable step, for the leader of a supposedly neutral nation, of meeting with Winston Churchill to draft and sign the Atlantic Charter. That document amounted to joint Anglo/American war aims, premised as it was on "the final destruction of the Nazi tyranny."[24]

LIES AND THE SOVIET ALLIANCE

Already by March 1939, when Nazi Germany swallowed the remainder of Czechoslovakia, there could be no question that the main threat to U.S. interests and values was headquartered in Berlin and not Moscow. Hence, announcement of the Nazi-Soviet Pact on August 23, 1939, shocked and angered Roosevelt but did not shake his conviction that Germany posed a singular danger. However, the related Soviet invasion of eastern Poland, in late September, deepened anti-Soviet opinion among many ordinary Americans. Millions of Polish-Americans, in particular, reflected bitterly on another partition of their ancestral homeland. They were supported by other Catholics concerned for the welfare of Polish coreligionists, still bitter over the Spanish Civil War, or just following the severe line toward Moscow laid down by the popes since 1929.[25] Catholics were joined in anti-Sovietism by millions of other Americans, stunned at what they regarded as the naked cynicism of Stalin's deal with Hitler.[26] More than the assault on Poland, the Soviet Union's unprovoked aggression against Finland ("Winter War") in late 1939 had embittered relations with the United States, and deeply angered Roosevelt personally. FDR was in a quandary. He had not invoked the Neutrality Act to cover Moscow's participation in the partition of Poland in September 1939, fearing that would only drive Stalin deeper into Hitler's embrace. He similarly was reluctant to do anything over the invasion of Finland which might push the Soviet Union closer to Nazi Germany. On the other hand, he was moved by the plight of the Finns and personally angered by Stalin's naked and brutal opportunism. He decided to ban sales to the Soviet Union of certain strategic metals, appealed directly to Stalin not to bomb Finnish cities, revived his earlier call for a "moral embargo" on sales of aircraft to aggressor countries, and opened fresh lines of credit to enable Finland to purchase munitions.[27] Roosevelt decided against breaking diplomatic relations with Moscow, although the House of Representatives nearly took the matter out of his hands de facto when it came within three votes of denying appropriations for the Moscow Embassy. Lastly, FDR endorsed the expulsion of the Soviet Union by the League of Nations, a feeble moral gesture made at the final meeting of that tragically hapless organization.[28]

Roosevelt's desire to assist the Finns, however minimally, was at odds with America's still prevailing mood of isolationism. Congress thus resisted the effort to aid Finland, supported in its obstruction by a general public which disapproved of Soviet actions and admired Finland, but remained nervous about any measure which involved America in the war in Europe. In December 1939, one poll recorded that 88 percent of Americans had extensive sympathy for Finland. Yet a poll taken two months later revealed that 77 percent opposed entry into the wider European war even if it seemed likely that Nazi Germany would defeat Britain and France. And isolationists in the Senate vehemently opposed aid to Finland out of fear that the United States might be dragged by a Nordic side door into the larger war in Europe.[29] Roosevelt's anger at the Soviet Union and frustration over Senate myopia came together in February 1940, when he declared in a moment of rare public frankness: "The Soviet Union, as everybody who has the courage to face the facts knows, is run by a dictatorship as absolute as any other dictatorship in the world."[30]

A profound ambivalence ran through Roosevelt's thinking: deep anger toward and moral alienation from the Soviet Union, coupled with recognition that nonetheless he would have to work with Stalin if the Nazi threat was to be countered. That conclusion was not altered even by events of midsummer 1940. France fell under the German jackboot in a mere six weeks in May and June, following the even more rapid conquest of Norway and Denmark, and the Low Countries. Stalin took advantage of war in the west to occupy the Baltic States, in accordance with a secret protocol to the Nazi-Soviet Pact and a follow-up treaty in which he had traded rights to the Polish provinces of Lublin and Warsaw to Hitler, in exchange for Lithuania. He also forced Rumania to give up its provinces of Bessarabia and Bukovina.[31] Despite anger in Washington over these moves, strategic considerations outweighed the temptation to indulge in futile moral gestures, such as breaking diplomatic relations. As ruthlessly opportunist as Stalin appeared to be, Roosevelt and even the public realized Hitler's appetite for conquest was more immediate, and probably insatiable.[32] The conviction was deepened that Germany was a fundamental threat far outweighing the distant distaste most Americans felt for the Soviet Union.[33]

When Hitler unleashed Operation Barbarossa against the Soviet Union on June 22, 1941, Churchill and Roosevelt immediately decided to give all possible assistance to Stalin, including Lend-Lease.[34] Roosevelt's public education efforts over the previous years and months—in which he had played to anti-Soviet sentiments when necessary, but overall had sought to convince Americans that the main threat came from the Axis—were beginning to pay off, greatly aided by the force of events.[35] However, there was one large block of anti-Soviet opinion that neither Roosevelt nor Hitler could so easily dissolve. American Catholics continued to cling to such fierce anticommunist convictions that they posed a significant obstacle to getting approval of supplemental Lend-Lease appropriations for the Soviet Union through Congress. Roosevelt was hoist on his own petard: he had repeatedly stated that religious belief was a major source of "democracy and international good faith."[36] He had also counted freedom of religion among the "Four Freedoms" on which he said he wanted to base post-war order and reconstruction, in an expedient oversimplification that was comforting to millions and thus politically effective.[37] He could hardly now admit that antagonism to organized religion informed Soviet domestic law and practice. In September 1941, he thus began a sustained campaign to convince Americans that religious liberty was unfolding in the Soviet Union.

In September 1941, Roosevelt expressed convenient optimism about the future of religious liberty in the Soviet Union in a letter sent to Pope Pius XII to solicit papal aid in obtaining Catholic acquiescence in Lend-Lease to Stalin:

I believe there is a real possibility that Russia may as a result of the present conflict recognize freedom of religion. . . . I believe that the survival of Russia is less dangerous to religion, to the church as such, and to humanity in general than would be the survival of the German form of dictatorship. Furthermore, it is my belief that the leaders of all churches in the United States should recognize these facts clearly and should not close their eyes to these basic questions and by their present attitude on this question directly [sic] assist Germany in her present objectives.[38]

In this correspondence Roosevelt made use of his personal representative to the Vatican, Myron C. Taylor, appointed in December 1939, in anticipation of just such difficulties with American Catholics. The Pontiff, despite his deep failings with regard to the nature of Nazism and fascism in Europe,[39] knew better than Roosevelt the real conditions under which believers lived and labored in the Soviet Union. He replied with polite generalities, avoiding mention of conditions in Russia. FDR was satisfied because the Pontiff drew a fine distinction between wartime assistance to the Soviets and forbidden support for communism, which left the moral opening FDR wanted for American Catholics to back Lend-Lease.[40]

Roosevelt's natural skill at deceit now began to ill-serve him and the nation. Instead of pushing Lend-Lease through the narrow opening permitted by Pius's reply, Roosevelt adopted a broad tactic of lying about the real conditions for religious believers in the Soviet Union, in order to manipulate American Catholics (and some others) into supporting Lend-Lease. A baleful pattern now developed, wherein Roosevelt dissembled and deceived even when the possibilities of straight talk had not been exhausted. For example, in late September 1941, he suggested during a press conference that reporters acquaint themselves with the freedom of religion clause of the Soviet constitution (Article 124), which also declared the right of the state "equally to use propaganda against religion." He next described this limitation as "essentially what is the rule in this country, only we don't put it quite the same way." He concluded, "Since the Soviet constitution declares that freedom of religion is granted, it is hoped . . . an entering wedge for the practice of complete freedom of religion is definitely on its way."[41] Of course, he knew better. Just six months earlier his administration had privately protested NKVD[42] desecration of the Catholic Church in Moscow which serviced American Embassy officials, as sanctioned by mutual recognition agreements signed in 1933. Roosevelt had personally negotiated, and proudly trumpeted at the time, clauses in those agreements purporting to guarantee a right to religious worship for U.S. Embassy officers.[43] When an outcry arose over the inaccuracy of Roosevelt's characterization of Soviet domestic practice, the State Department sought to stifle it with a statement attesting that freedom of worship was denied equally by Communists and Nazis.[44] That was true, but entirely beside the point.

There can be no doubt that the clear intention behind Roosevelt's glib depiction of the state of religious affairs in the Soviet Union was an effort to forestall Catholic and other religious opposition to his extension of Lend-Lease to Stalin. He was quite explicit about this in private, as when he told Soviet Ambassador Constantine Oumansky, "If Moscow could get some publicity back to this country regarding the freedom of religion [in Russia] it might have a very fine educational effect before the next lend-lease bill comes up in Congress."[45] Embassy staff were then ordered to request formal Soviet assurances that freedom of religion would be respected in future. These were readily provided, since Stalin's need for Lend-Lease supplies was great and his intention to honor paper promises was nil. In transmitting the Soviet reply the Embassy warned, with considerable restraint and understatement, that "the Soviet Government will give lip service and make a few gestures to meet the President's wishes but is not yet prepared to give freedom of religion in the sense that we understand it." Pressure was also coming from outside the administration. House Majority Leader John McCormack advised Roosevelt that a great advantage could be had "from a psychological angle" if the United States intervened on behalf of a number of Polish priests being held in Soviet concentration camps. Assistant Secretary of State Adolf Berle agreed to press for their release, because he said it "would mean definite assistance in allaying some of the Catholic opposition to aid to Russia."[46] The Soviets were told that freedom for the Polish clerics was sought "not with the intention to interfere in Soviet internal affairs [sic]," but in the hope that Moscow would in turn facilitate Roosevelt's effort to extend it the maximum of assistance.[47] This remarkable exchange utterly ignored the fact that the Polish priests were arrested during the 1939 Soviet aggressive invasion of eastern Poland, made in accordance with the Nazi-Soviet Pact, and that the United States had never recognized the Soviet annexation as legal.

The most practiced student of Catholics and American foreign policy, George Q. Flynn, argues that Roosevelt's efforts were only superficially cynical, that

"the president seriously hoped to promote religious freedom in Russia."[48] While
that may have been true on one level—Roosevelt had a deep sentimental and
romantic streak—on another plane he was undoubtedly deliberately false. After
all, in 1942 he candidly admitted to Treasury Secretary Henry Morgenthau, "I
am perfectly willing to mislead and tell untruths . . . if it will help win the war."[49]
But there was more to it than that. As Robert Dallek noted:

> Roosevelt knew full well that there was no freedom of religion in the Soviet Union. Nor
> was he blind to the fact that he could extend Lend-Lease help to Russia without dem-
> onstrating her devotion to religious freedom. But . . . convinced that only a stark contrast
> between freedom and totalitarianism would provide the emotional wherewithal for Amer-
> icans to fight, Roosevelt wished to identify the Russians, regardless of Soviet realities,
> with Anglo-American ideals as fully as he could.[50]

The appropriate criticism thus is not that Roosevelt lied. The real problem was
that he may have lied *unnecessarily*, before he really tried an all-out campaign
of using the presidential bully-pulpit to convince anti-Soviet Americans that
massive material aid to Russia was in the direct and vital interest of the United
States—which, of course, it was. Instead, as the war progressed additional deceits built upon the first, until real damage was done to the long-term interest
of having a willing, because informed, public behind the great efforts of war
and peacemaking that lay ahead.

   After the Axis invasion of the Soviet Union, and Imperial Japan's attack on
Pearl Harbor and various British and Dutch outposts five months later, the American public naturally revised its opinion of the Soviet Union.[51] As also happened
in 1917, many Americans evidenced a need to regard their new Russian ally as
moved by democratic ideals similar to their own, whatever the truth about "Why
Russia Fights." Too many downplayed or dismissed entirely the bloody purges
of the 1930s, the persecution of religious and other minorities that had begun
under Lenin right at the outset of the Bolshevik Revolution, and more recent
Soviet aggression against Poland, Finland, the Baltic States, and Rumania. By
1943 the shift in public opinion occasioned by the German assault, but also
assiduously shepherded by FDR, was complete: majorities of Americans, of
nearly all class or religious backgrounds, reported favorable views of the Soviet
Union. They even upheld belief in a bright future of peaceful postwar cooperation with Stalin.[52] What brought about this remarkable change? Naiveté and
ignorance about the true character of Stalin and the nature of his terror regime
played a real part. So, too, did a natural sense of shared wartime burden and
common moral purpose with the peoples of the Soviet Union, who were indeed
engaged in a heroic defense against an utterly barbaric and genocidal enemy in
Nazi Germany. Whatever the real character of Soviet government, many Americans—including Catholics who, like their pontiff, otherwise remained deeply
suspicious of Moscow—looked mainly to the undoubted heroism, suffering, and
sacrifice of millions of ordinary Soviets. They just could not believe that such

appalling suffering and enormous effort to defeat one great tyranny would be cynically abused and magnified by another.[53] Yet, sharing enemies and wartime suffering does not fully explain how the Soviet Union came to be seen by a large majority of Americans not just as an ally in a mutual war against fascism, but as a viable partner in reconstruction of the postwar order along free and democratic lines.

The leading cause of this crucial change in public opinion was that Roosevelt set out to cultivate a false impression that Stalin endorsed Anglo-American ideals and war aims, as set out in the Atlantic Charter. Americans were repeatedly told that the Soviets accepted that the peace would be reconstructed according to Roosevelt's vaunted "Four Freedoms," of speech and religion, and from want and fear (of aggression). Just as he had earlier sought to mollify Catholics by claiming that freedom of religion was coming in Russia, Roosevelt next played to the tendency of the general public to oversimplify by Americanizing the objectives and interests of wartime allies, regardless of reality. In this he was joined by other administration officials. In *Mission to Moscow*, a bestseller published in 1941 and later turned into a smash Hollywood film, former Ambassador to Moscow (and apologist for Soviet purge trials and other "excesses") Joseph C. Davies wrote:

The Russia of Lenin and Trotsky—the Russia of the Bolshevik Revolution—no longer exists. . . . [The] Russian people, the Soviet government, and the Soviet leaders are moved, basically, by altruistic concepts. It is their purpose to promote the brotherhood of man and to improve the lot of the common people. They wish to create a society in which men may live as equals, governed by ethical ideals. They are devoted to peace. They have made great sacrifices attempting to achieve those spiritual aspirations.[54]

Davies elsewhere proclaimed that communism in the Soviet Union was established "after all, on the same principle of the 'brotherhood of man' which Jesus preached." Far from disagreeing about the internal nature of Soviet society and the putative altruistic and spiritual motivations of Generalissimo Stalin, Roosevelt endorsed Davies's views in private as well as in public.[55] At the same time, he ignored dissenting voices among the experienced officers of the State Department, such as George F. Kennan. Sometimes, this refusal to listen to opposing opinion extended to rejecting unpleasant facts, such as those attending Soviet responsibility for the Katyn massacre of thousands of Polish Army officers.[56] Powerful private citizens who embraced the President's policies, such as Henry Luce, editor of *Time Magazine*, reinforced the administration's distortions and willingly participated in his manipulation of public perceptions.

Nor was the administration alone in its belief in the expediency of misinformation about the Soviet Union. Encouraged by Roosevelt, some important Republican figures cooperated in the effort. Thus, after just two days in Moscow in 1942, Wendell Willkie told his Soviet hosts that the visit made him realize how unfairly their system had been represented to the American people. Ambassador William H. Standley reported back to Washington that Willkie said to the Soviets:

Enemies of the Soviet Union caused many Americans to believe that the Soviet Government did not permit freedom of religion . . . and was persecuting those who practiced religion. He now knew that the stories of religious persecution . . . were false. . . . It was now his understanding that the Soviet Government was opposed to priest craft [*sic*] as distinct from religion. He personally also had little respect for priest craft and . . . hoped that the American people could be brought to understand what the real situation was in the U.S.S.R.[57]

Willkie boasted that millions of Americans had confidence in him because "they knew that he was a man who frankly told the truth and the whole truth and that he could be trusted." Without blushing, he next promised to lie by omission, saying that "if he saw something which he did not like or which [if] made known in the United States might create an unfavorable impression, he would remain silent to it."[58] Willkie published *One World*, an account of his whirlwind global tour, the following year; it sold several million copies and had a huge impact on public opinion during World War II. In the chapter dealing with his brief sojourn in Moscow, he delivered a paean of praise for Stalin, whom he described as "a simple man, with no affectations or poses." He added: "Russia is an effective society. It works."[59] The top political leadership of the United States, led by the President, together presented to the American public a vision of easy cooperation with a rapidly, and genuinely, liberalizing Soviet ally. This great nation, Americans were told, was under the stern but deeply wise leadership of "Uncle Joe" Stalin, who shared their hopes for a postwar order of international peace and cooperation through the new United Nations Organization. After that, there would be hell to pay later when the truth finally came out about what "Uncle" had been up to at home and in the Baltic States, Poland, Silesia, and eastern Prussia. All these territories were liberated from the Nazi yoke by the Red Army's tanks and troops, but they were also immediately occupied by the ruthless secret police, informer network, and torturers and firing squads of the NKVD.

CONCLUSIONS

Roosevelt faced an unprecedented challenge to U.S. security at a time when American isolationism was deeper than it had ever been—and when there was a direct correlation between the degree of strategic threat and the deepening of the public's desire to avoid war. That situation went a long way to excuse his choice of manipulation and trickery to convert Americans to accept, first, the necessity of prudent self-defense measures, and eventually, to adopt an interventionist stance. In this case, the ends of rearmament and otherwise preparing the nation to face and defeat Hitlerism surely justified a few expedient means.

That said, not all his lies were defensible, even given the stakes involved. There was no good reason, for instance, to smear whole ethnic populations with presidential innuendo about disloyalty. Nonetheless, if Roosevelt deceived Americans about the long-term implications of his principled opposition to Nazism—and he did deceive them, often and deeply—he yet served the nation well. Those were extraordinary days, and the danger faced called for special dispensation from normal moral burdens.

Roosevelt should be commended for shouldering that most onerous of public duties: personal responsibility for morally ambiguous solutions to the problems of statecraft. He did not fear moral ambiguity as some might have (as Neville Chamberlain did, for instance), to the point of impaling the national interest on their personal principles and narrow conceptions of honor. Nor did he indulge in questionable practices for their own sake, or because he enjoyed power more—as some do—when it was exercised deviously. Instead, he accepted the paradox that in times of great and genuine emergency it may be the higher calling of a statesman to deceive in order to lead, and otherwise secure the nation. Like Abraham Lincoln before him—the only president to face a comparable or greater threat to the nation—he appreciated that *in extremis* it is sometimes necessary to violate the letter of the law in order to save the rule of law. Both men trod roughly on the Constitution at times, and Roosevelt trod also on the truth, in the name of higher good. Yet both thereby helped to preserve the idea and the rule of law for better days. If Roosevelt had one great flaw that Lincoln did not, it was that even with the United States definitely in the war and the enemy's defeat assured, he could never quite bring himself to stop dissembling and re-engage the truth. Lying is a requisite of diplomacy. But the best diplomats and national leaders nonetheless lie only rarely and in extreme cases, because they know that when deceit is overdone it destroys the essential ingredient of trust which is itself requisite to the effective implementation of policy. Roosevelt thus can be applauded for his early, essential lies, but also deplored for his later, petty ones. That said, he still may be properly judged to have been not only a great statesman on narrow, *Realpolitik* grounds, but, on the whole, also a moral practitioner of the ethically exacting art of statecraft.

NOTES

1. Sissela Bok, *Lying: Moral Choice in Public and Private Life* (New York: Pantheon Books, 1978).

2. Ibid., pp. 179–81. Original emphasis.

3. He did, on the other hand, believe that coexistence with the Soviet Union was unpleasant but entirely possible, as it had proved to be since 1920 and would again after 1945. On Roosevelt's view of the threat from Nazi Germany see Robert E. Herzstein, *Roosevelt and Hitler* (New York: Paragon House, 1989), pp. 215–403 passim; and Waldo Heinrichs, *Threshold of War* (New York: Oxford University Press, 1968). On FDR's view of the Soviet Union see Edward M. Bennett, *Recognition of Russia* (New York:

Blaisdell, 1970); idem, *Franklin D. Roosevelt and the Search for Security* (Wilmington, DE: Scholarly Resources, 1985); Robert Browder, *Origins of Soviet-American Diplomacy* (Princeton, NJ: Princeton University Press, 1953); and the author's *Principled Diplomacy: Security and Rights in U.S. Foreign Policy* (Westport, CT: Greenwood, 1993), pp. 45–89.

4. The "Little Entente" was an East European alliance that lasted from 1920 to 1939. To the original alliance between Czechoslovakia and Yugoslavia signed in 1920, there were added two additional bilateral pacts with Rumania in 1921. These separate agreements were incorporated into a single alliance treaty in 1929. The main purpose of the Little Entente (an informal, popular name echoing the prewar *entente cordiale* of France, Great Britain and Russia) was to prevent Austria or Hungary from attempting to reclaim the old Habsburg lands taken away in the Treaties of St. Germain (with Austria, 1919) and Trianon (with Hungary, 1919). With the rising threat from Hitler's Germany, efforts were made by the Little Entente powers to negotiate mutual defense arrangements with France. A turn to the hard right in Yugoslavia after the assassination of Alexander I, especially its willingness to collaborate with plans for aggrandizement by Nazi Germany, shook the Little Entente. The Munich Conference and then the occupation of the rump of the Czech lands by German forces gutted the Little Entente of any use it might have had to buffer Germany, by removing Czechoslovakia from the chessboard of Europe and drawing its other members closer to the Axis.

5. See Manfred Jonas, *Isolationism in America, 1935–1941* (Ithaca: Cornell University Press, 1966; Imprint, 1990). On the evolution of FDR's thinking about Nazi Germany see the essay by William E. Kinsella, "The Prescience of a Statesman: FDR's Assessment of Adolf Hitler Before the World War, 1933–1941," in Herbert Rosenbaum and Elizabeth Bartelme, eds., *Franklin D. Roosevelt* (Westport, CT: Greenwood, 1987).

6. Bennett, *Search for Security*, various passages.

7. George Q. Flynn, *Roosevelt and Romanism* (Westport, CT: Greenwood, 1976), pp. 29–62; Frank Freidel, *Franklin D. Roosevelt: A Rendezvous with Destiny* (Boston: Little, Brown, 1990), pp. 268–72.

8. Waclaw Jedrzejewicz, ed., *Diplomat in Paris, 1936–1939* (New York: Columbia University Press, 1970), pp. 168–70; Herzstein, *Roosevelt and Hitler*, pp. 244–45.

9. That is not to say there was no long-term threat, for there was. In 1940 Hitler instructed the German Navy to develop contingency plans for the seizure of Atlantic islands, preparatory to establishing bases within the Western Hemisphere. See Stetson Conn and Byron Fairchild, *The U.S. Army in World War II: The Framework of Hemisphere Defense* (Washington, DC: U.S. Government, 1960); and Alton Frye, *Nazi Germany and the Western Hemisphere, 1933–1941* (New Haven: Yale University Press, 1967).

10. Herzstein, *Roosevelt and Hitler*, p. 240ff; Robert Dallek, *Franklin D. Roosevelt and American Foreign Policy, 1932–1945* (New York: Oxford University Press, 1979), pp. 173–75; Freidel, *Rendezvous with Destiny*, pp. 209–20. Roosevelt continued to use this tactic after 1940, but by then, with Hitler's acquisition of the French coastal ports and Italian and German access to colonies and bases in North Africa, the threat was real.

11. Herzstein, *Roosevelt and Hitler*, p. 245.

12. See "Gallup and Fortune Polls," *Public Opinion Quarterly* (March and June 1940). More generally, see Robert A. Divine, *The Illusion of Neutrality* (Chicago: University of Chicago Press, 1962); and Jonas, *Isolationism in America*, pp. 244–72.

13. The strongest case made in this respect is in Herzstein, *Roosevelt and Hitler*, pp. 284–317. Roosevelt was not the only statesman to overestimate the resistance that

would be presented to Germany by France. Stalin too would make that mistake, with near fatal consequences for himself and his empire.

14. Quoted in Dallek, *Roosevelt and American Foreign Policy*, p. 250. Also see Herzstein, *Roosevelt and Hitler*, p. 352.

15. See Note 9, *supra*. For an idiosyncratic, revisionist viewpoint see Bruce Russett, *No Clear and Present Danger* (New York: Harper & Row, 1972).

16. On Roosevelt's titanic struggle with Congress see Jonas, *Isolationism in America*, pp. 206–72; Divine, *Illusion of Neutrality*, pp. 243–83 passim, pp. 297–303, 315–19; and John C. Donovan, "Congressional Isolationists and the Roosevelt Foreign Policy," *World Politics* (April 1951), pp. 299–316.

17. Dallek, *Roosevelt and American Foreign Policy*, pp. 243–47. On Roosevelt's stormy relations with the press see Graham T. White, *Roosevelt and the Press* (Chicago: University of Chicago Press, 1979).

18. Herzstein, *Roosevelt and Hitler*, pp. 347–48.

19. Heinrichs, *Threshold of War*, p. 20.

20. This episode is recounted in Herzstein, *Roosevelt and Hitler*, pp. 318–20.

21. "Gallup and Fortune Polls," *Public Opinion Quarterly* (March and June 1940).

22. The most comprehensive study of Lend-Lease is Warren F. Kimball, *The Most Unsordid Act: Lend-Lease, 1939–1941* (Baltimore: Johns Hopkins University Press, 1969).

23. Quoted in Herzstein, *Roosevelt and Hitler*, p. 357. Also see Henry L. Stimson (with McGeorge Bundy), *On Active Service in Peace and War* (New York: Harper & Row, 1947), p. 366.

24. Draft and final versions, along with a firsthand account of the Charter's composition, are in Winston Churchill, *The Grand Alliance*, Vol. III of his *The Second World War* (New York: Bantam, 1962), pp. 366–80.

25. Flynn, *Roosevelt and Romanism*, pp. 141–42.

26. See "American Institute of Public Opinion—Surveys, 1938–1939," *Public Opinion Quarterly* (October 1939), p. 596.

27. *Public Papers and Addresses of Franklin D. Roosevelt*, Samuel I. Rosenman, ed. (New York: Macmillan, 1941), Vol. VIII, pp. 586–94; and Robert Sobel, *Origins of Interventionism* (New York: Bookman Associates, 1960), pp. 91–94.

28. Alexander DeConde, *History of American Foreign Policy*, 3rd ed. (New York: Scribner's, 1978), Vol. II, p. 584.

29. "Gallup and Fortune Polls," *Public Opinion Quarterly* (March/June, 1940), p. 102. For a summary of press and other reactions to the attack on Finland, see Thomas R. Maddux, *Years of Estrangement: American Relations with the Soviet Union, 1933–1941* (Tallahassee: University Presses of Florida, 1980), pp. 114–27; also see Donovan, "Congressional Isolationists," pp. 299–316.

30. "Address to the American Youth Congress," February 10, 1940, *Roosevelt: Public Papers*, Vol. IX, p. 93; and see Dallek, *American Foreign Policy*, pp. 208–13, where this anecdote in placed in the broad context of Roosevelt's struggle with Congress and public opinion.

31. "Soviet/German Friendship and Frontier Treaty," September 28, 1939, in Jane Degras, ed., *Soviet Documents on Foreign Policy* (New York: Oxford University Press, 1951), Vol. III, pp. 377–79. The Baltic States were annexed in August 1940. For recently released documents from the Soviet archives see "The Baltic Countries Join the Soviet Union," *International Affairs* (March 1990), pp. 134–42; and (April 1990), pp. 97–124.

32. See Ralph B. Levering, *American Opinion and the Russian Alliance, 1939–1945*

(Chapel Hill: University of North Carolina Press, 1976), pp. 15–38; Thomas R. Maddux, *Years of Estrangement*, pp. 128–46.

33. *Inter alia*, see George Herring, *Aid to Russia, 1941–1946* (New York: Columbia University Press, 1974); Raymond Dawson, *Decision to Aid Russia, 1941* (Chapel Hill: University of North Carolina Press, 1959); and Robert Jones, *Roads to Russia* (Norman: University of Oklahoma Press, 1969).

34. Maddux, *Years of Estrangement*, p. 147; Heinrichs, *Threshold of War*, pp. 92–117. Text of the Lend-Lease agreement in Stanley Jados, ed., *Documents on Russian/ American Relations* (Washington, DC: Catholic University Press, 1965), pp. 86–88.

35. See "Gallup and Fortune Polls," *Public Opinion Quarterly* (Spring 1942), pp. 152ff. Following the Nazi-Soviet Pact, Stalin's invasions of Poland and Finland, and the additional annexations of neighboring territories in 1940, 35 percent of Americans polled (in October 1941) still believed the Soviet Union and Nazi Germany were equally detestable tyrannies. Another 32 percent thought there was little to choose between them internally but considered Soviet Russia slightly better than Nazi Germany. The key result came in answer to the question about which side Americans wanted to win the war; with Nazi panzers then surging toward Kiev, Moscow, and Leningrad, most Americans preferred a Soviet victory.

36. For example, see his "Annual Message to Congress," January 3, 1940, in Samuel I. Rosenman, ed., *Public Papers and Addresses of Franklin D. Roosevelt*, Vol. VIII (New York: Macmillan, 1941), p. 1.

37. Freidel, *Rendezvous with Destiny*, pp. 360–62.

38. "Letter from President Roosevelt to His Holiness," September 3, 1941, *Wartime Correspondence between President Roosevelt and Pope Pius XII*, Myron C. Taylor, ed. (New York: Macmillan, 1947), pp. 61–62.

39. Pius XII, né Eugenio Pacelli (1876–1958), was a career Vatican diplomat who rose to cardinal and then to secretary of state to the Holy See. He had lived in Germany, where he negotiated the Vatican's concordat with Hitler. His failure to speak publicly against the Holocaust has been bitterly criticized. Although Pius was informed about the genocide underway against Jews, Roma, and others under Nazi occupation, he did not speak openly against Nazism. Nor did he publish a major condemnation of anti-Semitism prepared by his predecessor, Pius XI. More pointedly, while tolerating the hiding of some Jews in Catholic monasteries and convents, he never commanded his clergy to speak against fascism, despite its antireligious and pagan philosophy. Nor did he command the faithful to oppose, to the best of their moral abilities and the limits of their personal courage, the murderous policy of the Nazi regime, not even when SS death brigades came into Rome itself in 1943 to cart off Italian Jews to the death camps. Pius's reticence was motivated by a complex of factors. He was, of course, concerned with political calculations relating to the vulnerable position of the Catholic Church in Nazi-occupied Europe. Second, he and the Curia were powerfully influenced by a deep detestation of communism and of the Soviet Union, probably more so than by any personal antipathy for Jews, though that possibility may not be discounted entirely. Finally, Pius feared the destruction of his life's work, which had been to consolidate papal power over national Catholic churches in Italy and Germany and worldwide. Even if all that is true, his silence still deafens. And there lingers the possibility that his passivity had darker, more sinful motivations of personal anti-Semitism. See John Cornell, *Hitler's Pope* (1999).

40. "Reply of His Holiness to President Roosevelt," September 20, 1941, Myron Tay-

lor, ed., op. cit.; and Freidel, *Rendezvous with Destiny*, p. 376. Also see George Q. Flynn, "Franklin Roosevelt and the Vatican," *Catholic Historical Review* (July 1972), pp. 171–94; and idem, *Roosevelt and Romanism*, pp. 165–69.

41. Press conference, September 30, 1941, *Roosevelt: Public Papers*, Vol. X, pp. 401–2. See Article 134 of the 1936 Soviet Constitution, in Ian Brownlie, ed., *Basic Documents of Human Rights* (Oxford: Clarendon Press, 1971), p. 27.

42. Narodnii Kommissariat Vnutrennikh Del (NKVD), or People's Commissariat of Internal Affairs. This was the name of the Soviet secret and political police from 1934 to 1954. In 1934 the OGPU (formerly the GPU, formerly the Cheka) was expanded into the NKVD. The NKVD carried out the great purges of the 1930s and during the war maintained Rifle Divisions numbering tens of thousands of political troops, whose principal task was to shoot Soviet soldiers who retreated or deserted, along with nationalist partisans or anyone else in momentary disfavor with their master in the Kremlin.

43. Department of State, *Papers Relating to the Foreign Relations of the United States*, 1941, Vol. I, pp. 998–1000. Hereafter cited as *FRUS*.

44. "Aid to Russia," October 13, 1941, *Roosevelt: Public Papers*, Vol. X, p. 418. On the protest against desecration of churches, see *FRUS*, 1941, Vol. I, pp. 998–1000; and Flynn, *Roosevelt and Romanism*, pp. 159–60 for an account of American Catholic and editorial reaction.

45. *FRUS*, 1941, Vol. I, p. 832.

46. Ibid., pp. 997–1005.

47. Ibid., p. 1004.

48. Flynn, *Roosevelt and Romanism*, p. 158.

49. Quoted in Dallek, *American Foreign Policy*, p. 336.

50. Ibid., p. 298.

51. Levering, *American Opinion and the Russian Alliance*, pp. 39–62.

52. Ibid., pp. 97–145; and see Warren B. Walsh's compilation of wartime polls, "What the American People Think of Russia," *Public Opinion Quarterly* (Winter 1944/45), pp. 513–22.

53. On the brief wartime lull in Catholic antipathy for the Soviet Union, see Miscamble, "Catholics and American Foreign Policy," op.cit., p. 236.

54. Davies, *Mission to Moscow* (New York: Simon & Schuster, 1941), p. 511. A rare, and mostly misguided, positive view of Davies is Elizabeth Maclean, "Joseph E. Davies and Soviet-American Relations, 1941–43," *Diplomatic History* (Winter 1980), pp. 73–93.

55. See John L. Gaddis, *The United States and the Origins of the Cold War, 1941–1947* (New York: Columbia University Press, 1972), pp. 35–36; quoted at p. 36.

56. For example, see the account of how Roosevelt treated dissent over his handling of the Katyn massacre, in Crister S. Garrett and Stephen A. Garrett, "Death and Politics: The Katyn Forest Massacre and American Foreign Policy," *East European Studies Quarterly*, XX, No. 4 (January 1987), pp. 429–46.

57. *FRUS*, 1942, Vol. III, pp. 645–46.

58. Ibid.

59. Wendell Willkie, *One World* (New York: Simon & Schuster, 1943), pp. 83, 53; also see his "We Must Work with Russia," *New York Times Magazine*, January 17, 1943.

CHAPTER 4

Political Leadership and "Dirty Hands": Winston Churchill and the City Bombing of Germany

Stephen A. Garrett

One of the perennial issues in the analysis of the moral conduct of political leaders, and perhaps especially so in the realm of international relations, is the concept of "dirty hands." Reduced to its essentials, the notion of dirty hands suggests that political authorities may be required to do things—or to tolerate things—that would be regarded both by them and by others as unacceptable, even as genuinely evil, if the actions took place in their private lives. Some would say that political leaders actually have little choice in the matter: if they *are* to exercise leadership, they must necessarily set aside their standards of personal morality in those cases where insisting on such standards may be obstructive in advancing the broader public interest. Stated in its most direct form, the political leader has no other alternative, and moreover *should* have no other alternative.

Two assertions are typically advanced to spare top officials from the burden of moral judgment, to allow them a realm of "freedom from morality" that is supposedly their special preserve and even right. The first has to do with their identity as representatives of the "collective." The idea is that a social unit, especially a nation, has needs and demands that perforce require the leader to set aside any personal moral doubts he may have about either these needs themselves or the means necessary to attain them. In this sense the foreign policy leader is not a creature of free choice but rather the servant of the primordial demands of his constituency, whether they be for territorial security, economic advantage, religious or ideological influence, or whatever. If he feels uneasy with what is necessary to achieve these, or with the goals themselves, his only legitimate recourse is to stand down from leadership of the nation and pass authority on to someone with less delicate sensitivities.[1]

There is also the argument that advances the special nature of the international system. It asserts that international relations is a peculiarly brutal and anarchic enterprise. Considerations of justice, fairness, or moderation that might be appropriate in dealing with domestic affairs have little if any place in confronting the realities of the world beyond one's shores. Machiavelli offered the basic point: "a man who wishes to make a profession of goodness in everything must necessarily come to grief among so many who are not good. Therefore it is necessary for a prince, who wishes to maintain himself, to learn how not to be good, and to use this knowledge and not use it, according to the necessity of the case."[2]

The implications of such an argument convey a rather melancholy judgment. They suggest that even the most well-meaning of individuals necessarily must set aside personal moral convictions in dealing with the grim realities of the world on behalf of the nation. Would that the world were a better place so that saints could direct the affairs of state. Since the world is not a better place, and indeed is a worse place than any but the most vivid imagination could conceive, the effective leader has to accept the essential tragedy of his position, which is that political power essentially *equates* with dirty hands. Such assertions as these cannot be easily set aside, and there is no claim here that they are not important aspects of the world of statecraft. Yet the essential argument of this chapter is that they represent only a partial truth about the duties, and even more the opportunities, of statesmen. No reasonable person would claim that the leader of a nation can apply exactly the same moral standards to his activities as public servant as he does to his own private life. Yet the legitimate gap between the two can be overstated. The public and private realms are indeed different, but that does not mean they are totally unconnected. It is simply to say that there is a necessity for reflection on what special moral principles may rightly be applied to public life in contrast with more intimate circumstances. In examining this issue, I propose to offer here a case study in applied ethics that involves the problem of political leadership and dirty hands in its most acute form, that is to say, during wartime itself. It has to do with Winston Churchill's role in the British bombing of German cities in World War II.

BACKGROUND

During the first few months of the war British long-range bombers did little more than make occasional forays over the Ruhr valley dropping propaganda leaflets, although there were a few strikes against German naval facilities on the Baltic. British restraint during this period may be accounted for in part by its relatively limited technical capability for massive air strikes against Germany. There was also concern about German retaliation in kind if the informal proscription against large-scale city strikes was abandoned. Also important, however, was the principle that civilized states were bound even in wartime to observe the crucial distinction between combatant and noncombatant. This standard had been emphasized by the so-called Hague Draft Rules drawn up in

1923, which denounced the indiscriminate bombing of civilian populations, and was reaffirmed as reflecting British policy by British Prime Minister Neville Chamberlain on the outbreak of war.[3]

Having considered the initial British stance on strategic bombing against Germany, it is instructive to consider the events of the night of July 27, 1943. That evening 787 planes from Bomber Command attacked the center of the German city of Hamburg with a combination of explosive and incendiary bombs. It had been a hot and dry summer in northern Germany, and this fact, combined with the unusually tight concentration of the bombs on the working class districts of the city, produced a firestorm that eventually covered an area of about four square miles. Temperatures at the center of the firestorm reached about 1800 degrees Fahrenheit, accompanied by winds of hurricane force. One British pilot described the scene: "It was as if I was looking into what I imagined to be an active volcano. . . . Our actual bombing was like putting another shovelful of coal into the furnace." Over forty thousand people died on that evening in Hamburg within a period of about two hours.[4]

The transition in British policy from a rejection of "indiscriminate" or area bombing to an apparent embrace of precisely this concept resulted over the course of the war in the progressive destruction of almost every major city in Germany. Over 500,000 Germans lost their lives as a result; about twice that number suffered serious injury. Some three million dwellings were destroyed. The British decision to adopt an unalloyed strategy of devastating German cities through air attacks seems to have derived from several factors which can only be briefly summarized here, but which nevertheless have their own importance in arriving at a moral judgment on the strategy itself. One supposed "goal" of the policy was to undermine German civilian morale sufficiently to make it impossible for Hitler to continue the war. How this goal was to work itself out in practice, given the totalitarian character of Nazi Germany, and whether German morale would really break under bombing, were items that were left basically unexamined. In actuality the move toward area bombing seems to have been dictated by technical factors as much as by any consideration of strategic airpower doctrine. At this stage of the war daylight strikes by Bomber Command had basically been abandoned because of the prohibitive losses that German air defenses could inflict on the attacking bombers. Moreover, the accuracy with which British aircrews could hit specific military targets even in daytime had been shown to be badly wanting. Under the circumstances, nighttime bombing of large cities seemed the only available alternative for Bomber Command, both in terms of limiting losses of aircraft and in terms of the crude aiming capabilities of these aircraft. Since those in authority were committed to a massive strategic air offensive of some kind against Germany, indiscriminate bombing of German cities followed almost as a matter of course.[5]

Winston Churchill had been Prime Minister of Britain since the previous May, and the move toward area bombing received his full support. Indeed, he may be regarded as one of the principal sponsors, if not the principal sponsor, of the new strategy. As early as July 8, 1940, he had written to Lord Beaverbrook, Minister for Aircraft Production, that there was only one thing that would bring Hitler down, and that was "an absolutely devastating exterminating attack by very heavy bombers from this country upon the Nazi homeland. We must be able to overwhelm them by this means, without which I do not see a way through."[6] In looking back on his decision to order the area bombing of Germany, Churchill insisted after the war that the adoption of such a strategy was both necessary and just. He commented to a former staff officer of Bomber Command that "we should never allow ourselves to apologize for what we did to Germany."[7]

STANDARDS FOR EVALUATION

Was such an apology necessary? More specifically, what moral judgment can be rendered on Churchill's supervision of the area offensive? Did he have dirty hands, and if so can we excuse his having them in this particular case? The first part of the question seems almost self-evident. Anyone who presides over the death and injury of thousands, or, in the case of area bombing, more than a million, may hardly be said to be an innocent. It is the second part of the query that is the really important—and relevant—one. In arriving at an assessment of Churchill's role in the area bombing of Germany, it is necessary to set out certain specific criteria for judgment. It may be tempting to argue that any political leader responsible for such destruction as was visited on Germany by area bombing is to be condemned outright. From this perspective, area bombing was inherently a crime and thus quite indefensible. If a weighing of Churchill's moral position with respect to area bombing is to have a more general significance, however, a rather more systematic set of standards has to be established by which an ethical verdict can be rendered both on him and on other leaders and other situations, especially ones somewhat less dramatic than the devastation of German cities.

Intuitive Values

The first of these has to do with what may be called the "intuitive values" of the leader. An intuitive value judgment regards a certain action as invariably wrong (or right) regardless of its effects, and reflects the pure dictates of conscience.[8] Even given the terrible responsibilities of leadership, particularly in wartime, one has the right to suggest that there are inherent differences between different kinds of policies, and that some are inherently more ethical than others. In the case of the practice of war, for example, the slaughter of innocents, that is to say, of noncombatants, is almost universally regarded as an evil in itself quite aside from whatever "utilitarian" calculations may be advanced for the necessity of violating this principle. A moral leader in wartime is thus one who constantly has the protection of innocents as a major consideration.

Even more important than this is the general sanctity of life itself: it is an intuitive requirement that leaders conduct military operations in such a way that not only their own troops but even those of the enemy suffer the least harm consistent with the search for victory. An enemy in uniform—just as an enemy noncombatant—does not lose all his rights. It cannot be said that he is subject to idle or vengeful slaughter simply because he is the enemy. This principle is indeed widely accepted. It accounts for the standard injunction that enemy prisoners of war are entitled to certain basic protections, even though their murder might actually be of some military utility to their opponent. In passing moral judgment on wartime leaders, therefore, a first test is the degree to which the leader in question displays an appropriate commitment to and awareness of the intuitive values discussed above. Such a test, for example, helps us to assess the ethics of a Napoleon Bonaparte, who is said to have boasted to Metternich that he could afford to "spend" 30,000 men a month. Also relevant was his comment that "I do not care a fig for the lives of a million men."[9] Whatever his other qualities, this virtual moral nihilism disqualifies (or should disqualify) Napoleon from our admiration.

There is nothing in the body of Churchill's public or private pronouncements that comes close to Napoleon's brutal lack of concern with his own men. Indeed he consistently had the welfare of the average British soldier very much in mind. Ironically, that was one of the reasons he supported the area bombing of Germany. Churchill was a veteran of the trench warfare of World War I, and it seems to have made a profound impression on him. He was virtually obsessed with finding a way of defeating Germany that would avoid the mindless slaughter of the first great struggle, at least insofar as the British armed forces were concerned. He evidently saw area bombing as a way to achieve this goal. Such attacks would hopefully weaken the German power of resistance sufficiently to make the ultimate Allied invasion of Europe a tolerable exercise in terms of casualties. Area bombing also had another related rationale: it was used by Churchill to deflect American and Soviet pressure for a *premature* invasion of the continent that would, in Churchill's view, carry the risk of quite exorbitant losses. The British resources and energy applied to strategic air strikes against Germany were a testament to the fact that Britain was committed to a vigorous prosecution of the war effort even if she balked at an early second front in Europe. This was an important factor in itself in Britain's relationship with its Allies.

In terms of certain other "intuitive" values, Churchill also presented many attractive qualities, including a capacity for generosity, human kindness and loyalty, that we commonly identify as primary virtues. He was particularly noted for his willingness to extend forgiveness to former enemies. He emphasized in the House of Commons in January, 1945, that the Allies had no plan to "exterminate or trample on the German people. . . . Not at all. We remain bound by our own customs and our own nature."[10] Yet this is hardly the whole story. There was a darker side to the Churchill persona as well, and it has to be considered in any moral evaluation of his role in the area bombing of Germany. An interesting incident in this regard came on October 17, 1940, when a Conservative Member of Parliament for Eccles (Robert Cary) confronted him in the smoking-room of the House of Commons and demanded that the Prime Minister authorize full-scale city bombing of Germany in retaliation for German attacks on Britain. Churchill's reply: "My dear sir, this is a military and not a civilian war. You and others may desire to kill women and children. We desire (and have succeeded in our desire) to destroy German military objectives." This was an admirable defense of standards of discrimination in wartime, and Churchill appears admirable for having offered it.

Unfortunately he didn't stop there. He went on to say to Cary that "I quite appreciate your point. But my motto is 'Business before Pleasure.' "[11] The coarseness of this remark was reflected in other comments that Churchill sometimes offered about the "character" of the German people, which seemed to suggest that all their suffering was not only militarily appropriate but even deserved in the bargain because of flaws in their personality. At one point he maintained that one of the purposes of area bombing was to make "the German people taste and gulp each month a sharper dose of the miseries they have showered upon mankind."[12] In April, 1941, he offered the sociological observation that "there are less than seventy million malignant Huns—some of whom are curable and others killable."[13] When confronted with the fact that the indiscriminate bombing of cities seemed to represent a significant rejection of previous restraints in the conduct of war, and especially British standards in this regard, he cavalierly remarked that "it is absurd to consider morality on this topic. . . . In the last war the bombing of open cities was regarded as forbidden. Now everybody does it as a matter of course. It is simply a question of fashion changing as she does between long and short skirts for women."[14]

In assessing this sort of language it is important to accept that it was offered during a period of extremely high stress and in some cases during a phase of the war in which the prospects of a German victory—with all that implied for the future of British democracy—were seen not just as a theoretical threat but as a very real one. Under the circumstances, as one of his close aides and unalloyed admirers argues, it may have been hardly surprising that "as time went on, and the accumulated horrors of the war hardened all our hearts, he grew indifferent to the sufferings of the German cities."[15] Some allowance also has to be made for Churchill's occasional affinity for hyperbole, a tendency with which those around him were quite familiar and which they took pains to minimize in the actual conduct of affairs. All the same, the above comments (as well as others that could be presented in the same vein) are troubling evidence that in certain key respects Churchill was quite unnecessarily and inappropriately callous about the consequences for German civilians of Bomber Command's nightly forays over their country. Even if he saw area bombing as a crucial component of a strategy for defeating the Nazis, our admiration of his wartime leadership can not help but be diluted by his frequent dismissal of the idea that

the suffering of enemy noncombatants was even a relevant item for consideration.

Consequentialism

But did Churchill really feel that area bombing was critical to the successful
prosecution of the war effort? There is a second test of the ethics of leaders,
and it may be broadly regarded as utilitarian or consequentialist rather than
intuitive. We have a right to expect that our leaders will examine all possible
alternatives in dealing with a policy problem, and, more than this, make a careful
assessment of the likely positive outcomes of certain actions balanced against
their negative side effects. As one study puts it, "Awareness of the consequences
of one's actions seems a necessary if not sufficient condition for moral conduct.
. . . The principle seems [especially] beyond dispute for public officials deciding
important policy issues. Officials have a duty to anticipate the important consequences of policies they advocate or implement."[16]

In some ways this may seem like a fairly commonplace injunction. Certainly
most, if not all, leaders do consider different ways of achieving their goals, and
pick the course of action which seems best calculated to contribute to the desired
end. In the case of international relations, however, and particularly during wartime, the consequentialist principle has a special application. Decisions taken in
this realm are often going to result not just in grumbles from some dissatisfied
interest group but in considerable human suffering, even (in wartime) in death
and destruction. It is thus that the principle of proportionality intrudes itself.
Simply put, this requires that for any given action taken in a (presumably) just
cause, the positive returns from that action must outweigh the evil side effects
that it may produce. To be sure this is often a difficult concept to apply in
practice. How *much* of a contribution does a specific action have to make to
counterbalance certain evil side effects? How do we define what *are* "evil side
effects"? In the case of war, however, the second question is perhaps more easily
answered. On an intuitive basis, *all* human death or suffering is *ipso facto* an
evil effect. The issue thus becomes how one can choose actions that are pro-
ductive or necessary in the search for victory, while at the same time limiting
such death or suffering as much as possible. From a somewhat different perspective, the standards of utility require that if the latter is to be great, the value
of the former must be pronounced and unmistakable.

What is striking about Churchill's role in the area bombing of Germany is
the apparent *inconsistency* in his analysis as to the practical effects of such a
strategy. Before the war began he was on record as being quite skeptical on the
matter. He went out of his way to denounce the concept of "terror" bombing in
an article for the American magazine *Colliers* in June, 1939, on both moral and
practical grounds. These doubts seemed to be washed away, however, once he
became Prime Minister. We have already recounted how in the grim days following the fall of France, when Britain stood alone against the might of the

German war machine, Churchill seemed to feel that there was only one possibility of reversing the fortunes of war. His minute to Lord Beaverbrook on July 8, 1940, referred to the massive bombing of Germany as the "one sure path" for the defeat of the Nazi menace.[17] In the succeeding months the Prime Minister was perhaps the principal voice arguing for the importance of Bomber Command as the key to victory.

By the fall of 1941, however, Churchill's views on the strategic bombing offensive seemed to take yet another turn. On October 7, he wrote to Sir Charles Portal, Chief of the Air Staff, along the following lines: "We all hope that the air offensive against Germany will realize the expectations of the Air Staff. . . . I deprecate however placing unbounded confidence in this means of attack. . . . The Air Staff would make a mistake to put their claim too high."[18] Some nine months later (in July 1942), with the United States now in the war, Churchill put the point even more directly:

In the days when we were fighting alone, we answered the question: "How are you going to win the war?" by saying: "We will shatter Germany by bombing." Since then the enormous injuries inflicted on the German Army and manpower by the Russians, and the accession of the manpower and munitions of the United States, have rendered other possibilities open.[19]

These other possibilities included diverting the aircrews of the Royal Air Force from attacking Germany to direct support of the ground campaign in North Africa, and subsequently in Sicily and Italy, as well as to the destruction of the German U-boat threat in the North Atlantic. Moreover, considerable resources could have been redirected away from the building of heavy bombers to the expansion of the army and navy (a possibility that many, although few within the Royal Air Force, strongly supported).

All of this seems to admit of only one interpretation. In the most desperate days of Britain's struggle with Germany, Churchill supported the area bombing of Germany as the one effort that held out even the smallest hope of preventing German victory. With the United States and the Soviet Union in the war, he saw quite clearly that Germany ultimately would be defeated and that area bombing was now hardly a "military necessity" in any real sense of the term—that is, the only real alternative available to the British war effort. Even assuming that considerable emphasis would continue to be placed on some type of bombing of Germany, moreover, he had in the latter stages of the war an option open to him that was far more attractive in both moral and also in military terms. In his minute of October 7, 1941, the Prime Minister had suggested that Bomber Command might prove to be a truly significant force in the war should the enemy's air defenses be so shattered that what was called precision daylight bombing of arms factories and other targets became a real possibility. In the event, this is precisely what happened during the spring of 1944, particularly with the introduction of long-range fighter escorts such as the Mustang, which made deep-penetration strikes into the Reich against precision targets an inviting strategy. Following the success of the D-Day operation, German air defenses became even more enfeebled. As of this date Bomber Command had also developed advanced navigational and aiming devices that at last made it possible for British aircrews to undertake precision air strikes in Germany with great accuracy.

The point is that precision bombing promised—and delivered—far more decisive military results than area bombing ever could claim. During the main period of British area bombing of Germany, there was no evidence that German civilian morale had been affected to the degree that it posed a real threat to the continuation of the war effort. Even more significant was the fact that Nazi arms production actually increased rather than decreased. Construction of aircraft of all types went from approximately 15,000 in 1942 to about 40,000 in 1944. The production of tanks increased sixfold. The overall output of weapons and ammunition was almost three times the level achieved at the beginning of 1942.[20] Precision bombing, on the other hand (as mostly practiced by the Americans), had quite opposite and devastating consequences, resulting, for example, in the reduction of German petroleum production to only 10,000 tons in September 1944, barely a fraction of what the German armed forces required for successful operations.

It is only fair to ask whether Churchill had information at the time which suggested the ineffectiveness of area bombing. The answer is almost certainly yes. From sources such as "Ultra," which allowed the British to read secret German military communications, as well as a number of other photographic and related sources, it was evident to all but the most stubborn eyes that area bombing was not only morally repugnant but ineffective in the bargain. Churchill himself was an avid consumer of such intelligence. The leading historian of British intelligence states flatly that "no British statesman in modern times has had a more passionate faith in the value of secret intelligence than Winston Churchill." So intense was his interest in the subject that he often demanded to see raw intelligence reports before they had been analyzed by the professionals.[21]

Despite all of the preceding information, in September 1944 Bomber Command was allowed to resume much of its massive area offensive against Germany (after being diverted to support the D-Day invasion) instead of being forced to concentrate on precision daylight strikes against specific military targets such as the German arms industry, petroleum facilities and the transportation network. It is well to recall in this regard that approximately 80 percent of all the bombs dropped on Germany came in the last ten months of the war, and cities remained the primary target of Bomber Command until the very end. In terms of the "consequentialist" standard, therefore, Churchill's role in the area bombing of Germany seems even more problematic. Relatively early in the war he had come to have doubts himself about the military utility of such a strategy, and subsequently he had even more information that area attacks were—quite aside from their being morally repugnant—ineffective in the war effort. Moreover, the alternative of precision bombing of German military targets was available to him no later than the summer of 1944. Given these facts, it is hard to explain or to excuse his continued support of, or at least condoning of, the ongoing devastation of German cities and German civilians until virtually the last days of the war. It may be unreasonable to expect wartime leaders to adopt policies simply because they are morally attractive even though they may have harmful military consequences. In this instance there was a compelling congruence between morality and efficiency.

Universalization

There is a third test that may be applied to the moral evaluation of political leaders (even in wartime), although it may be argued that it has somewhat less force than the other two. A standard philosophical principle in establishing moral conduct is the requirement of "universalization." This means that the action undertaken must reflect an appropriate sensitivity to the interests of *all* concerned parties—not just one's own personal interests, or that of the special community one represents.[22] From a somewhat different perspective, what is implicitly involved here is Kant's famous Categorical Imperative, which dictates that one should "act only on that maxim whereby thou canst at the same time will that it should become a universal law." It is evident that there is a prudential as well as an inherent argument behind the concept of universalization. By considering the effects of one's actions in their totality, one may contribute to a more positive or stable collective environment that in itself will benefit the specific community which one represents.

The requirement of universalization, or of the Categorical Imperative, of course presents complications when we consider the conduct of states as opposed to that of individuals. Some would assert the relevance of these concepts to individual life while at the same time doubting whether they really apply to the life of collectives, given the semi-anarchic and self-interested character of international politics. Even if we partially concede the point, however, it seems reasonable to suggest that, by definition, a leader of great moral authority will attempt to go beyond an exclusive focus on the narrow interests of his or her own society and give at least some attention to the broader welfare of the international community as such. This does not mean that the very life and future of one's country has to be mortgaged to the welfare of others; it does imply that there are numerous situations in which a little less for one means a great deal more for others, and there is some considerable moral imperative for recognizing such situations and designing appropriate policies as a result.

In deciding on an "appropriate" British bombing policy in World War II, Churchill was, as it turned out, not totally indifferent to the philosophical requirement of universalization (although it is highly unlikely that he approached the matter in such abstract terms). From the earliest days of his stewardship of the British war effort, he was to insist that due care be given to at least one group of civilians subject to the power of Bomber Command—those living in occupied Western Europe. The fact is that a good deal of British bombing during the war was directed not just at Germany itself but at a range of targets in France and the Low Countries, and to a lesser extent in Denmark, Norway and other places as well. In October, 1942, the Air Ministry issued a directive to the head of Bomber Command stating that deliberate attacks on the civilian populations in the occupied territories were forbidden, and that all such raids in this area had to be on strictly defined military objectives. More significant was the injunction that aircrews had to take all reasonable measures to insure that "accidental" loss of civilian life was held to an absolute minimum. The same directive added, almost as an aside, that such discrimination was not required in attacks on Germany itself.[23]

This concern with the welfare of others—even if it meant imposing certain restrictions on Bomber Command operations—was reflected most noticeably in the spring of 1944. Under the so-called Transportation Plan, the Allied Chiefs of Staff, at the urging of the Americans, decided to concentrate all British and American bombing prior to the D-Day invasion on the German rail system in France and Belgium. The theory was that if this system could be shattered, the ability of the Germans to bring reinforcements to the invasion front would be badly compromised, which in turn would increase the likelihood of a successful invasion of the continent. Churchill strongly objected to the Transportation Plan, however, not only on grounds of its possible ineffectiveness but on moral grounds as well. He even went so far as to appeal to President Roosevelt directly to limit what he called the anticipated "French slaughters" and "the apparently ruthless use of the Air Forces, particularly of the Royal Air Force, on whom the brunt of this kind of work necessarily falls, and the reproaches that would be made upon the inaccuracy of night bombing."[24]

Roosevelt rejected Churchill's appeal, and as it happened preinvasion bombing in the occupied countries had a less draconian effect on the civilian population than feared. Approximately 12,000 civilians lost their lives. This was a somber enough figure in itself, but what is striking is how Churchill displayed a concern in this instance about civilian suffering that was almost totally absent when it was a question of bombing Germany itself. How to account for the difference? Certainly there was a pragmatic concern in British circles about a very negative political backlash in London's relationship with the de Gaulle Free French government-in-exile if large numbers of Frenchmen were killed in Allied bombing raids. But Churchill asserted a broader moral theory as well when he suggested that the death of French civilians would involve "a friendly people who have committed no crimes against us, and not the German foe, with all their record of cruelty and ruthlessness."[25]

Such an attitude, however understandable, can not gainsay the fact that even in wartime the enemy population still retains certain rights and interests that require attention. To be sure it seems reasonable to suggest that these may rightly be regarded as less compelling than the rights and interests of one's own soldiers and civilians, or those of Allied nations. Yet they hardly disappear even in the carnage of war. The idea that the welfare even of the enemy should be a subject of concern inevitably rests (as we have already argued) on the premise that there is no essential difference in the sanctity of life. If, as has been asserted, this applies even in terms of the treatment of enemy soldiers, the principle seems especially important in balancing the welfare of, say, one's own combatants with that of the enemy civilian population who are not combatants. By what moral calculus can we say that the death and injury of enemy civilians is essentially irrelevant as long as there is at least some prospect that such suffering will marginally reduce the danger to one's soldiers? Merely because a state of war exists does not remove the legitimate claims of enemy civilians for a reasonable chance to go on living. In order to protect such rights, it may be necessary for the soldier to accept a *somewhat* higher degree of risk (no one is demanding that they simply sacrifice themselves for the sake of enemy noncombatants).

Air Marshal Arthur Harris, the head of Bomber Command, had no doubt about how to resolve this issue. He observed at one point that "I do not personally regard the whole of the remaining cities of Germany as worth the bones of one British Grenadier."[26] Of many extraordinary statements offered during the war by Harris, this must surely rank among the most extraordinary. Was he really arguing that the killing of indeterminate thousands of additional German civilians was morally counterbalanced by the saving of one British soldier's life? Churchill was relatively more discreet in commenting on this matter, but based on his actions it does not seem unfair to suggest that implicitly he shared Harris's basic premise. The fact that he allowed Bomber Command to continue its devastation of German cities even up to the last days of the war can only be interpreted as a willingness to set aside whatever marginal concern he may have felt for the German civilian in order to pursue indiscriminate bombing as one way in which to force the Nazi regime into submission.

CHURCHILL'S CONDUCT SUMMARIZED

To reiterate a point made earlier, there is no question but that Churchill did have "dirty hands" in his role as Britain's wartime Prime Minister. Can we go beyond this, however, and argue that Churchill was in some ways a genuinely "wicked" man for whom the dirty hands defense offers an inadequate rebuttal? Such a conclusion is certainly tempting given the fact that he presided over what seems to have been a militarily unnecessary visitation of great calamity on German civilians. The term "wicked," however, is open to various interpretations, and seems to admit of differing forms. Perhaps Churchill's conduct was an example of what S.I. Benn calls "conscientious wickedness."

Conscientious wickedness is rarely a case of pursuing an end unaware of attendant consequences as evils; it is more often a case of a single-minded pursuit of an objective which . . . can reasonably be seen as good, but at the cost of a callous insensitivity to evil done by the way. It is not that the person believes the incidental evil to be itself good but rather that, having reason to think it evil, he nevertheless systematically disregards it.[27]

The mark of the "non-conscientious" wicked person, Benn continues, is "that such choices are for him neither difficult nor painful since the considerations that would make them so are systematically neutralized."[28]

It would be going too far to say that Churchill was able to put the tribulations of the German civilian population in World War II totally out of mind—that is to say, he was not able to totally neutralize his opinion of their sufferings. On one occasion in June, 1943, according to an account by an Australian representative to the War Cabinet, Churchill was shown some actual bombing films of Germany, which were "very well and dramatically done." He suddenly "sat bolt upright and said to me, 'Are we beasts? Are we taking this too far?' "[29] Even if such reactions were comparatively rare, there is certainly no question but that Churchill was devoted to a cause that could "reasonably be seen as good," i.e., the defeat of the Nazi challenge to civilization itself. These two circumstances perhaps exculpate Churchill from the grosser charge that his policy of bombing Germany was an unalloyed wickedness. To be "non-conscientiously" wicked, moreover, it is necessary that the individual involved be quite unaware of the fact that any moral issue is presented by his actions. In a curious sense the existence of hypocrisy may be an important standard for judgment here. The hypocrite is at least aware that a moral query may be presented against his behavior, and thus he attempts to disguise its actual character. If he were not sensitive to the charge itself, why bother to engage in the hypocrisy itself? As the French sage la Rochefoucauld put it, "hypocrisy is the tribute that vice pays to virtue."

In advancing the concept of hypocrisy as a defense of Churchill's moral standing, we might refer to the memorandum he wrote following the destruction of Dresden. This was probably the most famous (or infamous) application of Allied bombing during the entire war. On the night of February 13, 1945, the British attacked Dresden in two waves totaling almost 800 Lancaster bombers, and a tremendous firestorm of the sort only seen previously at Hamburg developed. Estimates on casualties from the Dresden raid vary widely, from a minimal guess of about 35,000 dead to the most drastic estimate of over 200,000. Throughout the war, spokesmen for the British government had denied that Bomber Command was simply attacking the center of German cities, but for a variety of reasons the reality of what had happened at Dresden became quickly known and widely disseminated. Sharp questioning took place in the House of Commons as to the real nature of Bomber Command's strategy, and there were widespread doubts expressed in other quarters as well about the purpose of destroying Dresden. It was against this background that on March 31, 1945 (some six weeks after the Dresden raid), Churchill wrote to Sir Charles Portal as follows:

It seems to me that the moment has come when the question of bombing of German cities simply for the sake of increasing the terror, *though under other pretexts*, should be reviewed. . . . The destruction of Dresden remains a serious query against the conduct of Allied bombing. . . . The Foreign Secretary has spoken to me on this subject, and I feel the need for more precise concentration upon military objectives such as oil and communications behind the immediate battle zone, *rather than on mere acts of terror and wanton destruction, however impressive.*[30]

Now it is readily apparent from the historical evidence that Churchill had actually been a prime actor in the decision to attack Dresden, and in this instance even against the doubts of such champions of area bombing as Sir Arthur Harris. Given this fact, his memorandum can only be regarded as an attempt to "cleanse" the historical record. Subsequent histories of British strategic bombing in World War II would record that he had expressed doubts (*ex post facto*) about the destruction of Dresden. As an historian himself, Churchill presumably wanted to have evidence placed in the record about his concern over the effects of area bombing, and specifically its application to Dresden, even though such doubts were noticeably absent in his earlier directives on the devastation of German cities. One may recoil before this example of political dissimulation, yet accept that it represented a belated admission by Churchill that Bomber Command (and he himself) had done wrong, and that he was implicitly saying as much, even though it came at a very late date.

This retroactive acceptance (even indirectly) of guilt may be of some reassurance to those who cherish the memory of the former British Prime Minister and want to continue to do so. For many others, however, a more balanced view would be that Churchill's initiation of, and subsequent support for, the area bombing of Germany remains as a permanent blot on his moral escutcheon. Certainly he was a man of many admirable qualities, and he obviously performed a critical role in vanquishing the Nazi challenge to basic human values. Even so, his part in the destruction of hundreds of thousands of German civilians hardly stands as his finest hour. To accept dirty hands as the price of political leadership, particularly in wartime, is one thing. To excuse a crude indifference (in the case of area bombing) to those very values, to the fundamental requirement that the effects of differing policies be carefully considered, and to the obligation to respect the rights in wartime even of the enemy is quite another. Winston Churchill's role in the ordeal visited on German cities in World War II still stands as a serious indictment of his insensitivity to the enduring moral imperatives that should govern the actions of statesmen.

NOTES

1. These "primordial demands," moreover, are innately selfish and even brutal when compared to the sort of aspirations considered admirable in individual life. See Reinhold Niebuhr's *Moral Man and Immoral Society* (New York: Charles Scribner's Sons, 1932).

2. Niccolò Machiavelli, *The Prince and the Discourses*, Chapter XV (New York: The Modern Library, 1940), p. 56.

3. John Finnis, Joseph Boyle, and Germain Grisez, eds., *Nuclear Deterrence, Morality, and Realism* (Oxford: Clarendon Press, 1987), p. 39.

4. Gwynne Dyer, *War* (Homewood, IL: Dorsey Press, 1985), p. 93.

5. For a more detailed discussion of the factors leading to the area bombing of Germany, see my *Ethics and Airpower in World War II* (New York: St. Martin's Press, 1993), pp. 9–14.

6. R.V. Jones, *Most Secret War* (London: Hamish Hamilton, 1978), p. 183.

7. Max Hastings, *Bomber Command* (New York: Simon & Schuster, 1987), p. 107.

8. J. Hare and Carey B. Joynt, *Ethics and International Affairs* (New York: St. Martin's Press, 1982), pp. 4–5.

9. Michael Walzer, *Just and Unjust Wars* (New York: Basic Books, 1977), pp. 29, 136.

10. Sir Harold Nicolson, *The War Years 1939–1945* (New York: Atheneum, 1967), p. 429.

11. Ibid., pp. 121–22.

12. Angus Calder, *The People's War* (New York: Pantheon Books, 1969), p. 491.

13. Robert H. Ahrenfeldt, *Psychiatry in the British Army* (New York: Columbia University Press, 1958), pp. 13–28.

14. Barton Bernstein, "Why We Didn't Use Poison Gas in World War II," *American Heritage* (August–September, 1985), p. 42.

15. Sir John Colville, as quoted in Ronald Lewin's *Churchill as Warlord* (New York: Stein and Day, 1973), p. 7.

16. Mark Moore, "Realms of Obligation and Virtue," in Joel Fleishman et al., *Public Duties: The Moral Obligations of Government Officials* (Cambridge: Harvard University Press, 1981), p. 10.

17. Jones, *Most Secret War*, p. 183.

18. Winston S. Churchill, *The Grand Alliance* (Boston: Houghton Mifflin Company, 1951), pp. 507–9.

19. Winston Churchill, *The Hinge of Fate* (Boston: Houghton Mifflin Company, 1950), p. 770.

20. P.M.S. Blackett, *Political and Military Consequences of Atomic Energy* (London: Turnstile Press, 1948), p. 195.

21. Christopher Andrew, "Churchill and Intelligence," in Michael Handel, ed., *Leaders and Intelligence* (London: Frank Cass, 1989), p. 181.

22. For an interesting discussion of this principle, see G. Elfstrom and N. Fotion, *Military Ethics* (London: Routledge and Kegan Paul, 1986), p. 17.

23. Finnis, Boyle, and Grisez, *Nuclear Deterrence, Morality and Realism*, p. 40.

24. Winston S. Churchill, *Closing the Ring* (Boston: Houghton Mifflin Company, 1951), p. 529.

25. Ibid., pp. 529–30.

26. Dudley Saward, *Bomber Harris* (Garden City, NY: Doubleday, 1985), p. 601.

27. S.I. Benn, "Wickedness," in John Deigh, ed., *Ethics and Personality* (Chicago: University of Chicago Press, 1992), p. 197.

28. Ibid., p. 199.

29. Lord Richard Casey, *Personal Experience 1939–1945* (London: Constable, 1962), p. 171.

30. Noble Frankland and Charles Webster, *The Strategic Air Offensive Against Germany 1939–1945*, Vol. III (London: Her Majesty's Stationery Office, 1961), p. 112 (emphasis added).

CHAPTER 5

No End of a Lesson: Vietnam and the Nature of Moral Choice in Foreign Policy

David Armstrong

It would not be difficult to develop a narrative of American decisions relating to Vietnam that showed, at each crucial turn, successive administrations arriving at a choice of policy that was both morally wrong and, as things transpired, disastrously misguided in other respects too. In this narrative a clear moral parable would emerge: if statesmen strive to do the right thing according to widely accepted ethical norms, particularly those regarded as having a specific application to statecraft, they will find that they have also served their country's national interests better than if they had followed the injunctions of realists from Machiavelli onward about the necessity to disregard conventional moral principles in the name of the overriding principle of the security and survival of their own state. The supposedly higher value of *raison d'état* will be clearly be seen as no such thing and right and wrong as identical in public and private spheres. If valid, this parable would have profound implications. Although statesmen have frequently invoked "the lesson of Munich" to justify the threat and use of force on many occasions, they have been less inclined than this narrative suggests they should be to use "the lesson of Vietnam" to justify more pacific approaches.[1] More generally, it might give fresh force to Edmund Burke's injunction: "Justice is the great standing policy of civil society; and any eminent departure from it, under any circumstances, lies under the suspicion of being no policy at all."[2] Similarly, the parable gives some support to those who have queried the dominance of realism in the theory of international relations from various critical or postmodern perspectives which problematize the separation of the observer from the observed and theory from practice.[3] Realism would be revealed not as timeless wisdom, embodying fundamental verities about international politics expressed in scientifically rigorous axioms, characterized by their objectivity and value-neutrality, but as a mere discourse or interpretation that helps to constitute what it is supposedly explaining.

FIVE STEPS TO PERDITION

Such a narrative might begin with the first significant American encounter with Indochina, when, in 1945, the Truman administration decided to ignore several approaches from Ho Chi Minh's Vietminh, the most powerful of the Vietnamese nationalist groups that had been fighting the Japanese. National self-determination had been proclaimed by Truman's predecessor as one of the most important principles for which the United States was fighting,[4] an emphasis repeated by Truman in his first State of the Union Address in 1946. Yet for a variety of reasons, ranging from apprehension about the Vietminh's Communist identity to a concern for the impact of losing Vietnam upon French domestic politics, where the Communist Party was enjoying some success, Washington decided to align itself with French attempts to reassert control over Vietnam, albeit through a compliant indigenous government in the South rather than a return to pure colonialism. Although Truman had declared that self-determination should apply equally in Asia, Africa, Europe, and the Western Hemisphere[5] his administration was able to ignore the principle on this occasion. A recent Truman biography argues that his specific decisions relating to Vietnam "by no means predetermined all that followed under later, very different Presidents."[6] Truman's own memoirs make it clear, however, that although Indochina was not seen as holding any particular significance, it was already being viewed as one of a number of areas threatened by what was perceived as a monolithic and aggressive communism: the image that dominated American thinking throughout the first two decades of the Cold War.[7] Hence it is not unreasonable to place this, very early, example of America's preparedness to ignore its stated moral principles in the case of Vietnam within the larger context of our parable. Had American policy from 1945 to 1954, when U.S. support for the French war in Indochina grew to a point where it was funding 78 percent of the costs of the French war effort, instead been founded on support for Vietnamese independence, all the damaging consequences of American involvement might have been avoided. These include not only the casualties (58,000 Americans and one million Vietnamese), the financial costs, and the lasting damage to U.S. relations with France but also more intangible consequences such as the harm to America's reputation.

Reluctance to contemplate self-determination for Vietnam, except on terms agreeable to Washington, continued to characterize U.S. policy, for example when the United States encouraged the Diem regime in South Vietnam to ignore the 1954 Geneva Conference's requirements for nationwide elections and when it acted against South Vietnamese leaders when they were contemplating a neutralist path for their country in the early 1960s.[8] However, my concern in this section is to identify specific moral norms and illustrate their violation by American decision-makers in Vietnam, rather than to write a detailed account of their application or otherwise over the twenty-five years of the American involvement in the country. In that respect, the second major principle we might consider is the fundamental norm in international law relating to the sanctity of treaties, *pacta sunt servanda* (agreements must be kept), which is an international legal version of the more general admonition to people not to break promises. The agreement in question is the 1954 Geneva Accords, which partitioned the country (on terms less favorable than the North had won in battle) pending the holding of nationwide elections in 1956 and prohibited both sides from forming military alliances with other states and from permitting foreign troops and additional arms and munitions to be introduced.[9] Although the United States refused to sign the Accords, it issued a separate "unilateral declaration of its position" agreeing to "refrain from the threat or use of force" to disturb the Accords, supporting free elections to achieve unity in nations divided against their will, and repeating "its traditional position that peoples are entitled to determine their own future."

There is room to debate the precise legal status of these agreements and of the United States' declaration (as well as a similar declaration by the French-supported "State of Vietnam," which also refused to sign them).[10] It is also true that they were breached by all sides. However, a reasonable case can be advanced that South Vietnam and the United States were the first violators. Only two months after Geneva, the United States formed the Southeast Asia Treaty Organization (SEATO), whose name was clearly designed to imply parallels with NATO. This in itself was something of a provocative gesture, particularly as the U.S. Secretary of State, John Foster Dulles, had wanted South Vietnam to be a member of SEATO—which would have directly violated the Accords. Even the addition of a Protocol to extend the protection of the Treaty to Cambodia, Laos, and South Vietnam was, at the very least, against the spirit of the Accords, while the American introduction of a covert military unit in 1954 was equally difficult to reconcile with the principles expressed in its Geneva Declaration.

The third ethical-legal principle ignored by the United States, in this narrative, was the central norm of the Westphalian international order of nonintervention in the domestic affairs of other states. In practice, as the Pentagon Papers' account of the war makes clear, the United States became increasingly involved in South Vietnam's internal affairs from the moment it gave its strong support (against French opposition) to Ngo Dinh Diem's continuing leadership.[11] Insofar as the insurgency in the South was essentially a local affair—something that continues to be debated—America's growing commitment to support Saigon's resistance to it might also be deemed contrary to the nonintervention norm. Out of countless other examples, particular mention might also be made of what was at the very least American connivance in the coup against Diem.[12] A long-standing principle of international law in this context is that no state "shall organize, assist, foment, finance, incite or tolerate subversive, terrorist or armed activities directed towards the violent overthrow of the regime of another State, or interfere in civil strife in another state."[13] By one argument, which perceives the conflict in Vietnam as civil strife rather than externally supported aggression (the position of successive American administrations), the American involvement in its entirety violated this principle, but its toleration of the coup against Diem is a relatively clearcut violation of it. The United States was later to be specifically criticized on similar grounds by the International Court of Justice in 1986 over its conduct in Nicaragua.[14]

Nonintervention is conventionally regarded as, essentially, a legal rather than an ethical principle because it expresses a corollary of the legal foundation stone of the Westphalian system: the principle of sovereignty. Law and morality are, of course, not identical: although both may be defined as sets of rules, they serve different functions in society, and while a particular law may embody some more general moral principle, it does not necessarily do so.[15] "Thou shalt not kill" is both a moral and a legal rule; "thou shalt drive no faster than fifty miles an hour" is not. In the case of international society, it is, clearly, possible to argue a moral case *for* intervention on humanitarian grounds, and such arguments have been heard with increasing frequency since the end of the Cold War. However, that humanitarian intervention is generally seen as the *exceptional* case, requiring justification on overwhelming moral grounds, suggests that nonintervention continues to be regarded as the higher, or at least more fundamental, norm. Furthermore, it is a norm that in specific cases may itself need moral rather than strictly legal justification: for example, through the argument that an intervention might do more harm than good. Hence, one does not need to agree with Austinian notions of international law as merely "positive morality" to accept that some of the basic principles of international law—and, indeed, of domestic law—derive from or are closely associated with more general moral norms.[16] In this case, nonintervention may be seen as a particular case of the larger moral injunction to respect the freedom of the individual and of such ethical principles as live and let live.

The fourth moral offense of the United States was, at the least, using disproportionate force and, at worst, waging an aggressive war. War is, of course, the most controversial international activity of all so far as general morality is concerned because it may involve conduct that would, if it took place within a national society, be seen as violating several fundamental social values, including the prohibitions against coercion, aggression, cruelty, and killing. For these reasons, pacifists argue that all wars are immoral; states, which see themselves as having to live with the permanent security dilemma imposed by the anarchical nature of the international system, have tried to work out normative justifications for resorting to force in certain circumstances. If anything, international society has become more, rather than less, permissive so far as the use of force is concerned than the relatively restrictive terms of Article 2(4) of the UN Charter seems to imply.[17] However, governments resorting to force in pursuit of their objectives invariably try to ground their conduct in some principle of justice or morality, such as resisting aggression, righting a wrong, or liberating a people from oppression. This suggests that the international community still sees the need for some variant of "just war" criteria to be employed in interstate conflicts. Since the Nuremburg war crimes tribunals three categories of offenses against these criteria have been distinguished: the act of resorting to force in defiance of international law, or waging an aggressive war; crimes committed in the course of a war; and crimes against humanity. Together with the crime of genocide, these were the main categories adopted by the International Criminal Court set up in the first years of the new century, which the United States has refused to join.

Two points in particular are usually made in relation to the charge that the United States waged aggressive war in Vietnam: the commencement of the bombing campaign in the North in 1964–1965 and the extension of the war to Cambodia in 1970. The famous statistic that the American bombing campaign employed a greater explosive power than all the bombs dropped by all sides in World War II has sometimes been used by critics of the war to charge the United States with violating the just war principle that force used in a war should be proportionate to its objectives. However, "proportionality" is one of the murkiest aspects of just war theory. One authority suggests that "proportionality in coercion constitutes a requirement that responding coercion be limited in intensity and magnitude to what is reasonably necessary promptly to secure the permissible objectives of self-defense."[18] Unfortunately this begs rather more questions than it answers: clearly the intention of this doctrine is not to impose a criterion of equivalence, one that limited the degree of force used in self-defense to that employed by the enemy, which would simply be a recipe for prolonging a war indefinitely. The key phrases "reasonably necessary" and "permissible objectives" are essentially subjective ones: a military commander would define them in ways that enabled him to ensure the maximum security and minimum casualties for his men; civilian victims—including, in the Vietnamese case, families moved from their homes under the controversial and widely disliked "strategic hamlets" program—would have a different perspective.[19] Moreover, judgments about proportionality depend to a significant degree on prior judgments about the legitimacy of the war as such, in particular whether it might be seen as an aggressive war.

The bombing campaign and the related issues of American use of napalm and defoliants such as Agent Orange are considered in more detail elsewhere. Here we may briefly note that the American justification for bombing rested on the argument that the United States was assisting South Vietnam to resist aggression; the counterclaim: that it was the United States itself that was committing aggression is based on arguments that the bombing was a further, and much more serious, violation of the Geneva Accords and that it was undertaken not as a response to aggression but for a range of lesser reasons including the failure of South Vietnamese forces to deal with their Communist enemies and the need to bring pressure on Hanoi to accept a political solution. The charge of aggressive war in the context of Cambodia rests on more straightforward foundations. Cambodia had sought to maintain its formal neutrality during the war but had been unable to prevent North Vietnam from developing several bases along the eastern border of the country, which it used to supply its forces moving along the Ho Chi Minh Trail from north to south. The new Nixon administration began a secret bombing campaign in Cambodia in 1969 and in April 1970, with its South Vietnamese allies, launched a land attack across the border. Critics of the incursion—who use the less neutral word "invasion"—see it as a clearcut case of aggression against a neutral state, whose consequences included not only Cambodia's inexorable slide toward the murderous brutality of the Khmer Rouge regime but the worst moments of the war in the United States itself, when National Guard forces killed students who were protesting against the incursion at Kent State University in Ohio and Jackson State College in Mississippi.[20]

Crimes committed by soldiers during wars (which involve the just war norm of *jus in bello*, as opposed to crimes involved in the initiation of a war, which violate *jus ad bellum*) seem to be inseparable from war, and Vietnam was no exception. All forces on all sides committed such offenses; in this respect, the American troops were hardly more reprehensible than their allies or enemies, notwithstanding the publicity attracted by revelations of American atrocities at the village of My Lai, when more than 400 old men, women, and children were massacred. This is not to exculpate those or any other soldiers involved in such events: their moral guilt is clear enough when the extenuating circumstances usually advanced (heat of battle, ignorance, obeying orders, duress) are dismissed, as they can be in the case of My Lai.[21] But if the issue is whether, to what extent, and in what ways American conduct in Vietnam is particularly morally reprehensible, incidents like My Lai are not central to the specific case that we are constructing in this section. A more serious question in this regard is whether the war as a whole can be viewed as a crime against humanity. Not many, even among the critics of the war, go quite that far, but a few do argue that, taken together, the million deaths in Vietnam alone, the consequences of the Cambodian incursion, the long-term health effects, including continuing birth defects, of the use of Agent Orange, the use of napalm and other chemical weapons, and, most generally, the nature of the war as a conflict between the world's most powerful state and one of its poorest bring it close to the category of crime against humanity.[22]

The final moral charge against successive American administrations is that of lying—in particular, of lying in contexts that amounted to subverting the U.S. Constitution. When Robert S. McNamara, Defense Secretary under Kennedy and, for a time, Johnson, decided after years of refusing to write his own account of his controversial period in office, he did so because he had "grown sick at heart witnessing the cynicism and even contempt with which so many people view our political institutions."[23] He was well aware that such reactions had, to a significant degree, been caused by revelations about the various deceptions

employed by successive administrations during the Vietnam era, of which one
of the most crucial was the use of a report of an attack on two American vessels
in the Tonkin Gulf on August 4, 1964 (following an earlier attack on August
2), to secure a near unanimous vote in Congress giving President Johnson broad
powers to take whatever military actions he felt appropriate. McNamara's general verdict on American decisions relating to Vietnam is that "we made an error
not of values and intentions but of judgment and capabilities."[24] In the specific
case of the Tonkin Gulf Resolution, he continues to maintain, there was no
deliberate deception, although he accepts that Johnson abused the power granted
to him by the Resolution by hugely expanding the American presence in Vietnam far beyond anything Congress would have authorized had it been specifically requested to do so.[25] However, when the President sought the Resolution,
he was well aware (as was McNamara) of many factors that, at the very least,
made the events of August 4 far less than the unambiguous attack against American forces which was being portrayed to Congress: the fact that the administration had been looking for a pretext to increase military pressure on Hanoi for
some months, the existence of covert American and South Vietnamese naval
operations that would have been seen as provocative by the North, the proba-
bility that the American ships were in North Vietnamese territorial waters, and,
most of all, the strong possibility that no attack had taken place on August 4,
with the reported attack based on mistaken radar readings.[26] A Pentagon source
leaked some of this information late on August 4 to one of the two senators
who were to oppose the Resolution, Wayne Morse, but he was unable to persuade Senator William Fulbright, to whom Johnson had entrusted the task of
shepherding the Resolution through Congress, especially as McNamara flatly
denied one of his assertions, namely, that the American ships were part of covert
operations against the North.[27] Similarly, Fulbright (who was later bitterly to
regret his part in this affair) was able to dissuade another sceptic, Senator Gay-
lord Nelson, from proposing an amendment that would have had the effect of
limiting the President's powers, on receiving private assurances from Johnson
that he had no intention of embarking upon the open-ended land war that Nelson
feared.[28] Although the blackest interpretation of these events—that the administration was involved in a conspiracy with the aim of securing the freedom to
lead the country into a massive escalation of the war—is almost certainly in-
correct, the charge of deception is probably justified.

This, then, is one way of representing the war: as a parable, or moral fable,
enjoining leaders to act in accordance with fundamental and well-known values
as the best means of serving their country's national interests. There are, however, at least two other ways of interpreting the war (or two alternative narratives), one which depicts American statesmen as acting throughout in accordance
with other, equally fundamental, moral principles, the second which sees the
war essentially as a tragedy. This chapter considers each of these narratives in
turn before indicating problems with all three perspectives and reaching conclusions on ethical statecraft in general.

THE MORALITY OF U.S. DECISIONS

The strongest version of the argument that the United States acted with the noblest of intentions throughout its involvement in Vietnam sees the conflict there as essentially an aspect of a larger battle between good and evil: a battle, moreover, that the United States could have won had it not had its hands tied militarily and had it not faced so many domestic constraints. Unsurprisingly, perhaps, Richard Nixon presents the starkest outline of this narrative in his 1980 book, *The Real War*. At the time he wrote the book the United States, in his view, was still involved in "World War III," a confrontation, begun as World War II was ending, between a Soviet Union committed to spreading Communist ideology (seen by Nixon as a form of enslavement) around the world and a United States committed to the defense of freedom and democracy. Vietnam had been but one battleground in that struggle, but Nixon's administration had first created the conditions for victory with his Nixon Doctrine of making countries threatened by Communist aggression take primary responsibility for their own defense, then "by following the strategy I initiated in 1969, we and the South Vietnamese were able to win the war militarily by the time of the Paris accords of January 27, 1973. . . . But the public had been so misinformed and misled by unwise government actions and the shallow, inflammatory treatment of events by the media that morale within the United States collapsed just when the North was overwhelmingly defeated on the battlefield. We won a victory after a long hard struggle but then we threw it away . . . when Congress prohibited military operations in or over Indochina and cut back drastically on the aid South Vietnam needed to defend itself."[29]

There is, of course, more than a small element of self-justification in this, but the most striking aspect of this book is its insistence—ten years before the collapse of communism in Europe—on the continuing relevance of the image that had guided U.S. policy since the end of the war, namely, that the United States was involved in a global struggle between good and evil. Repeated American statements—in private as well as in public—were to emphasize the same essential points in support of a portrayal of U.S. foreign policy as a moral crusade. Freedom and democracy were indivisible, and a threat to those values anywhere was a threat to the United States itself: once one domino fell, many more would shortly follow. The "lesson of Munich" should never be forgotten: only firmness and strength in the face of the relentless onward march of totalitarian communism would halt and eventually turn back the tide. In the opinion of one archrealist, Henry Kissinger, it was precisely America's attempt to apply its values to the inappropriate case of Vietnam that was responsible for the disasters that ensued: "America's rejection of national interest as the basis of foreign policy had cast the country adrift on a sea of undifferentiated moralism."[30]

In a narrative that portrays American decision making as based firmly on ethical principles, all five charges against the United States discussed here may be turned on their heads. First, freedom and self-determination were illusory concepts in the context of a world Communist system that was controlled from Moscow and that relied on oppression, thought control, and restrictions on individual liberty to maintain its power. True self-determination could be achieved only within the "free world." This was the image at the heart of the Truman Doctrine, announced in 1947, when he declared an American policy "to support free peoples who are resisting attempted subjugation by armed minorities or by outside pressures."[31] It underpinned the American decision to go to war in Korea and the developing American commitment to Southeast Asia, as exemplified by a speech by John Foster Dulles in March 1954: "The imposition on Southeast Asia of the political system of Communist Russia and its Communist Chinese ally, by whatever means, must be a grave threat to the whole free community."[32] And, in what may also be seen as a brief summary of all American war aims in Vietnam, it remained central to a Joint Chiefs of Staff paper outlining the "Over-all US Concept for Vietnam" on August 27, 1965:

The RVN (Republic of Vietnam) is a politico/military keystone in Southeast Asia and is symbolic of U.S. determination in Asia—as Berlin is in Europe—to prevent communist expansion. The United States is committed to the defense of the RVN in order to assist a free people to remain free. In addition to the freedom of the RVN, U.S. national prestige, credibility and honor with respect to world-wide pledges, and declared national policy are at stake. Further, it is incumbent upon the United States at this stage to invalidate the communist concept of "wars of national liberation."[33]

As the Joint Chiefs' memorandum suggests, American policy was also strongly influenced by a determination not to be seen as breaking commitments that Washington believed it had undertaken on behalf of South Vietnam: the same *pacta sunt servanda* principle that the United States was accused of violating in the first narrative. Many statements emphasize specific American commitments to Vietnam, such as its SEATO obligations, but a far more frequently expressed concern was with America's reputation as a country that honored its promises to other states. The belief that "abandoning Vietnam" would have repercussions elsewhere in Southeast Asia was an aspect of the domino theory from the time the United States began to take over from France—as, for example, in a 1956 speech by Senator J. F. Kennedy saying that "our prestige in Asia will sink to a new low" if South Vietnam "falls victim to any of the perils that threaten its existence—Communism, political anarchy, poverty and the rest."[34] As the American involvement grew in size, so too did estimates of the potential damage to American prestige and hence to perceptions of the credibility and value of its alliance commitments around the world if it was forced to withdraw. For example, Richard Nixon cites with approval two opinions he received in late 1969: one, from the British counterinsurgency expert Sir Robert Thompson that "the future of Western civilization is at stake in the way you handle yourselves in Vietnam," the other from Henry Kissinger, that if the antiwar movement in the

United States succeeded in forcing an American withdrawal, "the Communists would become totally convinced that they could control our foreign policy through public opinion."[35]

So far as the third of the general principles considered in the first section is concerned, many of the leading American officials who were responsible for the escalating American involvement in Vietnam have since taken the view that the degree of their intervention in South Vietnamese domestic affairs was probably mistaken. This, however, is not because of a late conversion to nonintervention as a moral principle[36] so much as from a realization that nation building to the extent that Washington pursued this goal was not feasible in a state without a deeply entrenched commitment to democratic values among its leaders. The U.S. success in helping to recreate stable democratic societies, through Marshall Aid in Europe and occupation in Japan, was, in other words, not transferable to the completely different circumstances in Vietnam. At the time, however, the more American military and economic aid to Vietnam increased, the more Washington insisted on political reform, to the point in 1961 when the new Kennedy administration insisted that the price of a huge increase in aid was to be a substantial American role in almost every area of Vietnamese domestic politics.[37] Nonintervention was seen not as a moral principle in itself but, effectively, as the abandonment of morality for a cynical self-interest that disregarded the needs of others. Even the American collusion in changing the Diem regime could be justified on the fundamentally moral grounds that Diem was becoming increasingly autocratic and was clearly not the person to accomplish the high American purposes of building democracy in South Vietnam and holding the line against international communism.[38]

Similarly, the mirror image of the charge that America waged an aggressive war in Vietnam is the argument that the United States was simply defending the South against Communist aggression. Moreover, since the aggression faced by the South was part of a much wider scheme of world domination by the Soviet Union, a firm stand in Vietnam was a contribution to a larger global struggle against a new form of imperialism, one of whose weapons was "wars of national liberation." In this respect, the domino theory may be seen as an aspect of the larger "lesson of Munich" that runs through the thinking of successive American administrations from Truman to Reagan (and which continued during the 1990s with regard to Iraq).[39] Henry Kissinger and others point to the more assertive Soviet policies in Africa and Afghanistan following the American withdrawal from Vietnam as evidence of the validity of the domino theory. A perhaps subtler defense of American policies against the charge of aggression would be that their use of force, certainly when it was increasingly recognized that final military victory could not be achieved, was always designed to achieve the limited objective of forcing Hanoi to accept a negotiated settlement. The significant number of bombing pauses ordered by Johnson demonstrates clearly this essentially political purpose of the bombing. A similar argument may be deployed against charges that the scale of the American bombing campaign, in particular the use of napalm and Agent Orange, amounted to an American crime against humanity. The American strategy was based on the belief that only a war of attrition, in which the enemy became convinced of American determination to continue fighting, could achieve an acceptable political outcome. McNamara argues that in the 1966–1967 period the Johnson administration was far more concerned about pressure from the right to abandon America's self-imposed restraints in its conduct of the war than about the growing antiwar movement.[40] Air power was a means of deflecting such criticisms at the same time as reassuring South Vietnam of the extent of the American commitment and keeping up the pressure on the North.[41] Even the much-derided faith of the administration's "best and brightest" in the power of modern technology may be interpreted in light of the determination to prevent the war from escalating into a potential conflict with China or the Soviet Union. Given that constraint, and in the absence of significant numbers of military targets for the bombing campaign, napalm, and other weapons designed to hurt and maim rather than kill were seen as the most effective means of bringing the desired pressure to bear on Hanoi. Agent Orange—whose long-term effects on GIs as well as Vietnamese on both sides were not fully appreciated at the time—was seen as a means of denying the enemy the kind of terrain in which he operated most effectively. Similarly, the American incursion into Cambodia was seen as a response to increased aggression there by both indigenous and Vietnamese Communist forces, as well as sending reassuring messages about American will to Saigon at the same time as warning and pressuring Hanoi.[42]

The obvious answer to charges of lying is that the accused was telling the truth—or at least the truth in the light of available intelligence and contemporary understanding of events. Both have been argued strongly by those involved in the decision making relating to Vietnam. Where some degree of deception is acknowledged, as Kissinger (who was not a member of the administration at that time) does with the Tonkin Gulf Resolution, the similar lack of candor with the American people employed by Franklin Roosevelt in pushing his country toward confrontation with Germany is pleaded in mitigation: what most now see as the right policy in terms of larger global considerations excused the element of deception used by Roosevelt.[43] Whether events in Indochina had quite the same global significance as the struggle against Hitler is immaterial: they were seen in a similar light by successive administrations. Others point to the sheer complexity of the policy-making process to excuse the lack of transparency and reliance on spin that sometimes characterizes governmental communications, especially over foreign policy issues. Roger Hilsman, a member of the Kennedy administration, points to three elements in the American policy-making system that sometimes led at the least to an oversimplified presentation of decisions, if not to deliberate obfuscation. The first was that the highly specialized nature of the American bureaucracy meant that "complex problems arising out of [bureaucratic] interaction, as between military and political considerations" tended to end up being considered at the highest level.[44] Inevitably a hard-pressed President, facing numerous domestic and foreign problems and without the benefit of omniscience or the ability to see into the future, would tend to frame a complex but not initially enormously important issue, like Vietnam up to 1965–1966, in black-and-white terms and would present it in that way to the American people. Second, the need to win over a wide constituency in support of policies committing the lives of American forces might lead to "overselling a policy proposal in the sense of claiming too much for it," as Hilsman believes was the case of Kennedy's Vietnam policy. Finally, the same need for wide support might also, at times, create "an incentive *not* to communicate effectively, to be a little fuzzy in articulating policy and its possible outcomes."[45] The peculiarities of foreign policy, where sensitive intelligence sources or delicate aspects of negotiations with foreign powers sometimes need to be concealed, may also tend to lack clarity.

It is clearly possible, using the same facts and even the same moral principles, to argue completely opposite cases so far as the morality of American conduct in Vietnam is concerned. If the lesson of the first narrative was that, had America adhered to the version of moral behavior outlined there, it would have achieved a far more satisfactory outcome in all other respects, the lesson of the second might be that the United States was actually *too* concerned with acting in accordance with its deepest principles, where a colder calculation of its interests might have served it better. This is very much the point of view of Henry Kissinger, who sees American foreign policy since 1945 as based on the principles of resisting aggression and promoting democracy: a policy that fitted the reality in the European context but not in Vietnam, which had no democratic tradition. Kissinger sees Vietnam as "the most ambiguous moral challenge" faced by America since 1945.[46] But because Americans sought moral certainty, they were unable to perceive the ambiguity of the situation in Vietnam and hence opt for more flexible policies there until it was too late.

THE WAR AS TRAGEDY

By far the commonest portrayal of the war is in more value-neutral terms as an unfolding tragedy. In one version of this narrative, "Vietnam is a triumph of the politics of inadvertence. We have achieved our present entanglement, not after due and deliberate considerations, but through a series of small decisions. It is not only idle but unfair to seek out guilty men."[47] Variations on this theme may be found in the later reflections of many of the leading participants, such as Kissinger's analogy with a classical Greek tragedy, "in which the hero is led step by step to his destiny by seemingly random events."[48] Additional subthemes include the wildly exaggerated view of the importance of Vietnam held by several administrations; the fact that the American strategy of fighting a war of attrition was actually far better suited to the Asian Communist doctrines of protracted revolutionary war, allied to the North Vietnamese willingness to accept heavy casualties, than to the imperatives and limitations at work in an open, democratic society; the fact that Hanoi's very clear understanding of American motives and constraints enabled it to ignore or exploit at will the numerous American peace initiatives; the separation between political and military objectives in the United States, as compared with the close harmony between these in Hanoi; lack of coordination between administrative departments; a lack of on-the-ground expertise about Indochina of the kind that had guided American decisions relating to the Soviet Union; the inability of the Johnson and Nixon administrations to extricate themselves from a developing entanglement while retaining the degree of honor that a superpower was entitled to expect. Central to the "tragedy" narrative is the thesis that the United States acted throughout its involvement in Vietnam from the best of intentions, seeking first to help to create a thriving democracy, then to preserve it from aggression, and finally to find an exit strategy that would not fundamentally weaken its global standing. The domestic opponents of the war were themselves participants in the tragedy because they too perceived events through a lens of moral absolutism that precluded support for the combination of firmness and willingness to negotiate that characterized the Johnson and Nixon administrations. They became, inadvertently, a weapon in the hands of the Communist side and helped, paradoxically, to delay the solution they so desperately sought.

NO END OF A LESSON

Kissinger, McNamara, Nixon, and many others have attempted to draw out the larger lessons of the war, which, in general, they tend to see in terms of the third narrative. To McNamara it seems "beyond understanding, incredible" that he and others did not ask such basic questions as "Was it true that the fall of South Vietnam would trigger the fall of all Southeast Asia? Would that constitute a grave threat to the West's security?"[49] However, he rejects arguments such as those advanced at the time by the American socialist Norman Thomas that he "would rather see America save her soul than her face in Southeast Asia" by asking rhetorically "how do you save your soul? Do you save your soul by pulling out of a situation, or do you save it by fulfilling your commitments?"[50] In other words, he adheres in essence to the moral parable of the second section, which portrays America as sliding deeper into the Vietnamese abyss *because of* its high moral principles. He also lists eleven causes of the American failure in Vietnam, including misjudgments of adversaries, allies, and risks, and he draws the principal lesson that future American initiatives should take place within the multilateral framework of the United Nations.[51] In this respect as well, he tends still to be looking for general principles to guide future policy. Kissinger, in contrast, draws very different conclusions from the experience. His lessons: before the United States commits itself to combat, America needs to have "a clear understanding of the nature of the threat ... a clear military strategy and an unambiguous definition of what constitutes a successful political outcome." Moreover, "when America commits itself to military action, there can be no alternative to victory [because] prolonged stalemate will sap the endurance and hence the will of the American public."⁵² This, in broad terms, also characterizes the American neoconservative response to the "Vietnam syndrome" that, for a time, inhibited American use of force in a number of situations for fear of becoming entangled in another Vietnam.

There may, however, be problems with all three narratives outlined here as well as with the kinds of prescriptions offered by Kissinger and McNamara. The first two narratives, taken together point to the moral complexities involved in foreign policy decision making. This is especially so in the case of war, which in itself already encapsulates so many moral ambiguities. What this suggests is that moral absolutes can never be a reliable guide to policy making, but does that mean that principles have no part to play in foreign policy? The third narrative shows individuals not in control of events but swept along by a relentless tide of inevitability, which might be taken as evidence for the thesis that most of the time policy-makers cannot be held to account for their actions. It might also suggest that there is little point in seeking to act morally in such situations. Cool-headed realism of the kind advocated by Kissinger is more effective as a guide to action.

However, just as McNamara may be making one kind of mistake in trying to cling to the notion that American foreign policy can still be guided by moral principles, so Kissinger may be mistaken in believing that his cold rationality might enable his country to make more effective foreign policy choices. If moralism, as many including Kissinger argue, has been a perennial problem in U.S. thinking about foreign policy, another problem revealed by the Vietnam War was a misguided faith in science, both in its capacity to provide technological solutions to complex political problems and, in its guise as social science, to produce clear, unambiguous policy guidance. One effect of the "Vietnam as tragedy" narrative is help to remove moral responsibility for decisions from those who made them. They might, as in a Greek tragedy, have possessed one fatal flaw in their characters—usually represented by the participants as too much idealism—but once the train of events was underway, they were carried along without any clear means of disembarking. A similar detachment of individual from moral responsibility may be derived from the related notions that the nature of the policy-making process can be clearly understood and deconstructed in "rational choice" and behavioralist terms and that the same application of "science" can lead to "correct" policies. "Rational choice" perspectives create a picture of the enemy—whether it be monolithic communism or a relentlessly power-hungry Middle Eastern dictator—who, removed from constraints such as history, geography, economy, and indeed mortality, simply pursues whatever increments to his power he can lay his hands on because that is the "rational" thing to do.⁵³ As Anatol Rapoport wrote in 1964, "it was never necessary to inquire what the enemy wants to do, but only what the enemy *can* do. If he can blackmail us, he will. If he can do us in, he will."⁵⁴ The task of the American decision-maker is thus made simple: presented with a clear threat, he works out the most effective means of dealing with it, guided by the same "rational choice" assumptions about the enemy's probable conduct. If the enemy's behavior appears not to accord with these assumptions about his rationality—as was the case in Vietnam—the realists' response is to improve the science rather than question its underlying assumptions.

But if absolute morality and science are equally flawed, are any general principles available that can both guide decisions more effectively and provide at least some moral underpinning of the kind that public opinion in democracies is wont to insist upon? In fact from an early stage of the Vietnam War an alternative voice could be heard that was sufficiently well informed about the dilemmas of exercising power not to fall into the counterproductive blanket denunciations of some in the antiwar movement. Because he also identifies a third fundamental problem with American decision making, alongside excess moralism and faith in science, pride of place in this group may be given to Senator Fulbright and his critique of the "arrogance of power." Without a conviction that American military and economic power could overcome all obstacles—indeed, without sufficient power at their disposal to enable "rational choices" to be exercized that would not have been contemplated by a less powerful state—the United States would not have been drawn so deeply into a quagmire of its own making. Certainly, as Fulbright suggests, "power tends to confuse itself with virtue and a great nation is peculiarly susceptible to the idea that its power is a sign of God's favor."[55]

Fulbright explicitly refutes both moralism and behavioralism as ways of understanding international relations, offering instead what he terms "humanism," comprising an attention to human needs, magnanimity, an understanding of cultural differences and an understanding of the irrational elements in human nature.[56] In one of his most powerful passages, he further argues:

There are two Americas. One is the America of Lincoln and Adlai Stevenson; the other is the America of Teddy Roosevelt and the modern superpatriots. One is generous and humane, the other narrowly egotistical; one is self-critical, the other self-righteous; one is sensible, the other romantic; one is inquiring, the other pontificating; one is moderate, the other filled with passionate intensity; one is judicious and the other arrogant in the use of great power.[57]

Both, he suggests, are characterized "by a kind of moralism, but one is the morality of decent instincts tempered by the knowledge of human imperfection and the other is the morality of absolute self-assurance fired by the crusading spirit."[58] He sees the historical origins of this division as the contrast between the influence of the Puritans—"harsh, ascetic, intolerant, promising salvation for the few but damnation for the many"—and the other English heritage of "tolerance, moderation and experimentalism."[59]

He reaches a clear conclusion about the kind of American foreign policy style he would like to see:

For my own part, I prefer the America of Lincoln and Adlai Stevenson. I prefer to have my country the friend rather than the enemy of demands for social justice; I prefer to have the communists treated as human beings, with all the human capacity for good and bad, for wisdom and folly, rather than as embodiments of an evil abstraction; and I prefer to see my country in the role of sympathetic friend to humanity rather than its stern and prideful schoolmaster.[60]

Fulbright was far from the only American advancing views of this kind: Under-Secretary of State George W. Ball was similarly urging the need for a more nuanced American policy in Vietnam during 1965.[61]

Many kinds of lessons have been drawn from the Vietnam conflict, ranging from the need for a new American isolationism to the requirement for American interventions to employ overwhelming force. What emerges from the discussion above is that neither interventionist nor noninterventionist policies in themselves necessarily hold a monopoly on morality. Nor, however, can decision-makers escape responsibility—including moral responsibility—for their conduct. What Fulbright is calling for, in effect, is a return to the old-fashioned concept of statesmanship, which more clearly encapsulates the need for leaders to have and to exercise certain virtues than the more neutral terms currently in use, such as "decision-maker." The classic virtues of statesmanship are wisdom, insight, prudence, common sense, pragmatism, tolerance, willingness to compromise where necessary, a knowledge of history (but not blindly following lessons like the Munich analogy), and an ability to see things from other perspectives. In place of implacable moral or ideological certainties, statesmanship offers common decency, common humanity, and a preference for peace over war. This does not mean, however, that peace will be chosen over war on all occasions: the supreme virtue of statesmanship is judgment. However, in the words of a very young Winston Churchill, "The duty of government is to be first of all practical. I am for makeshifts and expediency. I would like to make the people who live on this world at the same time as I do better fed and happier generally . . . but I would not sacrifice my own generation to a principle however high or a truth however great."[62]

NOTES

1. Indeed, for many, including former President Nixon, the "lesson of Vietnam" was precisely the opposite: that force should have been used more effectively or in greater quantities. Richard Nixon, *The Real War* (New York: Warner Books, 1981), pp. 105–36.

2. Edmund Burke, *Reflections on the Revolution in France* (Indianapolis: Bobbs-Merrill, 1959), p. 180, cited in Robert W. Tucker and David C. Hendrickson, *The Imperial Temptation: The New World Order and America's Purpose* (New York: Council on Foreign Relations Press, 1992), p. 133.

3. One of the best works from such a perspective is David Campbell, *Writing Se-*

curity: United States Foreign Policy and the Politics of Identity (Manchester: Manchester University Press, 1998).

4. In fact, Roosevelt had already begun to back away from applying this principle to Indochina in the months before his death. Robert Dallek, *Franklin Roosevelt and American Foreign Policy, 1932–1945* (New York: Oxford University Press, 1979), pp. 512–13.

5. *The State of the Union Messages of the Presidents* (New York: Chelsea House Publishers, 1967), Vol. III, 1967, p. 2908.

6. David McCullough, *Truman* (New York: Simon & Schuster, 1992), p. 990.

7. Harry S. Truman, *Memoirs. Vol. II, 1946–1952: Years of Trial and Hope* (New York: Hodder & Stoughton, 1965), pp. 377, 433, 454.

8. See, for example, the account in George McT. Kahin, *Intervention: How America Became Involved in Vietnam* (New York: Anchor Books, 1986), especially chapters 7–10.

9. The main agreement—effectively a cessation of hostilities—was, strictly speaking, signed between the French and Communist military leaders, a technicality that gave Diem's government grounds for claiming that it was not bound by the agreement because it had not participated. However, the second main document, a Declaration by all participants in the conference except the United States, made it clear that the division of the country was to last no more than two years. For both documents and the U.S. Declaration, see Richard A. Falk, ed., *The Vietnam War and International Law* (Princeton, NJ: Princeton University Press, 1968), Vol. 1, pp. 543–60.

10. There is a vast literature on the international legal aspects of the war, but several opposing points of view are presented in Richard Falk, ibid., Vols. 1–2.

11. *The Pentagon Papers*, Senator Gravel, ed. (Boston: Beacon Press, 1971), Vol. 1, pp. 180–84, 213–39.

12. A recent account argues that, notwithstanding conflicting signals from different American decision-makers to those planning the coup, "the White House had promoted the attempt by exerting economic pressures on Diem and then assuring his enemies of help in a successful aftermath." Howard Jones, *Death of a Generation: How the Assassinations of Diem and JFK Prolonged the Vietnam War* (Oxford: Oxford University Press, 2003), p. 405.

13. This has appeared in several documents, including a 1970 UN General Assembly Resolution and the Helsinki Final Act of 1975. James Fawcett, *Law and Power in International Relations* (London: Faber and Faber, 1982), pp. 112–13.

14. Werner Levi, *Contemporary International Law* (Boulder, CO: Westview Press, 1991), pp. 84–88.

15. See, for example, the classic discussion in H.A.L. Hart, *The Concept of Law* (Oxford: Clarendon Press, 1992), pp. 180–207, 221–26.

16. See also Terry Nardin, "Ethical Traditions in International Affairs," and Dorothy V. Jones, "The Declaratory Tradition in Modern International Law," both in Terry Nardin and David R. Mapel, eds., *Traditions of International Ethics* (Cambridge: Cambridge University Press, 1993), pp. 1–22 and 42–61.

17. Anthony Clark Arend and Robert J. Beck, "International Law and the Recourse to Force: A Shift in Paradigms," in Charlotte Ku and Paul F. Diehl, eds., *International Law: Classic and Contemporary Readings* (Boulder, CO: Lynne Rienner, 1998), pp. 327–51.

18. Myres S. McDougal and Florentino P. Feliciano, *Law and Minimum World Public Order* (New Haven, CT: Yale University Press, 1961), pp. 242–43.

19. For a discussion of the proportionality issue in the context of the Vietnam War, see Eliot D. Hawkins, "An Approach to Issues of International Law Raised by the United States Actions in Vietnam," in Richard Falk, op. cit., Vol. 1, pp. 189–93.

20. For the most detailed account of the incursion in these terms, see William Shawcross, *Sideshow: Kissinger, Nixon and the Destruction of Cambodia* (London: Hogarth Press, 1986).

21. For a discussion of this issue in the context of the My Lai killings, see Michael Walzer, *Just and Unjust Wars: A Moral Argument with Historical Illustrations*, 2nd ed. (New York: Basic Books, 1992), pp. 306–16.

22. See, for example, William Blum, *Rogue State* (London: Zed Books, 2002), pp. 51–52, 71, 83–84, 105–6, 135, 228–29.

23. Robert S. McNamara, with Brian Van DeMark, *In Retrospect: The Tragedy and Lessons of Vietnam* (New York: Random House, 1995), pp. xv–xvi.

24. Ibid.

25. Ibid., pp. 127–43.

26. Opinions on the administration's response to the Tonkin Gulf incidents range from the straightforward view that Johnson, McNamara, and others were simply lying (for example, Eugene C. Windchy, *Tonkin Gulf* [New York: Doubleday, 1971]), through the similar but more nuanced opinion of David Halberstam that McNamara had been "disingenuous to the point of open dishonesty" about several aspects of the affair (David Halberstam, *The Best and the Brightest* [London: Barrie & Jenkins, 1972], p. 419) to a more recent study that concludes that they were essentially mistaken (Edwin E. Moise, *Tonkin Gulf and the Escalation of the Vietnam War* [Chapel Hill: University of North Carolina Press, 1996]).

27. Stanley Karnow, *Vietnam: A History* (New York: Penguin Books, 1984), p. 375.

28. David Halberstam, op. cit., pp. 418–19.

29. Richard Nixon, *The Real War* (New York: Warner Books, 1981), p. 130.

30. Henry Kissinger, *Diplomacy* (New York: Simon & Schuster, 1994), p. 658.

31. David McCullough, op. cit., p. 548.

32. Speech to the Overseas Press Club, New York City, March 29, 1954, in Marvin E. Gettleman, ed., *Vietnam: History, Documents, and Opinions on a Major World Crisis* (Harmondsworth: Penguin Books, 1965), pp. 96–98.

33. Memorandum from the Joint Chiefs of Staff to Secretary of Defense McNamara, JCSM-652-65, in *Foreign Relations of the United States (FRUS), 1964–1968, Vol. III, Vietnam, June–December 1965* (Washington, DC, 1996), pp. 356–63.

34. Cited in Anthony Short, *The Origins of the Vietnam War* (London: Longman, 1989), p. 209.

35. *The Memoirs of Richard Nixon* (New York: Warner Books, 1978), pp. 501, 504.

36. However, McNamara did later reflect that "we do not have the God-given right to shape every nation in our own image or as we choose." *In Retrospect*, op. cit., p. 323.

37. See, for example, National Security Action Memorandum, 52, May 11, 1961, which stated the American objectives as preventing Communist domination in the South and creating "a viable and increasingly democratic society" by means of military, political, economic, psychological, and covert actions. *Pentagon Papers*, Vol. II, p. 642.

38. In fact, by 1963 fears that the growth of domestic opposition to Diem would

weaken the war effort were predominant in American thinking. George McT. Kahin, op. cit., pp. 144–48.

39. For a discussion of the Munich lesson in the context of U.S. foreign policy decision making, see Ole R. Holsti and Kames N. Rosenau, *American Leadership in World Affairs: Vietnam and the Breakdown of Consensus* (Boston: Allen & Unwin, 1984), pp. 3–17.

40. Robert S. McNamara, op. cit., pp. 252–53.

41. Robert Buzzanco quotes Maxwell Taylor, then American Ambassador to Vietnam, to the effect that the air campaign was a means of "producing maximum stress in Hanoi minds." *Masters of War: Military Dissent and Politics in the Vietnam Era* (Cambridge: Cambridge University Press, 1996), p. 1922.

42. Henry Kissinger, *The White House Years* (London: Weidenfeld & Nicolson, 1979), pp. 433–521.

43. Kissinger, *Diplomacy*, p. 659. And see Cathal J. Nolan, " 'Bodyguard of Lies,' " in this volume.

44. Roger Hilsman, *To Move a Nation: The Politics of Foreign Policy in the Administration of John F. Kennedy* (New York: Delta, 1968), p. 547.

45. Ibid.

46. Kissinger, *Diplomacy*, p. 676.

47. Arthur M. Schlesinger, Jr., *The Bitter Heritage: Vietnam and American Democracy, 1941–1966* (London: Sphere Books, 1967), p. 44.

48. Kissinger, *Diplomacy*, p. 645.

49. McNamara, op. cit., p. 39.

50. Ibid., p. 217.

51. Ibid., pp. 321–26.

52. Kissinger, *Diplomacy*, p. 700.

53. Ron Robin, *The Making of the Cold War Enemy: Culture and Politics in the Military-Intellectual Complex* (Princeton, NJ: Princeton University Press, 2001) provides a powerful critique of the influence of behavioralism.

54. Anatol Rapoport, "Critique of Strategic Thinking," in Roger Fisher, ed., *International Conflict and Behavioral Science* (New York: Basic Books, 1964), p. 234 (cited in ibid., p. 7).

55. J. William Fulbright, *The Arrogance of Power* (Harmondsworth: Penguin Books, 1970), p. 15.

56. Ibid., pp. 157–72.

57. Ibid., p. 235.

58. Ibid.

59. Ibid., p. 239.

60. Ibid., p. 246.

61. For example, *FRUS*, pp. 16–21, 55–57, 62–66, 106–13.

62. Arthur M. Schlesinger, Jr., op. cit., p. 100.

III
PEACEMAKING

CHAPTER 6

Power and Principle: The Statecraft of Theodore Roosevelt

William N. Tilchin

In light of the discussion of the relationship between ethics and statecraft presented in the Foreword and in the opening two chapters of this volume, the diplomacy of President Theodore Roosevelt is a natural topic for investigation. Joel Rosenthal's contention that "decision-making always involves reconciling the desirable with the possible" would please Roosevelt, who consistently perceived himself as a "practical idealist" pursuing "realizable ideals."[1] Cathal Nolan's claim that "the most profound realist writers were always aware of the moral realm" applies as well to profound realist *actors*—of whom Roosevelt provides an illuminating example.[2] And by Robert Jackson's eminently fair standard—that the "conduct of state leaders" should be evaluated "in relation to what could reasonably be expected of a person of sound mind and good character in the circumstances"[3]—Roosevelt stands tall, far surpassing "reasonable expectations" both in the way he employed American power and influence and in the ethical component of his diplomacy. TR's foreign policy demonstrates the entire "constellation of political virtues"—prudence, judgment, vision, good faith, courage, and the others—identified by Jackson.[4]

Roosevelt understood keenly the centrality of the factor of power in international relations and was an adroit practitioner of power politics. At the same time, he believed deeply—and continually acted on the belief—that a proper American foreign policy must be firmly grounded in ethical precepts. What Frederick Marks has termed "the moral quotient" was an integral element in the assertive, dynamic statecraft of President Theodore Roosevelt.[5]

THE ROOSEVELTIAN WORLDVIEW[6]

By the time he assumed the presidency upon the assassination of William McKinley in September 1901, Theodore Roosevelt had already developed many of the major elements of the worldview that would guide his presidential state-craft. Born into a wealthy New York family in 1858, Roosevelt had traveled widely. Moreover, since his youth Roosevelt had been a voracious and remark-ably retentive reader, enabling him to acquire a great breadth and depth of knowledge about many subjects, history and international affairs prominent among them. In the 1880s and 1890s he had also become a prolific and accom-plished author; and the work he had done researching and writing his many books—notably including *The Naval War of 1812* (1882) and *The Winning of the West* (four volumes, 1889–1896)—naturally had broadened and deepened his knowledge. In these same decades—toward the end of which he had served with boldness and distinction as assistant secretary of the navy—Roosevelt had taken his place as a conspicuous figure within the coterie of leading American expan-sionist thinkers, an influential group of big-navy advocates who interacted fre-quently and who shared many ideas about strategy, American power, American political and cultural superiority, and American beneficence. Simultaneously Roosevelt had been building friendships and corresponding regularly with a number of Britons whose perspectives on the need for Anglo-American cooper-ation and on other matters were compatible with his own. All these factors had contributed to the shaping of the new president's outlook on international rela-tions and on America's role in the world in the century then just beginning.

President Roosevelt believed in the superiority of Western, and particularly Anglo-American, civilization. He viewed imperialism, at least its U.S. and Brit-ish varieties, primarily as a force for the advancement of this superior civilization and the betterment of the human condition, *not* as a vehicle for economic ex-ploitation. Roosevelt closely monitored the United States' experience in the Phil-ippines, finding in it unambiguous evidence of the high-minded character of American imperialism.

Roosevelt also believed in the necessity of active U.S. engagement with the world. As one of the Great Powers, the United States was affected by important events occurring around the globe; hence, Roosevelt considered it not only fruit-less but also harmful to U.S. interests to try to shield the country from major overseas developments. And the United States needed not only to engage but to take initiative; it needed to seek to influence and to shape important overseas events to its advantage rather than simply observing them passively and reacting to them later. Considering the deeply entrenched and potent legacy of President George Washington's farewell address of 1796 urging Americans to "steer clear" of foreign entanglements, TR's belief in active U.S. internationalism stands among the most radical departures of his presidency.

Although the president defined U.S. interests in a global context, he did so very thoughtfully and discriminatingly. In Roosevelt's scheme, the Western Hemisphere—particularly the Caribbean region, where he saw U.S. hegemony as a self-evident strategic imperative—and the western Pacific were the two areas of the world most vital to the United States. In other areas Roosevelt was especially attentive to situations where there was conflict or the potential for conflict among two or more of the Great Powers. While a steadfast proponent of the "just war" doctrine, Roosevelt harbored no illusions about the horrors and the unpredictable consequences of war and considered it his moral obligation to do all that he realistically could to prevent or to stop unnecessary Great Power wars. Therefore, he always kept an especially close watch on Europe. In contrast, in Africa and on the mainland of Asia (unless, as in the cases of the Russo-Japanese War and the Moroccan crisis, a Great Power contest was looming or playing out in those areas), TR was usually reluctant to engage the United States directly, perceiving U.S. interests on those continents to be peripheral. More-over, in defining vital interests, Roosevelt accorded a much lower priority to economic concerns than to strategic ones. Thus, maintaining the Open Door policy throughout China was not a vital American interest in Roosevelt's eyes; amicable U.S.-Japanese relations were far more important to TR and always took precedence.

Roosevelt looked upon arbitration as a useful device for resolving interna-tional disagreements, but only if they did not involve questions of vital interests, territorial integrity, or national honor. When a dispute did fall into one or more of these three excluded categories, he was adamant that the United States must be free to act as it saw fit. And not only free but sufficiently strong militarily—for ultimately, TR clearly recognized, it was power more than any other factor that determined the course of international affairs.

Consistent with this perspective, Roosevelt adhered to the doctrine of peace through strength, according to which the most civilized and most righteous nations (as Roosevelt defined these terms) should always be well armed and should take particular care to build up and preserve a preponderance of naval power in order to be able to deter aggression and defend their interests.[7] He considered the United States and Great Britain—which shared, in TR's view, a duty to extend civilization and an attachment to the principles of freedom and self-government—to be the two most civilized and most righteous nations. Moreover, he realized, the two countries' strategic interests tended to coincide. Britain, therefore, was an essential friend for America.

Indeed, the cornerstone of Rooseveltian statecraft was the cultivation and solidification of a special relationship between the United States and the British Empire. TR was both a proud American nationalist and, in important respects, an internationalist. But as his presidency moved along, and as his devotion to U.S.-British unity was continually reinforced by events, he became in a sense an *Anglo*-American nationalist as well.[8] Without reservation, therefore, Roose-velt considered the unrivaled power of the Royal Navy to be an asset to the United States, and in his private correspondence he frequently proclaimed his support for the maintenance by Britain of its overwhelming naval superiority.[9]

The one other power President Roosevelt came to view as highly civilized was France. Roosevelt's concerns over the Franco-Russian alliance and over the long history of unfriendly relations between France and Britain (an unfriendli-ness exacerbated by their confrontation over the Sudan in 1898) were largely mitigated by the establishment in April 1904 of the Anglo-French *entente cordiale*, which he very quickly came to perceive as a crucially important bulwark against German military adventurism. From 1905 on, TR had a very positive outlook on French diplomacy, considering it entirely unthreatening and looking upon it as an extremely useful asset to the Anglo-American special relationship he was so diligently working to construct.

In contrast, Roosevelt perceived Germany, Russia, and Japan to be potential enemies of the United States. Not only did their interests often clash with those of the United States, but they had not yet attained America's (or Britain's or France's) level of civilization.

TR viewed Germany as aggressive and militaristic and as having respect for the United States only insofar "as it believes that our navy is efficient and that if sufficiently wronged or insulted we would fight."[10] By the closing years of his presidency, his long-standing doubts about the emotional stability and rationality of Kaiser Wilhelm II and suspicions about the nature of German society in general had hardened. "The German attitude toward war," Roosevelt lamented in a letter of February 1907 to the British editor John St. Loe Strachey, "is one that in the progress of civilization England and America have outgrown."[11]

Regarding tsarist Russia—viewed by TR more as a long-term than as a short-term menace—Roosevelt foresaw "nothing of permanent good . . . , either for herself or for the rest of the world, until her people begin to tread the path of orderly freedom, of civil liberty, and of a measure of self-government."[12] In its diplomacy, Russia was guilty of "appalling, . . . well-nigh incredible mendacity"; and a Russian victory over Japan in their war of 1904–1905 "would have been a blow to civilization."[13]

As the foregoing quotation suggests, the case of Japan was somewhat more complex in Roosevelt's perception. In a letter of June 1905, TR admiringly called the Japanese "a wonderful and civilized people, . . . who are entitled to stand on an absolute equality with all the other peoples of the civilized world."[14] Moreover, Roosevelt heartily approved of (and informally linked America to) the Anglo-Japanese alliance. Yet even while he was pursuing a cooperative and friendly U.S.-Japanese relationship, the president was uncertain about Japan's motives and ultimate intentions. Thus, as he wrote to Whitelaw Reid, his ambassador to Great Britain, in June 1906, "my policy with Japan is to be scrupulously polite, to show a genuine good will toward her, but to keep our navy in such shape that the risk will be great for Japan if it undertakes any aggression upon us."[15]

Roosevelt's disparate assessments of the six Great Powers were reflected in his thinking about the balance of power. It would be inaccurate to assert that he saw "balance" as the key to stabilizing all areas of possible Great Power conflict. He did indeed desire such balance between Russia and Japan in Manchuria. But when Great Britain or the United States was a party to a dispute with another power, balance was the president's minimum objective. A better guarantee of peace—and therefore desirable from the standpoint of international morality as well as U.S. interests—was an *im*balance decidedly favorable to Britain or America or the two of them combined. As the world's most civilized countries, England and the United States would not abuse a position of military supremacy; and such supremacy would ensure against miscalculation on the part of a more selfish, less civilized, less mature power. Thus, Roosevelt was convinced, a preponderance of British or American strength in any region of the globe constituted a safeguard, not a danger.

Although Roosevelt was an ambitious statesman—as reflected in his fast-paced naval building program, in his many bold actions in the foreign policy arena, and in his expansive ideas about the international role the United States could and should play during and beyond his era—he possessed a keen sense of limits as well. "Practical idealism" was among TR's most important working principles, and—just as in his dealings with domestic affairs—he constantly endeavored to mesh realism and ethics in his foreign policy. TR's well-reasoned distinctions between vital and peripheral U.S. interests have already been pointed out. Where there was war or the potential for war (either involving the United States or otherwise), he was adept at evaluating power balances and at anticipating consequences and figuring out whether and how undesirable ones might be avoided. Roosevelt looked at the world through clear lenses (literally as well as figuratively) even while striving to better it: "We can only accomplish good at all," he wrote to the trusted diplomat Henry White in 1906, "by not trying to accomplish the impossible good."[16]

Military, cultural, geographical, international political, and domestic political realities combined to define the limits of the possible in Roosevelt's mind. The greater the stakes, however, the more willing the president was to test those limits by taking political, diplomatic, and military risks in an effort to attain his objectives. For example, he went out on a political and diplomatic limb in what turned out to be a highly successful effort to settle the Franco-German crisis over Morocco in 1905 and 1906 because he saw that situation as extremely dangerous. As Roosevelt wrote to Ambassador Reid shortly after the conclusion of the crisis, "it really did look as if there might be a war," which might "literally" turn into "a world conflagration," and Roosevelt "felt in honor bound to try to prevent the war if I could."[17]

A well-informed, carefully constructed, well-integrated, complex, sophisticated Rooseveltian worldview provided the conceptual foundation for a coherent, dynamic, successful presidential foreign policy. But such an outcome naturally would also require a high level of proficiency in the area of execution. There too Roosevelt would prove equal to the challenge.

STATECRAFT ROOSEVELTIAN STYLE

The style in which President Theodore Roosevelt practiced the art of statecraft suited his personality and facilitated the attainment of his foreign policy objectives. At the core of Rooseveltian statecraft were presidential domination, personal diplomacy, and the quintessentially Rooseveltian (and often misunderstood and caricatured) "big stick" diplomacy.

As is true of most successful leaders, Roosevelt was skillful both in selecting capable subordinates and in managing them. In many areas of domestic policy, he gave his top appointees substantial leeway in making decisions and in setting administration policy. In the arena of diplomacy, however, the self-confident and singularly knowledgeable twenty-sixth president for the most part held strong, well-defined views and was less willing to share authority. And when dealing with the foreign policy matters he saw as most important, Roosevelt charted the broad course of American diplomacy *and* attended personally to the significant details of its execution.

Two excellent secretaries of state, John Hay (inherited from McKinley) and Elihu Root (appointed following Hay's death in 1905), worked under Roosevelt, and time and again the president availed himself of their services. He did so because he had confidence in their abilities and because their ideas about foreign policy largely coincided with his own. Root, formerly Roosevelt's secretary of war and in the president's view an upgrade over Hay, functioned as a steady and clear-thinking presidential counselor, a superb administrator, and an extremely loyal, reliable, and effective diplomatic representative.

President Roosevelt developed a network of foreign policy advisers and operatives that extended well beyond his secretaries of state. Prominent figures in this Rooseveltian network included Senator Henry Cabot Lodge of Massachusetts (a very close friend since the 1880s), Secretary of War William Howard Taft, Ambassador to Russia George von Lengerke Meyer, Ambassador to Britain Whitelaw Reid, and the accomplished and versatile diplomat Henry White. A number of foreigners were also sometimes brought into this network, most notably the Britons Cecil Spring Rice and Arthur Lee and France's ambassador to the United States, Jean Jules Jusserand.

This sizable and varying network facilitated the informal, personal diplomacy conducted by the president, which in turn facilitated presidential domination of foreign policy. The trusted Root and Taft became Roosevelt's most intimate foreign policy associates, but TR really had no set inner circle of foreign policy advisers in the usual sense of that concept. Instead he would solicit the counsel of and assign diplomatic missions to different individuals at different times, as it suited his needs. And he generally would interact with them informally; even with the small number of overseas U.S. diplomats in whom Roosevelt had great confidence—particularly Meyer, Reid, and White—important communications tended to be in the form of private letters dispatched outside the established channels. Fundamentally, TR liked to "move with secrecy and quiet to shape events, letting only a few close friends know even a portion of the larger picture."[18] Indeed, often when Roosevelt appeared to be seeking advice, he was really looking for a stamp of approval for decisions he had already made. He intended to and did in fact maintain a tight grip on the reins of American diplomacy throughout his presidency.

Not only did informal, personal diplomacy facilitate presidential control of foreign policy; it offered Roosevelt a couple of other advantages as well. The president sometimes took diplomatic initiatives for which he believed it would be difficult to win domestic political backing; in such cases he could proceed quietly and without publicity in pursuit of his goals. (Conversely, when TR anticipated a favorable public reaction—to his acquisition of the Panama Canal Zone, for example—he would methodically orchestrate publicity for his diplomatic activities.)[19] And informal, personal diplomacy enabled Roosevelt to achieve important foreign policy victories without humiliating the losing side, a key tenet of big stick diplomacy.

As practiced by its architect, big stick diplomacy had at its foundation five central principles. The first was the possession of a formidable military capability, which during the opening decade of the twentieth century meant, especially, a large, well-equipped, well-trained U.S. Navy. "Diplomacy," Roosevelt declared before a Naval War College audience on July 22, 1908, "rests on the substantial basis of potential force."[20] The second principle was to act justly toward other nations. The third was never to bluff, and the fourth was to strike only if prepared to strike hard. Fifth and finally, as just mentioned, big stick diplomacy required its practitioner to allow an honorable adversary to save face in defeat. In a letter to Ambassador Reid of December 1908, President Roosevelt discussed big stick diplomacy in these words: "The foreign policy in which I believe is in very fact the policy of speaking softly and carrying a big stick. I want to make it evident to every foreign nation that I intend to do justice; and neither to wrong them nor to hurt their self-respect; but that on the other hand, I am both entirely ready and entirely able to see that our rights are maintained in their turn."[21]

The two-phase Moroccan crisis of 1905 and 1906 offers perhaps the most extraordinary example of Rooseveltian personal diplomacy in action. During the spring and summer of 1905, Roosevelt stayed completely out of the public eye as he stealthily worked through Secretary of War Taft, German Ambassador to the U.S. Speck von Sternburg, Ambassador Reid, and, with an astonishing degree of intimacy, Ambassador Jusserand—along with Spring Rice, Lodge, and others—to arrange a conference that headed off a Franco-German war. While willing to risk public exposure of an involvement for which only a tiny minority of Americans would have seen any justification, the president naturally preferred to avoid—and adroitly succeeded in avoiding—such exposure. During the second and somewhat less dangerous phase of the crisis, the Algeciras conference of January–April 1906 (at which U.S. participation was public knowledge but was downplayed by the administration), Roosevelt once again operated masterfully behind the scenes. Having appointed Henry White—considered by TR "the most useful man in the entire diplomatic service"[22]—as chief American delegate at Algeciras, the president then employed the thoroughly dependable Secretary of State Root as his agent for communicating with White. Meanwhile, Roosevelt was more directly in contact with the French and German governments through frequent personal interactions with Jusserand and Sternburg in Washington.

While in the end Roosevelt prevailed on behalf of France and Britain and to the dismay of Germany, and while the president leaned heavily on Germany to reach this outcome, the Moroccan crisis was not a classic case of Rooseveltian big stick diplomacy. For at no time during either phase of the crisis did the president even consider using, much less threaten to use, U.S. military force against Germany. "I did not intend to take any position," he explained to Reid in the aftermath of the crisis, "which I would not be willing at all costs to maintain."[23] Still, elements of big stick diplomacy were very much in evidence here. For one, the foregoing quotation affirms the no-bluffing principle. Moreover, judging correctly that Germany had willfully provoked the crisis, Roosevelt believed he was acting justly in upholding the position of France. And the face-saving principle was vividly in play. After deftly engineering Germany's capitulation (largely through invoking at just the right time Germany's June 1905 pledge to defer to the U.S. president in the event of a deadlock at the conference), TR did his best to persuade Germany that the outcome was actually a German victory; and he lavished public praise on the vain kaiser for Wilhelm's "brilliant" statesmanship.

The episode routinely cited as the epitome of Rooseveltian big stick diplomacy—the U.S. acquisition of the Panama Canal Zone—is in reality a very imperfect example. For TR's success in this instance was as much a product of exasperation and opportunism as it was of calculation and initiative. In addition, the president did not extend himself to shield Colombia, the big loser in the affair, from humiliation.

By September 1903, after many fruitless months of endeavoring in good faith to reach an agreement with the government of the backward-looking and obstructive "authoritarian ideologue" José Marroquín,[24] Roosevelt had lost patience with what he confidentially termed "the foolish and homicidal corruptionists in Bogota."[25] Hence, well aware of the strong and rising secessionist ferment in Colombian-ruled Panama, TR and Secretary of State Hay encouraged this revolutionary movement—but only in private and even then only by indirection.[26] Beginning on October 17, the president ordered U.S. naval vessels to sail toward Panama—not to take an active part in the revolution, but, as stipulated in a U.S.-Colombian treaty of 1846, "to 'maintain free and uninterrupted transit' across the isthmus and to prevent the landing of any armed force, whether Colombian or Panamanian."[27] The bloodless Panamanian rebellion was carried out in less than three days, ending on November 6. Richard Collin accurately apportions responsibility as follows: "Although Roosevelt and the Americans were hardly innocent, Panama was the most active agent of its own revolution."[28]

The United States promptly granted recognition to the new Panamanian government and beefed up its naval presence in the area to prevent Colombia from overturning Panama's separation; there would be no further pretense of American neutrality. The Hay-Bunau-Varilla Treaty, granting the United States sov-

ereignty "in perpetuity" over a ten-mile-wide canal zone and making Panama a
virtual protectorate of the United States, was signed on November 18, 1903,
and ratified by the Senate on February 23, 1904. The construction of the Panama
Canal, a mammoth undertaking in which President Roosevelt was deeply interested and became heavily involved, soon commenced.

Roosevelt was extremely proud of his statesmanship relating to the acquisition
of the Panama Canal Zone, believing that he had absolutely nothing to hide,
and that he not only had advanced the interests of the United States but also
had thwarted Colombia's attempt to impede the progress of humanity. He would
never cease to defend his actions vigorously, most notably in the autobiography
he published in 1913.[29]

As for Colombia, TR did meet personally on December 6, 1903, with Rafael
Reyes—the head of a Colombian mission seeking to regain control of Panama
and soon afterward Colombia's president—and did reply to a confidential letter
from President Reyes with a reasonably cordial confidential letter of his own in
February 1905. But Roosevelt never made any serious effort to mitigate Colombia's embarrassment, thereby appearing to violate an important principle of big
stick diplomacy. Perhaps, in light of Colombia's highly objectionable behavior
in 1903 and its military weakness, Roosevelt believed that such an effort was
both unwarranted and unnecessary. Or perhaps, as his letter to Reyes suggests,
he simply could figure out no way to implement the principle in this unique
instance.[30]

There were, on the other hand, three truly classic displays of Rooseveltian
big stick diplomacy. In chronological order, they were directed at Germany,
Great Britain, and Japan.

Joint Anglo-German military action against Venezuela for the purpose of debt
collection beginning in December 1902 led to a German-American confrontation. Blaming Germany for the expedition, and seeing the expedition as a challenge to the Monroe Doctrine, President Roosevelt dispatched a battleship
squadron to the waters near Venezuela, insisted on arbitration (for which the
Venezuelan government was calling), and privately issued in mid-December and
in early February two timely and stern ultimatums to the German government.[31]
By the middle of February 1903, Germany had agreed to Roosevelt's demand
for arbitration, and the crisis had ended. Adhering to all the tenets of big stick
diplomacy, TR had found Germany's conduct unjust and unacceptable, had read-
ied the necessary military forces, had personally issued unambiguous warnings,
and by keeping those warnings private had made it possible for Germany to
back down without losing face.

Right from the beginning of (and even before) his presidency, TR looked
upon the Canadian interpretation of the Alaskan-British Columbian border as
"an outrage pure and simple."[32] Thus, he saw the boundary question as an issue
of national honor and was adamantly opposed to abandoning any essential elements of the American claim. Yet the Anglo-American friendship he had been
cultivating was also immensely important to Roosevelt. The reconciliation of

these conflicting imperatives would require statecraft of the highest order. The president measured up to the test.

The story of the resolution of the Alaskan boundary quarrel reveals a determined American statesman adroitly employing personal diplomacy and big stick diplomacy to attain the result at which he was aiming. Having "quietly and unostentatiously" dispatched troops to the disputed region in 1902,[33] Roosevelt agreed early in 1903 to the establishment of an "impartial" six-person tribunal, including three Americans appointed by himself, to settle the boundary question. However, TR's selections—Secretary of War Root, Senator Lodge, and former Senator George Turner, upon all of whom Roosevelt could depend to sustain the U.S. claim—made it apparent that he looked upon the tribunal, in Charles Campbell's words, merely as "a device to help a friendly country, which had blundered through deference to an obstreperous colony, climb down from an untenable position."[34] The president then launched a multipronged diplomatic offensive, utilizing a number of personal agents—particularly Root, Lodge, Turner, Hay, Henry White, Ambassador to Britain Joseph Choate, and U.S. Supreme Court Justice Oliver Wendell Holmes—to drive home two crucial messages to British Colonial Secretary Joseph Chamberlain, Foreign Secretary Lord Lansdowne, Prime Minister Arthur Balfour, and Lord Chief Justice Alverstone, the lone Briton on the tribunal. First, in the absence of a settlement affirming all the essential aspects of the American stance, TR would deploy sufficient numbers of U.S. troops to "take possession of the disputed territory" and would ask Congress for "an appropriation which will enable me to run the boundary on my own hook."[35] But, second, there were "two or three lesser points on which there is doubt," and on these he was prepared to countenance U.S. concessions in order to provide England with a dignified way out.[36] The key American and British participants picked up Roosevelt's signals, and an agreement—supported by the one British and three American tribunal members but not by the two Canadians—was reached in October 1903.[37]

Just as impressive was Roosevelt's handling of the crisis in U.S.-Japanese relations that was sparked by the San Francisco school board's passage in October 1906 of a resolution segregating Asian school children and was stoked by the continuing immigration to the United States of substantial numbers of Japanese laborers. TR's well-conceived, multifaceted approach entailed pressuring the Californians to end the blatant discrimination (and accompanying violence) while emphasizing to Japan his disapproval of Californian behavior; working with Japanese officials to find an amicable way to halt the flow of Japanese workers to the American mainland; and strengthening and exhibiting the U.S. Navy both to deter Japan and to prepare for war should it prove unavoidable. Behind the scenes he engaged the services of Arthur Lee and Canada's commissioner of labor and immigration, William L. Mackenzie King, among others, in an attempt—only partially successful—to draw Great Britain, Japan's ally, into his diplomatic enterprise. In Roosevelt's single most illustrious act of big stick diplomacy, he sent the American battleship fleet (the "Great White Fleet") on a fourteen-month world cruise beginning in December 1907. Not a threatening word was spoken—indeed, Japan invited the fleet to its shores and extended it a grand welcome in October 1908—but the warning that America was strong and ready was unmistakable. Meanwhile, a "Gentlemen's Agreement"—structured in such a way as to spare Japan humiliation—finally brought the immigration problem under control by the middle of 1908. Then, in November of that year, the signing of the Root-Takahira Agreement, demonstrating to the world the achievement of respectful and friendly relations between the United States and Japan, marked a climactic triumph for the president's Japanese policy. Roosevelt immodestly but very accurately summed up his accomplishment in a letter to Lee of December 20, 1908: "My policy of constant friendliness and courtesy toward Japan, *coupled with sending the fleet around the world*, has borne good results!"[38]

THE DIPLOMATIC RECORD

President Roosevelt's foreign policy aspirations were extremely ambitious. Although TR pursued these aspirations simultaneously, seeing them as overlapping and mutually dependent parts of a whole, it may be useful to single out the following five as particularly important: (1) building and solidifying a singularly special relationship between the British Empire and the United States; (2) establishing U.S. hegemony in the Western Hemisphere, especially in the Caribbean region; (3) sharply expanding the international role played by the United States; (4) contributing to peaceful and stable relations among the Great Powers of the world; and (5) contributing to the progress of civilization.

Essential to the pursuit of this far-reaching foreign policy agenda, the president fully understood, was a powerful U.S. Navy. The author of *The Naval War of 1812* and former assistant secretary of the navy was an exceptionally well informed, attentive, enthusiastic navalist, who both knew what he wanted for the navy and possessed the political and managerial attributes needed to realize most of those desires. Between 1901 and 1905 Roosevelt pushed Congress into authorizing the construction of ten battleships among more than thirty total warships. Then, after slowing down temporarily, TR responded to the dreadnought revolution (marked by larger battleships carrying uniform batteries of big guns, of which the Royal Navy's H.M.S. *Dreadnought*, completed in December 1906, was the prototype) and to increasing tension in U.S.-Japanese relations by calling for a stepped-up pace of naval building, with an emphasis on adding dreadnoughts to the battleship fleet. The world cruise of the Great White Fleet not only waved a big stick at Japan but also functioned as a magnificent public relations spectacle that extracted from an antagonistic Congress in 1908 an authorization for two dreadnoughts (Roosevelt had astutely demanded four) and a commitment to fund two per year in the future. By 1907 the U.S. Navy, the world's sixth in size in 1901, had grown into the second largest. Moreover, by aggressively overseeing the implementation of a radical program of naval reform, President Roosevelt had greatly improved training (especially in gunnery), readiness, and overall efficiency. The proud outgoing president, as Stephen Howarth observes, "was fully aware that he personally could take the main credit for placing the United States' fighting ships in their new high position."[39]

Building and strengthening an Anglo-American special relationship was, as noted earlier, the cornerstone of Rooseveltian statecraft. Although relations between the United States and Great Britain were in reasonably good condition when Roosevelt assumed the presidency in September 1901 (owing especially to Britain's decidedly pro-American neutrality during the Spanish-American War of 1898 and to the United States' equally pro-British neutrality during the ongoing Boer War), the young Anglo-American rapprochement was still quite fragile, its future uncertain. Over the next seven and one-half years, with determination, lucidity, and a steady hand, President Roosevelt would take the lead in transforming this fragile rapprochement into a seasoned friendship and a deep-rooted informal partnership.

During the period 1901–1903, the president furthered the cause of Anglo-American amity in several ways. He began by continuing unchanged through the end of the Boer War in the spring of 1902 the McKinley administration's unpopular, but politically sustainable, pro-British neutrality policy.[40] In dealing with the crisis of December 1902–February 1903 over the joint Anglo-German attack on Venezuela, Roosevelt assessed British behavior as merely foolish and thus dealt harshly only with Germany, whose conduct he considered genuinely threatening. In the immediate aftermath of this crisis, TR did speak pointedly to Ambassador Michael Herbert, thereby making sure that the British government grasped the mistake of being "roped in as an appendage to Germany" and would never repeat it.[41] Most significant was the well-considered, hands-on presidential diplomacy, previously examined, that achieved a resolution in October 1903 to the very sensitive and complicated Alaskan boundary dispute. As he continued throughout his presidency to pursue his goal of building a strong special relationship between England and the United States, TR would encounter no more hurdles of such magnitude. As he claimed retrospectively in 1911, the agreement on the Alaskan border "settled the last serious trouble between the British Empire and ourselves."[42]

Advances in Anglo-American relations during the early years of Roosevelt's presidency paralleled and contributed to his progress in asserting U.S. hegemony in and around the Caribbean. First, the U.S.-British Hay-Pauncefote Treaty of November 1901 cleared the way for the United States to build, control, and fortify a trans-isthmian canal. Then, as discussed in the preceding section, Roosevelt opportunistically acquired the Panama Canal Zone from newly independent Panama in November 1903; the digging of the canal, of which the U.S. Navy would be a primary beneficiary, could now proceed. And the president aggressively pushed forward the development of Guantanamo, Cuba, as the United States' "main naval base . . . in the Caribbean Sea and the principal guard of the Atlantic entrance of the Panama Canal." Similarly, he began the devel-

opment of Pearl Harbor, Hawaii, "the key to the Pacific Ocean," as the U.S.
Navy's most important Pacific base; its many functions also would include defending the canal.[43]

Meanwhile, recovering quickly from its Venezuelan misadventure, in 1903
the British government began encouraging the United States to play a more
active part in the affairs of Latin America. The following year, spurred by
chaotic conditions in the Dominican Republic, TR issued the Roosevelt Corollary to the Monroe Doctrine, proclaiming the obligation of the United States to
counteract "gross wrongdoing" in the hemisphere: "If we intend to say 'Hands
off' to the powers of Europe, . . . we must keep order ourselves."[44]

Roosevelt was actually very reluctant to exercise this new international po-
licing authority, and he initially resisted the Dominican government's overtures
for U.S. intervention. By the beginning of 1905, however, the president believed
it was imperative to act, and he arranged to establish a U.S. customs receivership
in the Dominican Republic. And when partisan politics impeded Senate ratification of the Dillingham-Sanchez Protocol, the president fell back on his broad
constructionist principles and through an executive agreement with the Dominican government instituted a modus vivendi embodying the terms of the protocol. In the Dominican Republic the U.S. customs receivership was kept limited
by Roosevelt and functioned very well, enabling the Caribbean nation to repay
debts owed to foreigners and to finance government operations. Finally, early
in 1907, the Senate ratified a slightly modified U.S.-Dominican treaty.

For their part, Britain's leaders provided tangible evidence of their support
for the greatly expanded U.S. role by almost completely withdrawing British
naval forces from the Caribbean region, leaving the protection of British colonial
and other interests there in American hands. "South of us," TR could write with
conviction to King Edward VII in March 1905, "our interests are identical with
yours."[45]

TR's Dominican intervention was one of only two he undertook under the
terms of the Roosevelt Corollary. The second was in Cuba, for whose benefit
(and the validation of America's good faith) Roosevelt had won ratification of
a tariff reciprocity treaty back in December 1903 after a long struggle with
Congress. Roosevelt's Cuban intervention, lasting from September 1906 until
January 1909, was undertaken with particularly strong reluctance. Even with
both the Cuban government and the leaders of an armed uprising against it
requesting U.S. military intervention, Roosevelt exhausted the possibilities for
diplomatic mediation before ordering forces ashore and setting up a provisional
government. Roosevelt certainly had no imperial designs on Cuba; he privately
told Secretary of War Taft in January 1907, "Our business is to establish peace
and order on a satisfactory basis, start the new government, and then leave the
Island."[46] And, in essence, the U.S. intervention adhered to the president's prescription.[47]

As is suggested by both the infrequency and the restraint with which he
intervened under his corollary, Roosevelt considered it a priority to try to min-

imize Latin American resentment and suspicion of the United States. His most proactive initiative in this regard was Secretary of State Root's goodwill tour of seven Latin American countries during the summer and early fall of 1906. The highlight of this journey occurred July 31 in Brazil at the Third International American Conference, where Root declared: "We wish no victories but those of peace; for no territory except our own; for no sovereignty except the sovereignty over ourselves."[48] The president was delighted with his trusted secretary's "wonderful trip,"[49] following which Root continued to work hard and effectively on behalf of better U.S.–Latin American relations. By 1909, "Root had substantially improved the nation's ties with Latin America."[50]

In light of President Roosevelt's admirable record in the area of Latin American policy, it seems worthwhile to ask why the image of a heavy-handed and widespread interventionism persists in the popular mind and continues to be sustained even by some scholars. Part of the explanation is the controversy still surrounding the U.S. acquisition of the Panama Canal Zone. But, as has been explained, the Panamanian revolution of November 1903 was authentic, and the successful policy of TR, who unquestionably had become very frustrated by Colombia's obstructive behavior, was actually more reactive and opportunistic than calculated.[51]

Another, and probably more important, part of the explanation springs from the Roosevelt Corollary to the Monroe Doctrine. It is true that the Roosevelt Corollary provided theoretical cover for the rampant U.S. interventionism in Latin America of the 1910s and 1920s. But this was decidedly not its purpose, and it seems inappropriate to fault Roosevelt for the subsequent misuse by others of his prescription for encouraging orderly development in the hemisphere and persuading outside powers to steer clear. Roosevelt's concept was based on combining, as Richard Collin puts it, "power, responsibility, and especially altruism," and the president's actions validated his intentions.[52] The interventionist dollar diplomacy of William Howard Taft (and of Warren Harding and Calvin Coolidge) departed sharply from the approach of TR, who, while naturally desiring a level international playing field for U.S. business, conducted a foreign policy that elevated U.S. strategic interests and the "progress of civilization" (which required respect for and upright conduct toward weaker nations) far above the promotion of American economic advantage.[53] Likewise, the "moral interventionism" practiced in Latin America by Woodrow Wilson deviated markedly from the less ambitious, less intrusive, more respectful policy carried out by Roosevelt and Root. Yes, Roosevelt's Latin American policy was paternalistic (albeit quite beneficently so), but charges of graver misdeeds are historically inaccurate and should, at long last, be put to rest.

Roosevelt's goals of greatly expanding the international role played by the United States and of contributing to peaceful and stable relations among the Great Powers were advanced most notably by his extraordinary mediation of the Russo-Japanese War and of the Moroccan crisis. Although he was a close and keenly interested observer of the Russo-Japanese contest right from its onset

in February 1904, and although by December of that year he was already thinking seriously about trying his hand as a mediator, he did not step forward until
an opportunity arose in the spring of 1905 in the wake of major Japanese military successes. After plenty of discreet preliminary work by the president, the
door was opened in May when Japan—financially strapped and militarily over-
extended despite its victories—requested that Roosevelt offer mediation to Russia "on his own initiative." Then, through the intensive and extremely adept
application of personal diplomacy involving British, French, and German as well
as Russian and Japanese officials—using the summer White House in Oyster
Bay, New York, as his base of operations—Roosevelt arranged for the conven-
ing in early August of a Russo-Japanese peace conference in Portsmouth, New
Hampshire, and proceeded to overcome formidable obstacles as he shepherded
it to the triumphant conclusion of the Treaty of Portsmouth of September 2.
This treaty, which restored an Asian balance of power, earned TR the Nobel
Peace Prize for 1906 and may have been his foremost single achievement as a
statesman. If so, Roosevelt's equally remarkable mediation of the two-phase
Franco-German dispute over Morocco in 1905 and 1906, outlined earlier, would
have to rank a close second. For this highly flammable crisis very conceivably
could have brought on World War I nine years before it actually began.

The Theodore Roosevelt's work as a mediator par excellence during the two gravest international crises of his presidency also contributed to the strengthening of
the Anglo-American special relationship on which he was so intent. In both
instances, he bolstered the Anglo-American connection by his resolute preservation of the Anglo-French *entente cordiale*. Because England was allied with
Japan while France was allied with Russia, the Russo-Japanese War imperiled
the young entente, a threat exacerbated by wartime German diplomatic activity
aimed at undermining the French-British link. And for its part, the Moroccan
crisis represented a frontal German assault on the entente. So Roosevelt was
motivated to become involved not only by the lofty goal of restoring or preserving peace among the powers and by the desire to wield American influence
on the world stage but also by a determination to protect the Anglo-French
entente, which he considered a vital element in an international balance of power
favorable to the defense and promotion of Anglo-American interests.

The manner in which President Roosevelt dealt with the Newfoundland fisheries problem—"the longest dispute in the history of American foreign policy"[54]—spotlights the depth of his commitment to Anglo-American unity. When
this on-and-off dispute was renewed by Newfoundland in 1905 in retaliation for
the U.S. Senate's unfriendly treatment of a U.S.-Newfoundland reciprocity (bilateral tariff reduction) treaty, Roosevelt did not react hastily. Indeed, he considered his own country to be primarily to blame. America's course, he
explained to Henry Cabot Lodge, "has given deep offense to Newfoundland,
and most naturally. If the circumstances had been reversed, this country in its
turn would have been deeply angered." The United States, he continued, should
"try to show such patience and forbearance as possible until the exasperation

caused by our very unfortunate action has worn off."⁵⁵ When Newfoundland placed additional restrictions on American fishermen in 1906, Ambassador Reid, representing the president, worked out a temporary modus vivendi with the British government. And when negotiations reached an impasse in the summer of 1907, Roosevelt proposed to resolve the fisheries issue through binding arbitration by the Hague Tribunal. Britain agreed; formal arrangements were set early in 1909; the following year (after Roosevelt had left the presidency) the tribunal rendered a compromise verdict. TR's sense of proportion and fairness, along with his creativity and his thoughtful prioritization of U.S. interests, had brought to a satisfactory conclusion this previously intractable dispute with the best and most important friend of the United States. It was another impressive triumph for Rooseveltian statecraft.

In light of Roosevelt's highly partisan stance on the Anglo-German rivalry and his excellent record in building an Anglo-American bond, his success in maintaining amicable U.S.-German relations throughout his presidency is noteworthy—and praiseworthy. Good relations with Germany were naturally preferable to hostile ones, and, importantly, they gave TR a degree of influence over German foreign policy that he otherwise would not have wielded. Thus, the German government actively supported TR in his mediation of the Russo-Japanese War and, as already noted, ultimately acceded to the president's pro-French prescription for ending the Moroccan crisis. Crucial to his effectiveness with Germany was Roosevelt's adeptness at handling the mercurial Kaiser Wilhelm II. Aware of Wilhelm's "intense egoism," TR endeavored to be friendly to the kaiser and was careful to avoid giving him "legitimate offense." Even "where I have forced him to give way," the president explained confidentially to Henry White in August 1906, "I have been sedulously anxious to build a bridge of gold for him, and to give him the satisfaction of feeling that his dignity and reputation . . . were safe."⁵⁶

For Roosevelt, the most difficult foreign power with which to manage U.S. relations was Russia. The government of Tsar Nicholas II, Roosevelt clearly recognized, was brutal toward its own citizens and habitually mendacious in its foreign relations. In 1903 TR considered, but upon reflection decided against, actively resisting Russian encroachments in Manchuria; alongside his awareness of the serious impediment posed by domestic political realities, he concluded that no vital U.S. interests were at stake on the Asian mainland. Also in 1903 the president defied the Russian government's wishes by forwarding to Russia a U.S. citizens petition expressing outrage and calling for justice in the wake of large-scale government-sponsored anti-Jewish atrocities in Kishinev. This action accomplished three purposes: it conveyed to the Russian government Roosevelt's genuine feelings of repulsion; it strengthened support for the administration among Jewish Americans; and it intensified the pressure on Russia to moderate its policy in Manchuria.

Roosevelt's frustrating interactions with Russian officials during the Russo-Japanese peace negotiations in August 1905 did not improve his perspective on

Russia. Nonetheless, thinking strategically, TR believed that Russian power in East Asia served the important function of balancing Japanese power. Similarly, he indicated cautious approval in 1907 when, to bolster its defensive posture against Germany, Great Britain added a rapprochement with Russia to its 1904 entente with France. "I was glad to see your agreement with Russia," he informed Cecil Spring Rice, "but of course we are all perfectly ignorant of what Russia's future will be."[57]

In the area of U.S.-Japanese relations, Rooseveltian statecraft was by any standard strikingly successful. As mentioned previously, TR's mediation of the Russo-Japanese War occurred in response to a private Japanese request. In addition, the secret Taft-Katsura agreement of July 1905 provides incontestable evidence that Roosevelt unequivocally approved of and informally linked the United States to the Anglo-Japanese alliance.[58] And (again as pointed out previously) Roosevelt not only defused the hot-and-cold U.S.-Japanese immigration-racism crisis of 1906–1909; through a multifaceted policy highlighted by the fourteen-month world cruise of the Great White Fleet, he carried U.S.-Japanese relations to new heights of friendship, affirmed by the Root-Takahira Agreement of November 1908. In this accord, while giving lip service to "the independence and integrity of China," the governments of Japan and the United States "firmly" resolved "reciprocally to respect the territorial possessions belonging to each other" and to uphold "the existing status quo" in East Asia and the Pacific[59]: Japan would continue to stay away from the Philippines; the United States would continue to support Japanese control of Korea; and it was transparently implied that where Japan's predominant position in southern Manchuria clashed with America's Open Door policy in China, the former would take precedence. (TR's successors as president—beginning with Taft, despite Roosevelt's protests—would undo his fine handiwork in building friendly U.S.-Japanese relations.)

Nearly all the accomplishments so far presented—particularly TR's success in forging an Anglo-American special relationship—furthered in some measure Roosevelt's strong, idealistic desire to contribute to the progress of civilization. Policies specifically aimed at this objective were his work on behalf of the principle of arbitration, his efforts to prepare the people of the Philippines for self-government, and his encouragement of British leaders similarly to continue to pursue with confidence a wise and generous imperial policy focused on uplifting the native peoples in the dependent colonies of the British Empire.

As is suggested by his recourse to the Hague Tribunal to settle the Newfoundland fisheries problem, Roosevelt firmly believed in arbitration as a proper, civilized means of resolving non-vital international disagreements. In June 1905 he expressed his outlook in these words in a letter to Lyman Abbott: "It is neither possible nor desirable in the present stage of the world's progress to agree to arbitrate all questions that may come up between different nations. But it is entirely possible and exceedingly desirable to limit the classes of cases which it is not possible definitely to promise beforehand to arbitrate, and to

provide not only that all other questions shall be arbitrated, but so far as possible
the manner and method of proceeding to such arbitration."[60] On this issue, however, TR was blocked by the Senate from fully implementing his ideas.[61]

Roosevelt approached the question of U.S. rule in the Philippines with a
genuine sense of a civilizing mission and a paternalistic determination to act in
the interest of the indigenous population. After completing in 1902 the very
harsh suppression of the insurrection against the American takeover, the president pushed hard for, but failed to obtain from Congress, a large-scale tariff
relief bill for the Philippines; he did succeed, however, in sharply reducing the
influence and privileges of the Catholic parish priests in the Philippines, thereby
redressing an important grievance of the people of the archipelago. Roosevelt
paid close attention to all aspects of governance in the Philippines. In 1907 he
sent Secretary Taft there "to open the new Filipino assembly, the first major
instrument of self-government for the Islands."[62] Where the United States had
made mistakes, TR told the British writer and editor Sydney Brooks in 1908,
"I am steadily trying to advance and perfect remedies."[63] As he prepared to
leave the presidency early in 1909, Roosevelt was very proud of what had been
achieved under his watch, confidently asserting in an important speech that "we
are constantly giving to the people of the Philippines an increasing share in, an
increasing opportunity to learn by practice, the difficult art of self-government.
. . . We are leading them forward steadily in the right direction."[64]

Although at times critical of Britain's imperial performance in some of its
colonies, Malaya in particular, on the whole Roosevelt was immensely impressed with the size of the British Empire, generally approved of the way it
was run, and viewed it as a potent force for the maintenance of world peace
and for the advancement of civilization. For the most part he expressed his
admiration and offered his encouragement privately, as when he proclaimed in
a letter of December 1908 to John Morley, secretary of state for India, that
"English rule in India has marked one of the signal triumphs of civilization."[65]
Soon afterward, on January 18, 1909, in response to a little prodding (only a
little was necessary) from Brooks and other Britons, the president publicly addressed the same subject. His unambiguously laudatory, even celebratory remarks on this occasion not only enunciated Roosevelt's genuine sentiments but
also served his diplomatic agenda in two ways. First, TR's unstinting open praise
shored up British self-confidence during a difficult period for British rule in
India. And second, it brought to the leaders and citizens of Great Britain a new
level of awareness of and appreciation for the Anglo-American special relationship and the excellent work Roosevelt had been doing for more than seven years
to advance it.[66]

As he proceeded over the course of his presidency to build an outstanding
record of accomplishment as a statesman, the politically astute twenty-sixth president had to deal with the realities of a public tending to be ignorant of and
apathetic toward foreign policy issues and a Congress tending to be narrow and
unsupportive, even obstructive. Therefore, while he explained to the public as
much as he thought was politically feasible, he often intentionally oversimplified

when presenting his objectives and motives. As for Congress, where the approval of two-thirds of the Senate was needed to ratify treaties, and where majorities in both houses were required to enact legislation and to fund naval-building and other programs, TR employed a combination of reliance on friends, reasoned persuasion, cajolery, and political gamesmanship—along with resorting to the "bully pulpit" and staging public relations spectacles (most notably the world cruise of the Great White Fleet)—in order to extract as much as possible of what he was seeking. Naturally he was sometimes unsuccessful, but his political skills and intelligence and persistence and savvy usually enabled him to prevail. Moreover, there were some initiatives (most importantly Roosevelt's involvement during the first phase of the Moroccan crisis in 1905) that could be carried out in complete secrecy, and there were others (most importantly the administering through an executive agreement of the Dominican Republic's customs houses during 1905–1907) where the president found a way to circumvent congressional obstruction.

Criticisms of Roosevelt for failing to educate the public more fully and for his broad constructionist approach to foreign policy are not very convincing. In the successful pursuit of an expansive, sophisticated, farsighted foreign policy agenda that both enhanced the United States' position in the world and actively contributed to international stability and peace, TR did his best to educate without undermining his various diplomatic endeavors, and he operated according to a constitutionally legitimate, if controversial, theory of presidential authority. His record as a statesman would have been extraordinary even had he enjoyed a more congenial political climate. Without that climate, it was all the more extraordinary.

"The strength of will, reasoning power, and other mental dispositions and disciplines to do what is morally required in the circumstances" (Robert Jackson's words)[67] were exhibited in abundance in Rooseveltian diplomacy. Even more, in his conduct of foreign policy America's twenty-sixth president displayed a degree of perspicacity that transcended his era. It would take the disastrous failure of isolationism and appeasement and the terrible experience of World War II to revive TR's way of thinking about U.S. foreign relations and to bring his guiding precepts—formidable and credible deterrent power, broadly conceived U.S. interests, and Anglo-American solidarity and preeminence—into the mainstream, where they have been ever since.[68] In the final analysis, the statecraft of Theodore Roosevelt, featuring an exemplary blend of power and principle, produced great short-term and long-term benefits for the United States and the world.

NOTES

1. Joel H. Rosenthal, this volume, p. xvii; William N. Tilchin, "Morality and the Presidency of Theodore Roosevelt," *The Long Term View*, Vol. 3, No. 3 (Fall 1996), pp. 57–58.

2. Cathal J. Nolan, this volume, p. 11.

3. Robert H. Jackson, this volume, p. 19.

4. Jackson, this volume, pp. 27–28.

5. Frederick W. Marks III, *Velvet on Iron: The Diplomacy of Theodore Roosevelt* (Lincoln: University of Nebraska Press, 1979), pp. 89–128.

6. The three main sections of this chapter are in essence a condensed version of the first three chapters of a Praeger Press book manuscript-in-progress (William N. Tilchin, *Exemplary Statecraft: The Diplomacy of Theodore Roosevelt as an Enduring Model*).

7. "I believe in peace," TR wrote to Andrew Carnegie in 1906, "but I believe that as things are at present, the course not only of peace but of what is greater than peace, justice, is favored by having those nations which really stand at the head of civilization show . . . that they ask peace in the name of justice and not from any weakness." TR to Carnegie, August 6, 1906, Elting E. Morison, John M. Blum, and Alfred D. Chandler, eds., *The Letters of Theodore Roosevelt* (8 vols., Cambridge, MA: Harvard University Press, 1951–1954), Vol. V, p. 346. *The Letters of Theodore Roosevelt* is hereafter cited as *Letters of TR*.

8. See, in particular, William N. Tilchin, *Theodore Roosevelt and the British Empire: A Study in Presidential Statecraft* (New York: St. Martin's Press, 1997), pp. 227–28.

9. See, for example, TR to Arthur Lee, June 6, 1905, *Letters of TR*, Vol. IV, p. 1207; and TR to Lee, August 7, 1908, *Letters of TR*, Vol. VI, p. 1159.

10. TR to Oscar Straus, February 27, 1906, *Letters of TR*, Vol. V, p. 168.

11. TR to John St. Loe Strachey, February 22, 1907, *Letters of TR*, Vol. V, p. 596.

12. TR to Cecil Spring Rice, June 13, 1904, *Letters of TR*, Vol. IV, p. 829.

13. TR to John Hay, May 22, 1903, *Letters of TR*, Vol. III, p. 478; TR to Albert Shaw, June 22, 1903, *Letters of TR*, Vol. III, p. 497; TR to Henry Cabot Lodge, June 16, 1905, *Letters of TR*, Vol. IV, p. 1230.

14. TR to David Bowman Schneder, June 19, 1905, *Letters of TR*, Vol. IV, pp. 1240–41.

15. TR to Whitelaw Reid, June 27, 1906, *Letters of TR*, Vol. V, p. 320.

16. TR to Henry White, August 14, 1906, *Letters of TR*, Vol. V, p. 359.

17. TR to Reid, April 28, 1906, *Letters of TR*, Vol. V, p. 236.

18. Lewis L. Gould, *The Presidency of Theodore Roosevelt* (Lawrence: University Press of Kansas, 1991), p. 174.

19. See Serge Ricard, *Théodore Roosevelt: principes et pratique d'une politique étrangère* [Theodore Roosevelt: Principles and Practice of a Foreign Policy] (Aix-en-Provence, France: Université de Provence, 1991), p. 253.

20. Quoted in Morison et al., *Letters of TR*, Vol. VI, p. 1108n.

21. TR to Reid, December 4, 1908, *Letters of TR*, Vol. VI, p. 1410.

22. Raymond A. Esthus, *Theodore Roosevelt and the International Rivalries* (1970; reprint, Claremont, CA: Regina Books, 1982), p. 17.

23. TR to Reid, April 28, 1906, *Letters of TR*, Vol. V, p. 234.

24. See Richard H. Collin, *Theodore Roosevelt's Caribbean: The Panama Canal, the Monroe Doctrine, and the Latin American Context* (Baton Rouge: Louisiana State University Press, 1990), especially p. 312.

25. TR to Hay, September 15, 1903, *Letters of TR*, Vol. III, p. 599.

26. Apparently right after his first meeting with Philippe Bunau-Varilla, the leading figure in the Panamanian revolutionary drama, Roosevelt wrote these words to his friend Albert Shaw: "Privately, I freely say to you that I should be delighted if Panama were an independent State . . . ; but for me to say so publicly would amount to an instigation

of a revolt, and therefore I cannot say it." TR to Shaw, October 10, 1903, *Letters of TR*, Vol. III, p. 628.

27. Gould, *Presidency of TR*, p. 96. Actually, these orders reached Commander John Hubbard of the *Nashville* on November 3, the day the revolution began, only after Hubbard had permitted Colombia to land over 400 troops, nearly wrecking the revolution. See Collin, *TR's Caribbean*, pp. 262–66.

28. Collin, *TR's Caribbean*, p. 245.

29. Theodore Roosevelt, *Theodore Roosevelt: An Autobiography* (1913; reprint, New York: Da Capo Press, 1985), pp. 526–46.

30. TR to Rafael Reyes, February 20, 1905, *Letters of TR*, Vol. IV, p. 1124.

31. See especially Edmund Morris, " 'A Few Pregnant Days': Theodore Roosevelt and the Venezuelan Crisis of 1902," *Theodore Roosevelt Association Journal*, Vol. 15, No. 1 (Winter 1989), pp. 2–13; and Ricard, *TR: principes et pratique*, pp. 279–94.

32. TR to Hay, July 10, 1902, *Letters of TR*, Vol. III, p. 287.

33. TR to Elihu Root, March 29, 1902, quoted in Richard H. Collin, *Theodore Roosevelt, Culture, Diplomacy, and Expansion: A New View of American Imperialism* (Baton Rouge: Louisiana State University Press, 1985), p. 178.

34. Charles S. Campbell, Jr., *Anglo-American Understanding, 1898–1903* (Baltimore: Johns Hopkins University Press, 1957), p. 311.

35. TR to George Turner, August 8, 1903, quoted in Campbell, *Anglo-American Understanding*, p. 327; TR to Oliver Wendell Holmes, July 25, 1903, *Letters of TR*, Vol. III, p. 529.

36. TR to Holmes, July 25, 1903, *Letters of TR*, Vol. III, p. 529.

37. For a much fuller discussion of Roosevelt's masterful management of the diplomacy of the Alaskan boundary dispute, see Tilchin, *TR and the British Empire*, pp. 36–48.

38. TR to Lee, December 20, 1908, *Letters of TR*, Vol. VI, p. 1432 (emphasis in original).

39. Stephen Howarth, *To Shining Sea: A History of the United States Navy, 1775–1991* (New York: Random House, 1991), p. 288.

40. See William N. Tilchin, "The United States and the Boer War," in Keith Wilson, ed., *The International Impact of the Boer War* (Chesham, England: Acumen Publishing, 2001), pp. 107–22.

41. Tilchin, *TR and the British Empire*, p. 34.

42. TR to Alfred Thayer Mahan, June 8, 1911, quoted in Campbell, *Anglo-American Understanding*, p. 347.

43. TR to Charles Warren Fairbanks, February 21, 1908, *Letters of TR*, Vol. VI, p. 951.

44. TR to Root, June 7, 1904, *Letters of TR*, Vol. IV, pp. 821–22.

45. TR to King Edward VII, March 9, 1905, *Letters of TR*, Vol. IV, p. 1136. The cooperative Anglo-American handling of the troublesome Jamaica incident of 1907 underlined the fundamental accuracy of Roosevelt's observation. This incident and its diplomatic aftermath are recounted in detail in Tilchin, *TR and the British Empire*, pp. 115–68. A briefer version is provided in Tilchin, "Theodore Roosevelt, Anglo-American Relations, and the Jamaica Incident of 1907," *Diplomatic History*, Vol. 19, No. 3 (Summer 1995), pp. 385–405.

46. TR to William Howard Taft, January 22, 1907, *Letters of TR*, Vol. V, p. 560.

47. See especially Collin, *TR's Caribbean*, pp. 529–42.

48. Quoted in ibid., p. 491. Along with the Dominican and Cuban episodes, evidence of the sincerity and veracity of Root's statement can be found in the benign, well-reasoned circumspection with which, in partnership with Mexico, the Roosevelt administration attempted (with mixed results) to help resolve Central American conflicts involving Guatemala, El Salvador, Nicaragua, and Honduras in 1906 and 1907.

49. TR to Lodge, October 2, 1906, *Letters of TR*, Vol. V, p. 440.

50. Gould, *Presidency of TR*, pp. 251–52.

51. Roosevelt's critics (and, for that matter, defenders) long assumed that he boasted in a speech delivered in California two years after leaving the presidency: "I took the Canal Zone." But a careful analysis presented by James F. Vivian in 1980 strongly suggests that TR made no such public statement. Instead, Vivian demonstrates, Roosevelt more likely claimed rather innocuously that he "took a trip to the Isthmus" and that he "started the canal." Vivian, "The 'Taking' of the Panama Canal Zone: Myth and Reality," *Diplomatic History*, Vol. 4, No. 1 (Winter 1980), pp. 95–100.

52. Collin, *TR's Caribbean*, p. 547.

53. In a well-researched essay focused on the Dominican intervention, Cyrus Veeser argues that "Roosevelt's Corollary . . . , an interventionist manifesto, provided a rationale for [Dollar Diplomacy]." But Veeser simultaneously—and revealingly—makes clear the failure of the corrupt, self-serving Santo Domingo Improvement Company and its devoted and talented agent, John Bassett Moore, to manipulate Roosevelt: "By the spring of 1905, Moore and the Improvement Company realized that the special status they had long enjoyed in Washington was being overwhelmed by Roosevelt's commitment to harmony among the Great Powers and stability in the Dominican Republic." Veeser, "Inventing Dollar Diplomacy: The Gilded-Age Origins of the Roosevelt Corollary to the Monroe Doctrine," *Diplomatic History*, Vol. 27, No. 3 (June 2003), pp. 301, 321.

54. Alexander DeConde, *A History of American Foreign Policy* (3rd ed., 2 vols., New York: Charles Scribner's Sons, 1978), Vol. I, p. 365.

55. TR to Lodge, August 19, 1905, *Letters of TR*, Vol. IV, pp. 1305–6.

56. TR to White, August 14, 1906, *Letters of TR*, Vol. V, p. 358.

57. TR to Spring Rice, December 21, 1907, *Letters of TR*, Vol. VI, p. 871.

58. On behalf of the president, Secretary of War Taft informed the Japanese that "the Government of the United States . . . could be counted on by [Japan and Great Britain] quite as confidently as if the United States were under treaty obligations." Taft to Root, telegram, July 29, 1905, quoted in Howard K. Beale, *Theodore Roosevelt and the Rise of America to World Power* (1956; reprint, Baltimore: Johns Hopkins University Press, 1984), p. 157.

59. Quoted in Henry Steele Commager, ed., *Documents of American History* (9th ed., 2 vols., Englewood Cliffs, NJ: Prentice-Hall, 1973), Vol. II, p. 53.

60. TR to Lyman Abbott, June 8, 1905, *Letters of TR*, Vol. IV, p. 1208.

61. See Tilchin, *TR and the British Empire*, p. 260, n. 8.

62. Morison et al., *Letters of TR*, Vol. V, p. 742n.

63. TR to Sydney Brooks, November 20, 1908, *Letters of TR*, Vol. VI, p. 1370.

64. TR, "Address of the President at the celebration [sic] of the African Diamond Jubilee of the Methodist Episcopal Church, Washington, D.C., January 18, 1909," pp. 28–29, Theodore Roosevelt Collection, Harvard College Library, Cambridge, MA.

65. TR to John Morley, December 1, 1908, *Letters of TR*, Vol. VI, p. 1402.

66. See TR, Address to Methodist Episcopal Church, January 18, 1909, pp. 17–24; Reid to TR, January 22, 1909, Theodore Roosevelt Papers, reel 87, Library of Congress,

Washington, D.C., and Harvard College Library, Cambridge, MA; and Lee to TR, January 29, 1909, TR Papers, reel 88.

67. Jackson, this volume, p. 26.

68. See William N. Tilchin, "Theodore Roosevelt and the Guiding Principles of U.S. Cold War Diplomacy," *Theodore Roosevelt Association Journal*, Vol. 23, No. 3 (1999), pp. 5–7.

CHAPTER 7

The Higher Realism of Woodrow Wilson

Arthur S. Link

On March 4, 1913, a gaunt man walked to the stands outside the east front of the Capitol in Washington to take the oath of office as twenty-eighth President of the United States. Although his face was somber with a sense of high seriousness, it radiated strength and determination, and there was thrilling power in his voice as he summoned the American people to the tasks of national reconstruction. Eight years later, in 1921, he assisted in the rituals inaugurating his successor, Warren G. Harding. Now he was broken in body, and his drawn face reflected the pain that came from his recent repudiation at the hands of the people during the election of 1920.

He was Woodrow Wilson, born in Staunton, Virginia, on December 29, 1856, reared in Presbyterian manses in Georgia and the Carolinas, educated at Davidson College in North Carolina and Princeton University, trained in the study of law at the University of Virginia, and prepared for a career in teaching and scholarship at the Johns Hopkins University. He had taught successively from 1885 to 1902 at Bryn Mawr College in Pennsylvania, Wesleyan University in Connecticut, and Princeton, and had served as president of the latter institution from 1902 to 1910. Plunging into the sea of politics in 1910, he had won the governorship of New Jersey and had gone on with almost irresistible power to capture the presidency in 1912. Then he had guided the destinies of the American people from 1913 to 1921 and helped to direct the destinies of the world during eight of the most critical years of the modern epoch.

This chapter was the Founder's Day address to the Presbyterian Historical Society in Philadelphia on October 12, 1962. It appeared in *Journal of Presbyterian History*, XLI, number 1 (March 1963), pp. 1–13, and is reprinted by permission.

I am happy to come before this particular audience in this venerable city to talk about the man who has been the subject of my main thought and work for twenty years. I must confess at the outset that I have prepared this paper with a definite purpose in mind. It is neither to praise Woodrow Wilson nor to bury him. The record of his contribution has its own integrity, and what little I could say would neither add to nor detract from it. It is not to bring you any new view of President Wilson, for I doubt that I could say anything really new about him at this point. My purpose is, rather, to attempt to pull together a number of thoughts and convictions that have been coursing through my mind during the past few years, in brief, to clarify my own conclusions about the subject of my life's work.

I have felt impelled to this undertaking in part by many conversations with English and German historians which have challenged my own emerging view of President Wilson. My experiences during a year abroad in 1958–59 have brought home the fact that Europeans on the whole still view Wilson very much as many of them viewed him forty years ago at the end of the Paris Peace Conference and the great struggle in the United States over ratification of the Treaty of Versailles. This European image is, I think it is fair to say, one of a well-intentioned idealist, a man good by Christian standards, but essentially a destructive force in modern history because he was visionary, unrealistic, provincial, and ignorant of European problems, zealous and messianic in conceit, but devoid of either practical knowledge or the humility to follow others better informed than he. I do not think that this is an essentially unfair statement of the European point of view. It was, of course, the image propagated by John Maynard Keynes, Georges Clemenceau, and many persons among the thoughtful European public at the end of the Peace Conference. It is the view still largely held by English, French, and German scholars alike, if for different reasons.

I have felt impelled to my subject not only by recent forceful reminders of the strong survival of the old European image of President Wilson, but also by the emergence in our own country during the past few years of a new school of historical critics, and by their work in constructing an image of President Wilson that is remarkably like the older European one. Calling themselves realists, and drawing their inspiration from the distinguished diplomat-historian, George Kennan, and the Austrian-trained authority in international relations, Hans J. Morgenthau, now at the University of Chicago, these new American critics have found Wilson wanting because he did not think in terms of strategy, bases, and armed power, but dwelt too much in ethereal realms.

Are the old European and new American critics right, I have asked myself over and over during the past few years: is this the image that I also see, the Wilson that I know? Were the Austrians right in thinking that his irresponsible preaching of a slogan, "self-determination," was primarily responsible for the destruction of the Habsburg Empire? Were the Germans right in holding him responsible for what they regarded as the monstrous betrayal of Versailles? Were the French right in thinking that he prevented the imposition of the only kind of peace settlement upon Germany that could endure? Were the English and new American critics near the truth when they portrayed him as a tragic figure irrelevant in the modern world?

I must confess that I have sometimes been tempted to agree. No one who has ever given any serious attention to President Wilson's life could fail to agree that he was *primarily* a Christian idealist. By this I mean a man who almost always tended to judge policies on a basis of whether they were right by Christian standards, not whether they brought material or strategic advantages. I mean also a man whose foreign policies were motivated by the assumption that a nation as much as an individual should live according to Judeo-Christian ethics, and by a positive repudiation of the assumptions of the classical "realists" about international behavior.

No one who has given serious study to Wilson's career, moreover, could fail to agree that there is at least an appearance of reality about the old European and new American image. Wilson was not merely an idealist, but a crusading idealist. An orator of enormous eloquence and power, he was also a phrasemaker who more than once fell victim to the magic of his own words. In international relations, he did not give undue weight to material forces or base his policies upon the assumption that nations must always act selfishly. At times, he did seem to give the appearance of believing that he was a kind of messiah divinely appointed to deliver Europe from the tyranny of history.

I have myself made all these criticisms and others more elaborately in my own writings. But they have never really satisfied me and do not satisfy me now. I do not think that they add up to a historical image that is accurate. Indeed, I cannot escape the conclusion that they altogether miss the main point and meaning of President Wilson's career. The point, in my opinion, and the theme of this paper, is that, among all the major statesmen and thoughtful critics of his age, President Wilson was in fact the supreme realist, and that because this is true, what he stood for and fought to accomplish has significant meaning for our own generation.

This is, to be sure, a very broad, perhaps even an audacious statement, one that does not mean very much unless we are careful to define our terms. A realist, I take it, is one who faces life and its situation without illusions, in short, one who can see realities or truth through the fog of delusion that normally shrouds the earth-bound individual. If the European and American critics of President Wilson who thought mainly in strategic and material terms, who measured national power by army divisions, naval bases, and the like, if *they* were realists, then President Wilson was a realist of a different sort. Sheerly for purposes of convenience, let us call his view of the way individuals and nations should cope in dealing with situations a "higher realism," higher because more perceptive, more in accord with ultimate reality, more likely to win the long-run moral approval of societies professing allegiance to the common western, humane, Judeo-Christian traditions.

We still have not passed beyond the statement of a thesis and a definition of elementary terminology. There now remains the much more important task of seeing to what degree the evidence of Wilson's career supports my generalization. We obviously do not have time to review all the important events of Wilson's long and active career in a brief essay. On the other hand, we cannot concentrate our attention on one aspect without running the risks of distortion. President Wilson actually had three separate public careers: as university president and educational statesman, as a domestic leader concerned with problems of political and economic reconstruction in the United States, and, finally, as a world statesman who attempted to give leadership to a movement for the reconstruction of the international community. He made large and seemingly different contributions in each field. And yet we must try to view his career and labors as a whole, for he was fundamentally the same man throughout. His "higher realism" was no less a force in his leadership at home than abroad.

It was evident in a striking way in the first contributions that he made as a public leader, as president of Princeton University from 1902 to 1910. There were, first, the things that he did and tried to do for Princeton: his introduction of a systematic and meaningful course of undergraduate study, and his positive repudiation of a chaotic free-elective system; his creation of the preceptorial, or conference, method of instruction to supplement the lecture system; and his proposal for the reorganization of undergraduate social life in order to elevate the intellectual life of the university. By such plans and by his own inspiration, he not only transformed Princeton, but also helped to transform higher education in the United States.

And yet Wilson made his greatest contributions in the field of education more by the things that he stood for than by what he did. For one thing, he stood for standards and academic integrity. For another, he had an exalted concept of the university and college and the role that they play in preparing men and women for the nation's service because they were dedicated to the cause of truth and the intellectual enrichment of mankind. Finally during an era of increasing specialization and degradation of undergraduate curricula by the introduction of all sorts of so-called useful programs of study, Wilson never ceased to remind fellow teachers and administrators that their first job was to help to perpetuate the cultural traditions upon which western civilization rested, not to teach students how to make money.

Who, we are entitled to ask, were the true "realists" in educational policy? Were they the alleged realists of Wilson's time, the sincere devotees of the new so-called progressive concepts and faddists, who were then beginning their long attack upon traditional studies and destroying the unity of university curricula? To ask the question is almost to answer it. The entire drive in American higher education during the past twenty years toward recovery of standards and unity in curricula and against the vulgarization that followed the widespread introduction of so-called useful courses of study—this entire movement, so full of promise, is testimony to the higher realism of Wilson's leadership in the academic world.

It was the same, I would suggest, with Wilson's leadership during his second career as governor of New Jersey from 1911 to 1913 and President of the United States from 1913 to 1921. He came to political leadership at one of the most critical junctures in American history, at the high tide of what American historians call the progressive movement. For more than a quarter of a century, the American people had been in revolt in city, state, and nation against corruption and venality among officeholders, irresponsibility on all levels of government, and, above all, the emergence and spread of great aggregations of economic power among railroads, banks, corporations, and so on, which were uncontrolled and often repudiated any responsibility to the people as a whole. This revolt was at the point of culmination at the very time Wilson was catapulted into political life in 1910. And because this was true the American people were now confronted with certain choices that would determine their future political system and the role that government would hereafter play in making fundamental economic decisions.

There was, first, the choice concerning the reconstruction of the American political system. Some so-called realists of the time argued cogently from the facts that the very concept and structure of representative government were fatally defective, and that the answer lay either in direct democracy or in concentration of political power in fewer hands. "Realists" on the other side, eager to preserve a status quo that benefited their own economic interests, argued just as convincingly that the American constitutional system, with its diffusion and separation of powers, was the most nearly perfect form of government on earth.

There was, second, the choice concerning the role that government should play in economic life. At the one extreme were the "realists" who, talking in terms of immutable economic law, defended traditional American policies of laissez faire in an effort to protect their privileged position. At the other extreme were "realists" with a greater popular appeal—men who demanded a sweeping extension of the power of government to bridle all hitherto uncontrolled economic interests. Some of these were socialists, ready to abandon capitalism in the major sectors of the economy altogether. Others were progressives who believed in capitalism but argued that it had reached a permanent phase of semimonopolistic maturity in the United States and could be saved only by instituting sweeping and rigorous public controls over all important areas of national economic life.

It was Woodrow Wilson's privilege to play a decisive role in the determination of these choices. To the "realists" who had despaired of representative government in the cities and states, he replied more by example than by precept—by giving a spectacular example of responsible leadership in action as governor of New Jersey. By making representative government work on the local level, he, along with the company of other leaders at the time, guaranteed its survival. To the "realists" (and he had earlier been among them) who had proclaimed the incapacity of the presidential-congressional system to cope with the great problems of national administration, Wilson responded both by reasoned word and striking deed, by transforming the office of President from that of an aloof presiding official into incomparably the most powerful force in the American constitutional system—the force that gave unity and direction not only to the other branches of the federal government but to public opinion as well. This, we can now see, was the "higher realism" of a man who well understood the weaknesses of the American institutional structure but who knew the fundamental strength of the American democracy far better than most so-called realists of his time.

I think that it is fair to say that President Wilson demonstrated the same kind of long-run wisdom, or "higher realism," in leading the American people to adoption of new policies for the regulation of economic life. He rejected the arguments both of defenders of the status quo and of proponents of violent change as being unsound in principle and unacceptable to the majority of the people. And he (along with his supporters in Congress) instituted a series of measures to impose increased public direction and control, but also to balance private initiative with public regulation in order to stimulate the enormous latent competitive energies of the people. In short, he laid the solid foundations of the present mixed American system of political economy, which, to the amazement and bafflement of many Europeans, works so curiously and so well. Viewing the subsequent development of the American economy within the framework erected by President Wilson and his colleagues, I think that we would have to conclude that Wilson's solution was the only "realistic" one that could have been adopted. It saved American capitalism by making it socially responsible and hence acceptable to the people, without, however, impeding the forces that are essential for growth in the capitalistic system.

I am sure that in talking about Wilson's "higher realism" in meeting domestic challenges, I have simply been saying things and making judgments with which virtually every historian of the United States would readily agree. It is precisely this "higher realism" that has entitled Wilson to rank, by the agreement of American historians, among the four or five most successful presidents in our history. In talking about Wilson's policies and contributions in the realm of foreign affairs, I am, I know, on more controversial ground. Wilson was magnificently prepared for leadership in internal affairs by long study of American history and institutions. He had little if any preparation for leadership in the world at large; indeed, at the outset of his tenure in the White House he had no serious interest in foreign affairs. At the outset and later he made mistakes that still seriously impair his record. Even so, I cannot but conclude that President Wilson on the whole showed the same kind of wisdom and long-range vision and understanding—in short, "higher realism"—in his third career as international statesman as he had already revealed in his first two careers at home. This, I know, is a big statement, and I would like to preface it with a few generalizations about Wilson's thought and character as a diplomatist in order to lay foundations for some later observations.

The first is the most obvious and the one with which most historians would agree, namely, that President Wilson was, as I have already said, above all an idealist in the conduct of foreign affairs, one who subordinated immediate goals and material interests to what he considered to be superior ethical standards and moral purposes. His idealism was perhaps best revealed in his thinking about the purposes that the United States should serve in the world. The mission of America, he said over and over and sincerely believed, was not a mission of aggrandizement of material power but one of service to mankind. It was a mission of peace, of sacrifice, of leading the nations into a new international community organized to achieve right ends. Second, all of Wilson's thinking about international relations was conditioned, in general, by a loathing for war and, in particular, by a conviction that physical force should never be used to achieve selfish and material aims. Third, Wilson was actually in many ways "realistic," even by conventional standards, in his thinking about and methods in the conduct of foreign relations. For example, he used armed force in the classic way to achieve certain diplomatic objectives in Mexico and the Caribbean. He understood the meaning of the term "balance of power." He was keenly aware of the relevance of material interests and had few illusions about the fundamental bases of international behavior. It is, one must say, the sheerest nonsense to talk about him as an impractical idealist and visionary. Fourth, while admitting that there were times when a nation has no recourse but to use armed force in international disputes, and while using force himself on behalf of the American government on certain occasions, President Wilson never permitted war's neuroses and fascinations either to derange his reason or to obscure the political objectives for which force was being used. Hence he was never the victim of that greatest twentieth-century delusion, that it is necessary to win wars even at the risk of losing everything for which wars are fought.

This is a very imperfect characterization of the thought and character of Wilson the diplomatist, but it may help us to understand his policies during the greatest tragedy of the modern epoch and the event that raised the gravest challenges to his leadership—the First World War. It was for Wilson a period with three distinct stages: the period of American neutrality, from August 1914 to April 1917; the period of American belligerency, from April 1917 to November 1918; and the period of peacemaking, from November 1918 to June 1919. The challenges of each period were different, but he met them all, on the whole, with the same "higher realism" that had characterized his leadership at home.

His policies during the first period can best be briefly described by saying that, from the outbreak of the war in Europe to the beginning of the German unlimited submarine campaign in early 1917, President Wilson tried as hard as any person could have done to be neutral, to make the necessary accommodations to the exercise of belligerent power, and to engage in stern defense of American rights only when they could not, because fundamental human principles were involved, be compromised.

Some of the recent American "realists" have joined the older English and French critics in charging Wilson with impractical idealism precisely because he did follow such a course—because he did not rally the American people to preparation for what they have said was an inevitable participation; because he conducted long and patient negotiations to avoid a break with Germany; because he did not undertake large and early measures of assistance to the Allies and thus help to shorten the duration of Europe's agony; because he refused throughout the period of American neutrality even to align the American people and their government morally on the Allied side.

Looking back upon the final outcome, as we are entitled to do, we well might wonder who the true realists were during this period: so-called realists, or President Wilson, who in an almost uncanny way kept himself immune from the emotional hysterias and passions that seized other men; who believed that the causes of the war were so complex and remote that is was impossible to assess the blame for it; who, overborne by the tragedy of the event, fought desperately to preserve American neutrality so that he could perform the healing task of reconciliation once the nations of Europe had come to some sense; who believed that an enduring peace could come only through a "peace without victory," a "peace between equals"? Who were the deluded men who had lost sight of reality? The European leaders who thought that they could win decisive victories on the battlefields and on or under the seas, and who thought they could impose their nations' wills upon other great peoples? Or Wilson, who thought that they were momentarily mad?

The climactic confrontation, the supreme reckoning between so-called realists and the alleged impractical idealist, came once the United States had been forced into the conflict and Germany was defeated. It did not occur earlier, because the British and French leaders had refused to permit it to occur before the Armistice was safely signed. But it could not then be long postponed, for the Allied leaders had matured their plans, and President Wilson had meanwhile formed a peace program of his own and announced it to the world in the Fourteen Points address and other speeches.

There is no need to review the turbulent events of the Paris Peace Conference here. They are familiar enough, to begin with; but a detailed account of them now would obscure my larger purpose—to look back upon the Paris settlement and, while looking back, to attempt to see who the true realists were. The supreme task of the victors at Paris in 1919 was, obviously, to work out a peace settlement and reconstruct an international order that could endure. It had to be a peace that could survive the ebbing of passions and hatreds that consumed Europe in 1919. It had to be a peace that could survive because it could command the approval of the German people. Above all, it had to be the kind of settlement that would endure because it could retain the long-run support of the American and English peoples, even the French people. The necessity of constructing this kind of settlement was, as we can now see clearly, the supreme reality of peacemaking in 1919. We must, therefore, judge men and measures at the Paris Conference according to whether they met this test or not.

By this criterion I do not see how any fair historian can but conclude that the so-called realists at Paris—the dedicated if cynical Clemenceau, concerned only about the future security of France; the well-intentioned Lloyd George, who had given so many hostages to war passions at home and to the Commonwealth that he was no longer a free man; and the Italians, Sonnino and Orlando, eager only for spoils—how could they be called anything other than sublime irrationalists and dreamers? Theirs was a dream, a nightmare, of unreality. Given the task of reconstructing Europe and preventing a future war, they would have responded by attempting to perpetuate the division of Europe and by making a new war almost inevitable.

On the other side and standing usually in solitary if splendid isolation was the alleged impractical idealist fighting for the only kind of settlement that had any chance of survival—for a peace of reconciliation, for disarmament by victors as well as vanquished, against annexations and indemnities, and for a new international organization that would include former enemy states as active members from the beginning. Over and over he warned that this was the only kind of peace that would prove acceptable to the American people in the short run and to the moral opinion of the world in the long run, in short, the only kind of settlement that could endure. It should require little reference to events that followed the Paris Conference to demonstrate the "higher realism" of President Wilson's views.

If proof is needed on specific points, one could cite, for example, Wilson's point of view on the problem of reparations. Over and over he insisted, and with a steadfast consistency, that reparations should be compensation for specific willful damage only, not indemnity; that the Germans should not be saddled with a debt that was heavier than they could carry; and that there should be a time limit to the obligation that the German nation should be forced to assume. What the Allied leaders demanded and finally obtained is well known to this audience. What the realistic solution of this problem was is now too obvious for comment. Or, as a second example, one might cite Wilson's attitude toward the Russian Revolution—how he saw the deeply rooted causes of that cataclysm and the futility of any western effort to suppress it by military force; and how the realism of his attitude contrasted with the egregious folly of so-called realists who thought that it lay within their power to change the course of Russian history.

The result of the clash between European so-called realism and Wilsonian so-called idealism was of course the Treaty of Versailles, that compromise that violated some of the terms of the agreement by which the Germans had stopped fighting and made a mockery of some of the principal planks in the American President's peace program. Why, it is fair to ask, did President Wilson permit such a peace to be made and sign the treaty embodying it? The answer, I submit, is that it was "higher realism" that drove him to this difficult decision. Having won many of the things for which he had been fighting, he had to give as well as to take, for he could not impose his will upon his colleagues. He signed the Versailles Treaty in the conviction that the passage of time and the Treaty's new creation, the League of Nations, would almost certainly operate to rectify what he knew were the mistakes of the peacemakers. He signed the Versailles Treaty, in short, because he believed that it was the best settlement possible in the circumstances of 1919.

What President Wilson hoped would occur did of course in large part take place during the 1920s and early 1930s, even though alleged realists in the United States combined with authentic visionaries to repudiate Wilson's work and prevent their government from playing the role of mediating leadership within the League of Nations of which Wilson had dreamed. The great tragedy of the postwar period was not that the Versailles Treaty was imperfect. It was that the forces of reconciliation could not operate rapidly enough without American leadership in the League, that France and Great Britain lacked the will to defend the treaty alone during the 1930s and, above all, that the German people submitted to demonic forces that promised a speedy rectification of all the alleged injustices of Versailles. But this is precisely what President Wilson, in another flash of "higher realism," predicted would occur if the so-called realists, both in the United States and in Europe, continued to have their way.

That is the age-old question, whether the so-called realists or the higher realists shall have their way in determination of national and international policies. President Wilson survives as a more powerful force in history than when he lived because he gave us the supreme demonstration in the twentieth century of higher realism in statesmanship. This, obviously, was no accident. Woodrow Wilson's "higher realism" was the product of insight and wisdom informed by active Christian faith. He was not, fundamentally, a moralizer, as he so often seemed to be, but a man who lived in faith, trying to be guided by the Holy Spirit in meeting the complex problems of a changing nation and world. Using one of his own metaphors, we can say that the light of Heaven gleamed upon his sword. His precepts and ideals will be relevant so long as democracy endures and so long as men seek after a new international community organized for peace and the advancement of mankind.

AFTERWORD

After twenty-five years of additional research on Wilson and his time, I have concluded that this chapter still stands as a fair evaluation and that I have no desire to revise it, except to make a few mainly stylistic changes. A number of fine monographs and biographical studies since 1970 have, it seems to me, elaborated and confirmed the interpretation of Wilson set forth in "The Higher Realism." This is true of such books (to mention only a few) as John Milton Cooper, Jr., *The Warrior and the Priest: Woodrow Wilson and Theodore Roosevelt* (1983); the essays by eminent Wilson scholars in Arthur S. Link, *Woodrow Wilson and a Revolutionary World, 1913–1921* (1982), to which I contributed only a foreword; Arthur S. Link, with the assistance of Manfred F. Boemeke, translator and editor, *The Deliberations of the Council of Four (March*

24–June 28, 1919): Notes of the Official Interpreter, Paul Mantoux, 2 vols.
(1992); Antony Lentin, *Lloyd George, Woodrow Wilson and the Guilt of Germany: An Essay in the Pre-History of Appeasement* (1984); Betty Miller
Unterberger, *The United States, Revolutionary Russia, and the Rise of Czechoslovakia* (1989); David R. Woodward, *Trial by Friendship: Anglo-American Relations, 1917–1918* (1993); Thomas J. Knock, *To End All Wars: Woodrow Wilson and the Quest for a New World Order* (1992); and August Heckscher,
Woodrow Wilson: A Biography (1991). If anyone wants a good illustration of
Wilson's higher realism in dealing with Central Europe and Russia, let him or
her read Professor Unterberger's book. Also, cautionary for those who still believe that Wilson was a naive idealist are two books by Frederick S. Calhoun:
Power and Principle: Armed Intervention in Wilsonian Foreign Policy (1986)
and *Uses of Force and Wilsonian Foreign Policy* (1993).

This historiographical tidal wave has, if I may say so, expanded and complemented what I said in "The Higher Realism of Woodrow Wilson." But most
gratifying to me are the recent words by George F. Kennan, one of the early
"realist" critics of Wilson:

I now view Wilson . . . as a man who like so many other people of broad vision and
acute sensitivities, was ahead of his time, and did not live long enough to know that
great and commanding relevance many of his ideas would acquire before this century
was out. In this sense, I have to correct or modify, at this stage of my own life, many
of the impressions I had about him at an earlier stage. In his vision of the future needs
of world society, I now see Wilson as ahead of any other statesman of his time.[1]

As we enter the post-Cold War era, when international leaders are struggling to
establish a new and better world order, even Wilson's critics agree that he set
the agenda for future foreign policy initiatives. That agenda is undergirded and
motivated by the following Wilsonian assumptions:

• Aggressive war cannot be tolerated and has to be met and forcefully overcome by the
  collective action of peace loving nations through the United Nations.

• Every people with a common history, language, geographical identity, etc., enjoy the
  inherent right to self-determination, that is, independence and the right to govern themselves without the threat of intimidation, subjugation, or of being bartered about (in
  Wilson's words) in the now discredited game of the balance of power.

• As for the United States, its foreign policy should be devoted to the advancement of
  democracy and human rights and the cooperation of nations and the preservation of
  peace through the United Nations.

• Most important, nations, and the men and women who lead them, are subject to the
  rule of law and high ethical standards just as individuals are.

This incomplete list of assumptions does not encapsulate Wilson's "higher realism" in statecraft and foreign affairs. But their acceptance by right-minded people makes it clear that the main elements of Wilson's "higher realism" are still standards by which we judge the relations of nations one to another.

NOTE

1. Comments on the paper entitled "Kennan versus Wilson by Professor Thomas J. Knock," in J.M. Cooper, Jr., and Charles E. Neu, eds., *The Wilson Era: Essays in Honor of Arthur S. Link* (Arlington Heights, IL: Harlan Davidson, 1991), p. 330.

CHAPTER 8

The World Outlook of
Dag Hammarskjöld

Dorothy V. Jones

Dag Hammarskjöld's approach to the problems of ethics and statecraft was a reflection of his views of the United Nations, and of his duties to the world that had placed its hopes in that organization. His reputation when he came to the post of UN Secretary-General (1953–1961) was that of a competent civil servant with some experience in international affairs. At the time of his election he was the Minister of State in the Swedish Foreign Office, which made him, in effect, the deputy foreign minister. In addition, he had served on the executive committee of the Organization of European Economic Cooperation, the group that administered the Marshall Plan, and he had been acting head of the Swedish delegation to the UN General Assembly in 1952.[1] This solid but unspectacular background was reassuring to those who supported him for the office of Secretary-General. After the stormy tenure of Trygve Lie, the first to hold that office, what was wanted was a quiet and competent administrator. As it turned out, the choice of Hammarskjöld meant that the organization got somewhat more than it bargained for, and the world got somewhat more than it was ready for.

The office of Secretary-General, the role of international law, and the very character of the United Nations came under the new Secretary's immediate scrutiny. Quietly, over time, profound changes were made. Hammarskjöld turned administrative tasks into executive action. He recast international law from a set of constraints on behavior to a collection of possibilities and guidelines for action. As for the character and authority of the United Nations itself—that, of course, said Hammarskjöld, was for the member governments to choose. Only they could decide if the organization was to function chiefly "as a static conference machinery for resolving conflicts of interest," or "as a dynamic instrument of governments" to develop more effective means of international cooperation.[2] There was no doubt which was Hammarskjöld's view of the

United Nations. He kept a dynamic view of the organization before the members
and the public as both the goal of actions taken in the present, and the standard
by which those actions could be judged. He always set the problem of the
moment within the larger framework of the future toward which the world was
moving, whether it would or not. The question was, What kind of future would
it be?

Here, then, is a clue to Hammarskjöld's contribution to ethics and statecraft.
His words and actions show how important in ethics is the effect of the temporal
perspective. It is not enough to know the goal of action. We need also to know
the time frame for accomplishment of that goal: An upcoming election? A lifetime? The next generation? Or some distant future the shape of which will be
determined by actions taken in the present? Whatever the temporal perspective,
it will be a strong influence on the means that are chosen to reach the chosen
goal, and it may well affect the choice of the goal itself.

In many respects, Hammarskjöld was unique among the leaders considered
in this volume. His freedom to take action in light of a world outlook was greater
than that of national leaders such as Winston Churchill or Woodrow Wilson,
who had to keep one eye always on the electorate and on the opposition party
at home. He was, however, constrained by the quarrels and pride of his constituency, the member states of the United Nations. Within those constraints, he
worked steadily toward long-term goals. He took action in the short-term world
of international conflict and crisis, but his eye was always on the long-term
effect. Would this or that action help or hinder the international community as
it groped its way toward an uncertain future? From Hammarskjöld's perspective,
it was necessary to do more than just contain a conflict or defuse a crisis. It
was essential that the actions taken also encourage those habits of consultation
and cooperation that could—some day—develop into reliable institutions for
the achievement of international goals.

REHEARSAL FOR THE UNITED NATIONS

Before examining how Hammarskjöld's concern for the future worked out in
actual practice, it will be useful to look briefly at Swedish foreign policy in the
early 1950s and at a man with whom Hammarskjöld worked closely during
those years, Osten Unden, longtime Swedish Foreign Minister. There is a striking similarity in the two men's approaches to foreign affairs. Clearly, Hammarskjöld learned much from Unden. He learned much also in the hard school
of a constant watch over the national interest of a small neutral state. In the
world of the 1950s, neutrality had to be created anew each day in response to
changing conditions, and it had to be ceaselessly maintained against the pressures that came from both the East and the West. Hammarskjöld was not a
political man in the sense of party membership and activities, but when he came
to the United Nations he was not a political innocent. He knew what it was to
maneuver between heavily-armed giants whose strutting displays threatened the

very existence of small, neutral states. He knew how much and how little a
small state could do when, for example, two of its aircraft were shot down by
the Soviets over the Baltic in 1952: formal protests and an exchange of diplomatic notes; a proposal to take the dispute to the International Court of Justice
(refused by the Soviets); and then an appeal to the public and the international
community through publication of the relevant documents and distribution to
the delegations of UN member states.[3]

All of this adds up to what? From a purely national perspective, not much
had been accomplished by Swedish efforts. There was neither apology nor res-
titution from the Soviets, who argued that the planes had not been over international waters, as Sweden claimed, but, rather, had violated Soviet airspace.
There was little that Sweden could do to force the issue, but when Foreign
Minister Unden spoke to the UN General Assembly in October 1952, he did
not talk as if Sweden had a hopeless case. Instead, he presented the facts of the
incident, as Swedish authorities had reconstructed them. His approach was that
of one reasonable human being to other human beings who also had the gift of
reason, and his talk was an invitation to use that gift. Civility was the hallmark
of Unden's speech, and of his approach to foreign affairs. So would Hammarskjöld cut through the Cold War rhetoric that filled the Assembly Hall in the
1950s, and depend on civility to create an atmosphere where the parade of
pejoratives could give way to reasonable discourse. Civility accompanied him
on his many journeys into the uncivil world and, except in the Congo, served
him well. Or—as he would surely have put it—served well the purposes of the
UN Charter whose servant he was.

Unden did more, however, than lay out the Swedish case. Quietly, and without
emphasis, he did what Hammarskjöld was to do many times in the future. He
used discussion of a particular incident as a starting point for a discussion of
more general issues. His general remarks served the larger purpose he had in
mind when he took Sweden's case to the Assembly. He knew that no action
was likely to be taken there. So he used the occasion for a discussion of arbitration as a means of resolving international disputes, particularly when questions of fact were involved, as in Sweden's dispute with the Soviet Union.
Finally, in a vein that Hammarskjöld was to make thoroughly his own, he looked
toward the future. He pointed out that over the past fifty years many states had
changed their attitudes toward the principle of arbitration. Instead of viewing it
as a reflection on their sovereignty, they now saw it as a useful tool of international life. It was to be hoped, Unden said, that such an attitude would eventually be adopted by the countries of the Eastern bloc because, "The principle
of arbitration cannot, in the long run, be put aside."[4]

"In the long run." This was Hammarskjöld's favorite theme, the bedrock on
which all his actions were based. Again and again he responded to questions
about his immediate aims with an answer that looked down the long vistas of
time. At a meeting of the Organization of American States in 1954 he spoke of
the "human struggle for peace and progress which may never end. Only partial

results can be expected in each generation." To impatient reporters in 1955, he pointed out that progress was not made overnight: "I feel that this is a problem into which we must grow." And again, in 1960, "We, like our ancestors, can only press against the receding wall that hides the future."[5] This long-term view shaped Hammarskjöld's attitude toward the UN Charter, the document that was the legitimating source for all actions by the Secretariat. It was, he felt, only a beginning stage in the long journey that the states were taking toward international cooperation.

Hammarskjöld often used an evolutionary metaphor to convey his sense of growth and change, a view that was expressed most fully in an address at the dedication of a new University of Chicago law school building in 1960. The nations of the world, he said, had so far only developed an institutional system of *coexistence*, not cooperation. This was not a cause for despair nor yet for grandiose schemes of world government. Weak and inadequate as that system of coexistence was, it still held great promise for the future:

However primitive a basic institutional pattern may be, it carries within it seeds for the growth of higher social organisms, covering wider areas and groups of peoples. To use my terminology of a moment ago, such an institutional system for coexistence, stage by stage, may be developed and enriched until, on single points or on a broad front, it passes over into a constitutional system of cooperation. When that happens, we get in a first, necessarily rudimentary form, a form of society which, while preserving and protecting the lives of the nations, points toward an international constitutional system surmounting the nations, utilizing them to the extent that smaller units are more efficient instruments for evolution, but creating rules which limit the influence of the nations in fields where bigger units present greater possibilities for development and survival.[6]

Here, in a typically convoluted form, was the philosophy that guided all of Dag Hammarskjöld's actions. His eye was always on the future system of international cooperation toward which, he felt, the present international organization had to evolve if nations and peoples were to survive. He rarely used the apocalyptic language of doom so popular with many commentators in the 1950s. Indeed, when he once used the word *nightmare* to describe the situation of stalemate in disarmament, he felt compelled to explain that even though this was the kind of language he seldom used, he felt it was the only word that adequately described the threat hanging over people everywhere.[7]

For the most part, he was much on the pattern of Swedish Foreign Minister Unden: principled, civil, educative, with one eye on the present and the other on the future. What set him off from Unden and from his own past in the Swedish Foreign Office, was his vision of what that future might be. The vision grew as he grew into his office and began to use abilities that had not been called on in the service of a single state. His personal growth was paralleled by institutional growth as new methods, such as the UN Emergency Force, were devised to handle international problems. In both instances, growth was stimulated by the crises that had to be dealt with as they arose, crises such as that in 1958 in the Middle East, where the daily fare of domestic turmoil had taken on international implications that could not be ignored.

LEBANON, 1958

Two worlds met in the small state of Lebanon in 1958 when civil war wracked the country, and the United States, at the request of Lebanese president Camille Chamoun, dispatched U.S. Marines to the area. One world was the traditional world of states pursuing their own interests, confident that they could control the consequences. The other world was that which Hammarskjöld and others in the United Nations were trying to bring into being, a world of cooperative endeavor where an impartial investigation of facts and the passage of time could work together to cool passions and allow reason to prevail.[8] Since the interdependence of the world made a purely national interest hard to define and even harder to defend, the states involved in the Lebanese crisis cast their actions on a larger screen. Thus, Egypt and Syria (as the United Arab Republic) spoke not of Egyptian and Syrian interests in events in Lebanon, but rather of Arab rights and aspirations. The Soviet Union's gloss on its traditional push for influence in the area was its support, in varying degrees, for struggles of national liberation. And the United States, on behalf of free peoples everywhere, was out to contain communism wherever it might appear. Here was the traditional power struggle in new international dress. The element that distinguished it from struggles in the past was the United Nations.

There were established procedures for Lebanon to file a formal complaint with the Security Council, and thus to gain an international hearing for any grievances it might have. In May 1958 it did just that, charging that the United Arab Republic had instigated the armed clashes that were turning Lebanon into a battle zone, and that men, weapons, and supplies were being infiltrated daily across the Syrian-Lebanese border. Since this constituted a threat to international peace and security, Lebanon asked the United Nations to intervene. The Soviet Union said publicly what many people privately thought: that Lebanese president Chamoun was trying to internationalize an essentially domestic conflict to justify remaining in office beyond the single term prescribed in the Lebanese constitution. Whether or not this was true, it was certainly true that Chamoun was trying to strengthen his domestic position. He had already received private assurances from Washington that if the independence of Lebanon were threatened by armed attack, the United States would come to its aid.[9] Having tried what the world of national-interest politics could do for him, Chamoun turned to the United Nations and the world of international endeavor. There he encountered ideas of internationalism that were very different from the kind of support that he had in mind. The ideas were still in the formative stages, still partially tied to the power plays of various member states, but out of UN experiences in Palestine, Indonesia, the Kashmir, Korea, and Egypt, methods were being devised to make impartiality more than just a theory embedded in the UN Charter. Chamoun, like many another national leader, did not like the results.

After the Arab League failed to find a solution that was satisfactory to all concerned, the UN Security Council authorized the establishment of an observer group.[10] Specifically, it authorized the Secretary-General to take the necessary steps to establish such a group, which would then report to him: he, in turn, would report to the Security Council. From this strong position, Hammarskjöld could operate with relative freedom. His actions were guided by an awareness of the political realities that had created the Lebanese situation and the world as it was, and a determination to see the possibilities in that situation for moving the world toward what the UN Charter envisioned that the world might be. In this instance he resisted pressure from President Chamoun, from Israel, and from the United States to turn the UN presence in Lebanon into a military force that would seal the border between Syria and Lebanon. He pointed out that such an action would go far beyond the terms of the Security Council's authorization, which was for the dispatch of observers only. Further, it would prejudge the very situation that the observers were being sent to investigate. Finally, and most importantly, if it turned out that the fighting in Lebanon was chiefly domestic in origin and personnel, such a move would risk involving UN personnel in a civil war—a situation to be avoided at all costs. Their effectiveness depended not on numbers or firepower, but on the perception of them as being neutral in situations of conflict.

Early reports from the United Nations Observer Group in Lebanon (UNOGIL) displeased Chamoun greatly. The reports indicated only a small amount of infiltration across the border, and even that was reduced after Hammarskjöld visited the Middle East for intensive talks in Cairo, Amman, and Beirut. UN observers managed to gain access to areas where the Lebanese government had lost control—stimulating Beirut to accusations of UN collusion with its enemies—and reported that the people in the area were in opposition to Chamoun because of what they saw as his illegal maneuvering to succeed himself. Since they felt cut out of the parliamentary process, they took to the streets and hills in protest. This was a ready-made *cause célèbre* for the protesters' Muslim "brothers" among Middle East militants. There was a great outburst of inflammatory broadcasts and editorials. That, in itself, was enough to worry those Western powers who saw the devious hand of Moscow in every Middle Eastern ripple. The worst tendencies of the world of interests were being played out in Lebanon in 1958, where the internationalization of essentially local conflicts threatened to bring on the Great Power confrontation that was dreaded by all, including the Great Powers themselves.

In this dread lay Hammarskjöld's freedom of maneuver, such as it was. He could consult in confidence with leaders who dared not climb down from their public stance on this or that principle. With their private backing, he could then take actions and risks that they could not afford to take. "What the Secretary-General may find it up to him to do is still partly unexplored," he had said that spring in response to a question at a press conference. Much of his activity in the Lebanon crisis, as in the other crises that occurred during his tenure, was an exploration of what it was the Secretary-General could, in fact, do. The outcome of such efforts, as he never failed to point out, "depends entirely on the judgment of governments as to the wisdom of his move."[11]

Little by little then, in the summer of 1958, Hammarskjöld and his co-workers nudged participants in the Lebanon crisis out of their pattern of confrontation and conflict. Chamoun finally announced that he would step down at the end of his term, and that new elections would be held at the end of July. Radio Cairo softened its tone. Fruit and vegetables became the primary cargo in truck traffic across the Lebanese-Syrian border. Then in mid-July, a military coup overthrew the pro-Western government of Iraq, and the West's worst fears seemed realized: revolutionary nationalism, or Communism, or both, were now on the move in the Middle East, and had to be stopped. Chamoun called for aid, the United States sent in the Marines, and the situation again assumed crisis proportions.[12] Henry Cabot Lodge, U.S. Ambassador to the United Nations, assured the Security Council that the United States had acted under Article 51 of the Charter, an article that affirmed the inherent right of individual and collective self-defense. He added that the United States would withdraw its troops as soon as the United Nations could assure the integrity and independence of Lebanon.

Since Lebanon was not under attack, Article 51 was a very small fig leaf with which to cover the actions of the United States. Hammarskjöld was careful not to disturb it, however, since the article also affirmed the primary authority and responsibility of the Security Council for international peace and security. The first task for the United Nations was to attempt to smooth out the shock waves caused by the landing of U.S. Marines in Lebanon, and of British paratroops in Jordan—at the request of a nervous Jordanian government. Jordan's and Lebanon's fears of Iraq were not generally shared in the Middle East, where the overthrow of Iraq's pro-Western monarchy had been hailed as a blow for freedom. With the landing of troops in Lebanon and Jordan, the tone of public debate went from celebration to near-hysteria. Memories of Suez, with the invasion of Egypt by the Israelis, French, and British, were still fresh in everyone's mind. This new incursion of Western troops seemed to confirm the worst fears of Arab nationalists: the imperialists were on the march again, and they had to be stopped.

The whole situation was a classic case of fear and mistrust. Here, in Hammarskjöld's view, was one of the worst problems of the international system as it existed in 1958: the distrust that made it impossible for one group to see any other group's point of view; the distrust that saw threat around every corner and a show of strength as the first and most obvious response. For Hammarskjöld, this world of threat and response, of move and countermove, was not simply political, it was existential. Distrust was the curse of the twentieth century, not just between states in the international system, but between people in their daily lives as well. He had responded with great sympathy to an explication of that

theme by the philosopher Martin Buber in a collection of essays that Hammarskjöld read shortly before the situation in Lebanon was brought to the United
Nations. Buber spoke of the necessity of genuine dialogue in life, and of its
difficulty in modern times because of

> the demonic power which rules our world, the demonry of basic mistrust. What does it
> avail to induce the other to speak if basically one puts no faith in what he says? The
> meeting with him already takes place under the perspective of his untrustworthiness. And
> this perspective is not incorrect, for his meeting with me takes place under a correspond-
> ing perspective. The basic mistrust, coming to light, produces ground for mistrust, and
> so forth and so forth.[13]

The situation in Lebanon in 1958 was very much one of "and so forth and so
forth."

Earlier that year, at Cambridge University, Hammarskjöld had spoken of the
"walls of distrust" dividing the peoples of the earth, so that even though political
horizons had expanded to embrace the whole world, the expansion "has, paradoxically, led to new conflicts and to new difficulties to establish even simple
human contact and communication." What could be done? "All of us, in whatever field of intellectual activity we work, influence to some degree the spiritual
trend of our time. All of us may contribute to the breakdown of the walls of
distrust and toward checking fatal tendencies in the direction of stale confor-
mism and propaganda." Freedom of inquiry and freedom of expression were
essential in that task. "So, attitudes in line with the liberal traditions of this
university emerge as a deeply significant element also in our efforts to master
the political difficulties."[14] The political difficulties in Lebanon in 1958 were,
in the end, mastered by what Hammarskjöld was later to call "preventive United
Nations diplomacy."[15] One part of that diplomacy could scarcely be discussed
in public, but it was a function at which Hammarskjöld excelled. It consisted
of providing ways for states to back down from the heights where pride and
mistrust had landed them, while making it appear that they had secured their
position in triumph. Thus, the United States and Great Britain could withdraw
their troops, confident that it was their show of force that had given the
communist-nationalists pause. The nationalists, whether communist or not, could
plume themselves on beating back the imperialist threat. Chamoun could point
out that he had put love of country before personal position. And the new
government of Iraq, which had apparently had designs on no one except the
deposed monarchy, could seek and get recognition from all concerned.

The road to this outcome was twisting, and tedious in the extreme. Hammarskjöld had the patience to stay the course through meeting after meeting, diatribe
after diatribe, suggestions that sought solutions, and suggestions that sought
advantage. At last the struggle came to rest in a special session of the General
Assembly in August 1958, at which everyone managed to agree on an Arab-
sponsored resolution. Beyond requesting the Secretary-General to consult with

the governments concerned, make "practical arrangements," and so forth, which he had been doing all along, the resolution renewed the commitment of the Arab states to certain international principles.[16] This, in itself, was unremarkable. The principles were taken from the UN Charter and from the Pact of the Arab League. They included such high-minded and uncontentious goals as tolerance and living together in peace. Presumably the Arab states and the other member states had already agreed that they would respect each other's integrity and independence, not interfere in each other's internal affairs, work together for the common good and, as the Charter put it, "settle their international disputes by peaceful means in such a manner that international peace and security, and justice, are not endangered."[17]

Arab recommitment to these principles was an almost perfect example of what, on another occasion, Swedish Foreign Minister Unden had called "the contradictions between declarations of principles and the political reality."[18] The political reality in this case was obvious enough. Arabs and non-Arabs alike had sought for three months to turn the Lebanese turmoil to their own advantage while denying advantage to anyone else, including the Lebanese. The euphoria that greeted agreement on the Arab resolution was in part sheer relief that the world had not stumbled into a major war over Lebanon. For the contending states, the value of the Arab resolution lay in the "practical arrangements" the Secretary-General was to make, after consultation with the concerned governments, to "facilitate the early withdrawal of the foreign troops from the two countries [Lebanon and Jordan]."[19]

For Hammarskjöld and like-minded allies, withdrawal of the troops was only part of the story. Hammarskjöld, especially, saw the unexceptional principles that the Arab states had reconfirmed as an important part of the world that was coming into being. In his last annual report to the General Assembly, he noted that the purposes and principles set out in the Charter "lay down some basic rules of international ethics by which all member states have committed themselves to be guided."[20] Hammarskjöld felt deeply about those rules and about the Charter in which they were embodied. The Charter was many things to Hammarskjöld: guide, legitimating source for all his actions, blueprint for the future, inspiration for the present. To it and all it stood for he had pledged himself and his best efforts in this life. One of the documents that was found in his briefcase after the plane crash that took his life was a small copy of the UN Charter. The New Testament, the Psalms, and a copy of the Charter had always gone with him as he traveled the world of the present on behalf of the world of the future toward which he always pressed.

RULES TO LIVE BY

What can we say about the ethics that guided Hammarskjöld's initiatives in the international sphere? Since he was explicit about basing his actions on the UN Charter, it is natural to look there for the answer to the question. And at first glance, the answer appears clear enough. Specific principles are enumerated in the Charter, and certain actions are prescribed for member states in order to give effect to those principles in international life. Thus, to make the equal rights and self-determination of peoples an effective principle, states are to develop their relations with each other with respect for that principle, recognizing that it is one of the ways to strengthen universal peace. Similarly, the basic principle of statehood—that every state has the right to be politically independent and to maintain its territory intact—is to be given practical effect through two separate measures: a prohibition against either the threat or the use of force, and a commitment to the peaceful settlement of disputes. As for international agreements, which provide the foundation for the entire structure of international relations, these are to be made a living reality by the faithful fulfillment of state obligations. One particular obligation laid down in the Charter is for states to promote "universal respect for, and observance of, human rights and fundamental freedoms for all without distinction as to race, sex, language, or religion."[21]

Taken together, these statements of principle and prescriptions for action constitute, as Hammarskjöld had said, a set of "basic rules of international ethics by which all member states have committed themselves to be guided." As the servant of those states, and particularly as the servant of the Charter by which they had bound themselves, Hammarskjöld was, in theory, subject to guidance by the same basic rules of international ethics. We have, then, a rule-based system of ethics, articulated by the states themselves, and derived, in part, from their long experience in dealing with each other. This seems simple enough. The Charter principles are clear. The prescriptions for action are unambiguous. But, as Osten Unden had noted, actions take place in the world of political realities, and it is there that divergences from the world of the Charter begin to appear. In this respect the international situation differs little from any situation where behavior diverges from the goals set out in various covenants and constitutions. The difference lies in the means for authoritative interpretation of those documents. Internationally speaking, the means scarcely exist for defending the larger issues in which national interest or honor is at stake. Hence, the many exceptions to the jurisdiction of the International Court of Justice, and the relative paucity of means to determine how rules should be understood and which rule should apply.[22]

In Hammarskjöld's hands, this situation became another tool to be used in the struggle to contain present conflicts so that future possibilities would not be foreclosed. He made the interpretive vacuum into a space for maneuver, and he constantly enlarged that space, all the while referring back to the Charter as authorization for his actions. His ingenuity in justification was such that during the special Assembly session on Lebanon, one Saudi Arabian delegate was prompted to remark that Mr. Hammarskjöld's very able statements always "mean much more than what they say." Half ruefully, half in admiration, the delegate noted that Hammarskjöld's statements had to be read, not line for line, but in between the lines, and they could not be understood by reading only part.

They had to be read in their entirety, for: "Mr. Hammarskjöld represents by himself an international entity."[23]

It was a fair summing up of the role that Hammarskjöld was creating in the United Nations. The Charter's discussion of that role was brief. Besides making the Secretary-General the chief administrative officer of the organization, it also gave him the right to "bring to the attention of the Security Council any matter which in his opinion may threaten the maintenance of international peace and security."[24] The founders of the United Nations could scarcely have imagined the seriousness with which this particular Secretary-General would view those few words, nor could they have foreseen that, on the strength of them, he would take up the watch-care of the entire international community. His care was tempered by a regard for the political and social realities of the time. While not retreating an inch from the principles set out in the Charter, he also did not think that there was any quick solution to the problem of giving them international substance. Instead, he set them within his vision of the long-range development of attitudes and institutions that would eventually achieve the world envisioned in the Charter. Thus, with human rights:

Fundamentally, the rate of progress will be determined by the degree to which the developing social conscience of the peoples of the world is able to find expression not only in national legislation and international treaties but also in the climate of opinion in the various regions of the world. . . . It should not be surprising that, having laid down universal standards in an area where cultural differences are so wide and fundamental, the United Nations should experience some difficulties in finding practical methods to enhance the adoption and implementation of these standards on a world-wide basis.

This was not a cause for frustration or despair. Instead, the United Nations should simply keep trying, and "favor initiatives leading forward."[25]

As always, it is the temporal perspective that gives a distinctive cast to Hammarskjöld's words and actions. His perspective was that of the future. He was always *looking* forward, and he tried to make the post of Secretary-General one that favored "initiatives *leading* forward." In so doing, he gave the office more weight than many states were comfortable with, and certainly gave it a more active role than anything suggested in the Charter. Hammarskjöld was aware of this, and aware, too, of how cautiously he had to move. When, in 1960, he spoke of the Secretary-General's office as a one-man executive in the UN organization, he put the word *executive* in quotation marks, and noted that this "executive" had "explicit authority in the administrative field, supplementary to, but not overlapping the authority of either the Council or the Assembly."[26] For some, Hammarskjöld's definition of "supplementary" was a convenient way to move more rapidly into the future than their own constituency would allow; for others, it was an outrageous usurpation of the powers reserved to member states. In the final analysis, the office reflected the character of the man. He believed that work in the international sphere, like work in any sphere of life, was a matter of personal ethics. He had elaborated on this in a speech at Johns Hopkins University where he warned, "Politics and diplomacy are no play of will and skill where results are independent of the character of those engaging in the game." In the end, in politics, as in any other endeavor, "the results of the work of the most brilliant mind will ultimately find their value determined by character."[27]

Once, at a press conference, Hammarskjöld was asked, "Mr. Secretary-General, do you feel that the United Nations would have greater influence and impact on the world if there were stronger emphasis in the UN organs on moral condemnation of wrongdoers?" Hammarskjöld replied, "I am perhaps not a moralist."[28] Yet the political world of the 1950s was replete with moralists who denounced those who disagreed with them, and declaimed their own versions of the truth.[29] Hammarskjöld worked quietly in their midst, a moral man, if not a moralist. He worked always to nudge the world closer to that constitutional system of cooperation that he had spoken of in Chicago in 1960. He worked with the sense that, as a Swedish friend of his had said in a poem that meant much to Hammarskjöld: "The past is always with us, and to the coming days we are those who carry the past centuries, and also our own few days."[30]

In comparison with the centuries of development that had gone before, and the millennia that lay ahead, the few days of the present were insignificant in themselves. They gained importance from their place in the long progression of time. As Hammarskjöld put it to a gathering of correspondents at the beginning of his second term, "those days are really nothing in comparison to what is back of us, and what is in front of us. But they get their sense from what is back of us, and they get their sense in what they mean for the future; that is to say, what we can hand over after our time of work is not just what we have managed to add to the heritage, it is the whole heritage with the little we have managed to add."[31] Dag Hammarskjöld's long-term perspective reached well into the past as well as far into the future, that future of order and justice that he foresaw as the time when people could finally respond to the poet's question, "will the day ever come when joy is great and sorrow is small?" with the answer: "Yes. The day has come."[32]

NOTES

1. Brian Urquhart, *Hammarskjöld* (New York: Alfred A. Knopf, 1972), pp. 22–23. Urquhart had long experience in the UN Secretariat, and worked closely with Hammarskjöld throughout the Secretary-General's tenure. While writing this work, he had access to Hammarskjöld's private papers, and to unpublished documents as well as official records of the United Nations. His biography of Hammarskjöld is unlikely to be superseded in the near future. Emery Kelen, *Hammarskjöld* (New York: G.P. Putnam's Sons, 1966) is a pleasantly anecdotal account by the then director and producer of television at the United Nations. Bo Beskow, *Dag Hammarskjöld, Strictly Personal* (New York: Doubleday, 1969) succeeds in personalizing this formidably accomplished man through reminiscences of their times together, especially in Sweden.

2. Introduction to the sixteenth annual report, 17 August 1961, in *Public Papers of the Secretaries-General of the United Nations* (hereafter, *Public Papers*), Andrew W. Cordier and Wilder Foote, eds., 8 vols. (New York: Columbia University Press, 1969–1977) Vol. 5, p. 542. For a thorough study of Hammarskjöld's conception of the United Nations, see Mark W. Zacher, *Dag Hammarskjöld's United Nations* (New York: Columbia University Press, 1970).

3. Swedish Institute of International Affairs, *Sweden and the United Nations* (New York: Manhattan Publishing, 1956), pp. 1–8, 11, 128–37.

4. Speech by the Minister for Foreign Affairs in the General Assembly of the United Nations, 16 October 1952, in Swedish Royal Ministry for Foreign Affairs, *Documents on Swedish Foreign Policy, 1952* (hereafter, *Swedish Documents* with date), N.S.I: C: 2 (Stockholm, 1957), p. 91.

5. *Public Papers*, Vol. 2, pp. 274, 633; Vol. 4, p. 585.

6. *Public Papers*, Vol. 4, p. 584.

7. *Public Papers*, Vol. 4, pp. 71, 78.

8. The UN role in Lebanon in 1958 can be followed in *Public Papers*, Vol. 4, pp. 96–221. Editorial notes throughout this section give an excellent and detailed summary of events from May, when Lebanon brought the matter to the United Nations, through November when U.S. and British troops and then the members of the UN observer group were all withdrawn.

9. Telegram from U.S. embassy in Beirut to U.S. Department of State, 13 May 1958, and Secretary of State John Foster Dulles to Ambassador Robert A. McClintock, 13 May 1958, in U.S. Department of State, *Foreign Relations of the United States, 1958–1960* (hereafter, *FRUS, 1958–60*), Vol. 12, *Lebanon and Jordan* (Washington, DC: Government Printing Office, 1992), Vol. 42, pp. 49–50. The U.S. role in Lebanon in 1958 can be followed in detail in this volume.

10. *Public Papers*, Vol. 4, p. 98. For accounts of the UN observer group in Lebanon, see the UN Dept. of Public Information's *The Blue Helmets: A Review of United Nations Peacekeeping* (2nd ed., United Nations, 1990), pp. 180–85, and David W. Wainhouse, *International Peace Observation* (Baltimore, MD: Johns Hopkins University Press, 1966), pp. 373–86.

11. *Public Papers*, Vol. 4, p. 79.

12. Telegram from U.S. embassy in Beirut to U.S. Department of State, 14 July 1958, and the several meetings on 14 July at which the U.S. response was formulated, *FRUS, 1958–60*, Vol. 12, p. 207–40. For the views of the man sent to the area as a special U.S. envoy, see Robert Murphy, *Diplomat among Warriors* (Garden City, NY: Doubleday, 1964), pp. 396–418.

13. Martin Buber, *Pointing the Way* (New York: Harper & Bros., 1957), pp. 222–23. For Hammarskjöld's reaction to Buber's essay, see *Public Papers*, Vol. 4, pp. 69–70.

14. *Public Papers*, Vol. 4, pp. 91, 94.

15. *Public Papers*, Vol. 5, p. 132.

16. *Public Papers*, Vol. 4, pp. 169–70.

17. UN Charter, Art. 2(3).

18. Speech by the Minister for Foreign Affairs in the General Assembly of the United Nations, 24 September 1953, in *Swedish Documents, 1953*, N.S.I: C: 3 (1957), p. 33.

19. *Public Papers*, Vol. 4, p. 170.

20. *Public Papers*, Vol. 5, p. 543.

21. UN Charter, Art. 55(c). See also Art. 1(3).

22. Hammarskjöld did not inquire deeply into the source for these rules. It was enough for him that they were included in the Charter, and that the states had agreed to them. Their development can be followed in Dorothy V. Jones, *Code of Peace: Ethics and Security in the World of the Warlord States* (Chicago: University of Chicago Press, 1991). For a perceptive discussion of the link between power and the adoption of certain rules of international behavior, see Charles De Visscher, *Theory and Reality in Public International Law* (Princeton, NJ: Princeton University Press, 1957), pp. 133–56. Discussion of interpretation in international law texts is usually limited to interpretation of treaties, as in Louis Henkin, Richard C. Pugh, et al., *International Law: Cases and Materials* (2nd ed., St. Paul, MN: West Publishing, 1987), pp. 440–51.

23. *Public Papers*, Vol. 4, p. 167.

24. UN Charter, Art. 99.

25. *Public Papers*, Vol. 2, pp. 77, 556.

26. *Public Papers*, Vol. 4, p. 588.

27. *Public Papers*, Vol. 2, p. 507. Any discussion of the sources of some of the facets of Hammarskjöld's character would need to deal with the role of religion in his life. The posthumous publication of his diary, *Markings* (New York: Alfred A. Knopf, 1964) revealed the depth of his thoughts on the subject. Much can be learned from the writings of Nathan Soderblom, the Swedish religious leader who was a frequent visitor in the Hammarskjöld home in Uppsala. See, for example, Soderblom, *The Nature of Revelation* (1933; pbk. ed. Philadelphia: Fortress Press, 1966) and the discussion on p. 109 of human longing for the ideal. A starting point is Henry P. Van Dusen, *Dag Hammarskjöld, The Statesman and His Faith* (New York: Harper & Row, 1967).

28. *Public Papers*, Vol. 4, p. 329.

29. U.S. Secretary of State John Foster Dulles is one example, although recent scholarship credits him with more subtlety of thought than might be guessed from his strident public statements. See Richard H. Immerman, ed., *John Foster Dulles and the Diplomacy of the Cold War* (Princeton, NJ: Princeton University Press, 1990).

30. Quoted in *Public Papers*, Vol. 4, p. 63.

31. Ibid.

32. *Public Papers*, Vol. 4, p. 68.

IV

TRANSFORMATION

CHAPTER 9

Realism and Idealism in Historical Perspective: Otto von Bismarck

Otto Pflanze

A few years ago I attended a conference of historians, political scientists, and foreign policy experts on the subject "The Realist Tradition in U.S. Foreign Policy" that focused on three presumed "realists": Hans Morgenthau, Reinhold Niebuhr, and George Kennan. In the course of the afternoon the speakers came to the conclusion, with some disappointment (or so it seemed to me), that there was an undercurrent of idealism to be found in the writings of all three. On reflection, I could think of no historical figure with a reputation for realism of whom the same is not true. Was there ever a realist so pure as to be untouched by ethico-ideological concerns? And is not the opposite question also valid: was there ever an idealist unconcerned about power and its uses?

To arrive at a conclusive answer to these questions within the scope of a chapter would, of course, be impossible. What can be done is to sketch out in broad strokes the relevant early history of European diplomacy and then examine in greater detail the thought and practice of one of its most gifted practitioners.

First, it is necessary to clarify the terms being used here. In this essay "realism" and "idealism" identify models or ideal types derived from common political usage rather than from philosophical definitions. Realism concerns the actual or real; idealism, the abstract or speculative. The realist focuses on what is; the idealist, on what ought to be. To the realist, governments are primarily motivated by self-interest or the "interests of state"; to the idealist, governments should focus on the interests of Mankind as a whole, whose welfare is best served by the application of absolute values and standards. In political life, realists and idealists alike wrestle with the problem of power, its use and misuse. The realist accepts both the legitimacy of force and its practical limitations for the actualization of political goals; the idealist may decry coercion and violence and yet recognize its necessity for the achievement of ideal ends. Idealism can also take the form of fanaticism, in which case any means can be justified to achieve the desired end.

UNIVERSAL MONARCHY OR BALANCE OF POWER?

Historically these models are seldom to be found in their pure state, whether in the form of theory or conduct. Consider, first, the case of Niccolò Machiavelli, often regarded as the prototypical realist. Machiavelli was long misunderstood because his readers judged him on the basis of the amoral political tactics that he recommended in *The Prince*, but ignored his views about the conditions that seemed to make such tactics necessary: namely, the moral depravity of Renaissance rulers, the disunity and weakness of Italy under the city-state system, and the desirability of creating order out of chaos. His other works, furthermore, show that Machiavelli was a convinced republican dedicated to the principle of individual liberty. Realism and idealism coexisted in his political thought, but not always at the same place in his writings.[1]

Machiavelli's greatest contribution to the development of political realism was to divorce the study of politics from theology. That was possible in the largely secular society of fifteenth century Renaissance Italy, whose city-states developed foreign policies based upon reasoned self-interest and the balance of power in a largely self-contained peninsular state system.[2] As a model for all Europe, however, the Italian system was premature.

The growth of large territorial states in France, Spain, and Austria in the sixteenth century ended Italy's self-containment. After 1494 the peninsula became a sideshow of European politics, in which the main event was a long duel between the Habsburg and Valois-Bourbon dynasties for supremacy in Europe. That conflict, which continued intermittently for nearly two centuries, had a power-political character. The Habsburgs of Spain and Austria sought to consolidate their hold on Italy, Germany, and the Netherlands in the quest for a "universal monarchy" like those of Charlemagne and the Roman Empire. At the court of Charles V and Philip II, universal monarchy was not only a dynastic but also an ideal goal; it was the first step toward restoration of the unity of Christendom, riven since 1517 by the Protestant Reformation. In the religious wars of the sixteenth and seventeenth centuries realism and idealism, the simultaneous quests for universal power and universal faith, were again joined. When Habsburg Spain declined in the late sixteenth century, the Austrian Habsburgs took up the cause. In 1629 the goal seemed attainable, when at a climactic moment of the Thirty Years' War Catholic armies under Habsburg leadership conquered northern Germany and Jutland.

The response of the Valois and Bourbon kings of France from Francis I onward was to support any power willing to oppose the Habsburgs, whether Catholic, Protestant, or Muslim. When Gustavus Adolphus of Sweden assumed leadership of the Protestant cause by entering the Thirty Years' War in 1630, he was assisted financially by France. Under the leadership of Cardinal Richelieu, France remained out of the conflict until a compromise peace, signed at Prague in 1635, threatened to end the war before France had achieved its objectives against the Habsburgs. Catholic France, in alliance with Sweden and the Protestant princes of the Holy Roman Empire, went to war against Catholic Austria. Hitherto a struggle for both power and religion, the Thirty Years' War now lost its religious component.

As the statesman most responsible for this consequence, Richelieu is often regarded as the progenitor of a new age of political realism, of undisguised power politics divorced from all ideological concerns. William Church has shown that this image is simplistic by tracing the connections between Catholic faith and *raison d'état* in Richelieu's thought. His belief in the divine right of the Bourbon dynasty led naturally to the suppression of internal opposition, the quest for defensible frontiers, and the liquidation of Habsburg encirclement. Religious conviction and reason of state were inseparable in the cardinal's mind; the Protestant heresy was of secondary importance.[3]

By the time Louis XIV launched his bid for universal monarchy at the end of the seventeenth century, the European state system had reached a stage of development that made this goal much more difficult to achieve, at least with the means then available. Although Louis XIV ruled the wealthiest, most populous country in Europe, the wars he launched from 1667 to 1713 ended largely in failure, for they triggered the formation of defensive alliances among the threatened states that ultimately frustrated the French attack. Out of these struggles came the European balance of power.[4]

THE "CLASSICAL SCHOOL" AND ITS ETHOS

In the history of politics, whether internal or international, reality tends to be validated by theory. The idea of universal monarchy was derived from the realities of the Roman empire, universal church, and *res publica Christiania* of medieval Europe. Out of the struggles against universal monarchy came, first, the reality of the balance of power and, then, its idea or principle in political thought. In 1648 the Treaty of Westphalia confirmed in law the sovereignty of individual states, a development which had matured over the course of two centuries, and in 1714 the Treaty of Utrecht declared that the lasting "peace and tranquility of Christendom" was to rest on "an equal balance of power."[5] The balance of power had become the regulative principle of the European states system.

The problems of war and peace engaged the active minds of the Enlightenment, to whom the discovery of nature's laws constituted an intellectual endeavor of the highest priority. Among "enlightened" rulers and statesmen the conviction grew that the balance of power was not only a natural phenomenon of political life but also a desirable bulwark against tyranny. By its means European powers, great and small, could prevent any one power from destroying the liberty and sovereignty of others. It appeared to provide the only practical assurance of safety in a politically divided continent. But it was also seen as a guarantee that rulers would pursue rational foreign policies. They would abandon the unbridled pursuit of personal and dynastic aggrandizement typical of the past. Instead, they would pursue the calculated "interest of state" within the restraints imposed by the European equilibrium. Greed would be restrained by reason as well as by the threat of retaliation.

But most *philosophes* were subjects, not rulers, and they concerned themselves primarily with issues of human freedom, social equality, the social contract, and international peace. *Philosophes* of this orientation rejected the doctrines of *raison d'état* and balance of power, which sanctioned war as an instrument of state policy. Why, they asked, should relations between states not be governed by the same moral principles expected of relations between individuals?[6] "Foreign affairs," wrote Felix Gilbert, "showed most clearly the ills of a world not yet ruled by reason."[7]

The balance of power was the prevailing system of European politics from 1714 to 1792, yet this era of "cabinet politics" was hardly tranquil. In fact, it was marked by frequent tensions, as rulers calculated, ministers plotted, and generals planned. Increasingly, diplomacy was professionalized[8]—and likewise armies. Among the Great Powers, standing armies became common; the soldiers were uniformed, drilled, and disciplined; the weaponry improved and standardized. The ranks were mostly filled with mercenaries without patriotic attachment to the governments and countries they served. Frederick the Great thought that his subjects should take no notice when the king went to war; the affair was his, not theirs.[9] At peace conferences, territories were bartered away with little or no attention to the wishes of the inhabitants. What has been dubbed the era of "classical diplomacy" could only prosper in a society dominated by absolute monarchies served by an aristocratic elite common to all Europe and motivated by the same social mores, values, and interests.[10]

The careers of Frederick the Great, king of Prussia, and Prince Wenzel Anton von Kaunitz, chancellor and foreign minister of Austria under Empress Maria Theresa, exemplify the classical school of foreign policy. Frederick—ruler, general, and *philosophe*—embodied both the realistic and idealistic sides of the Enlightenment. His studies of recent European history and politics had convinced him that *raison d'état* and balance of power required Prussia's expansion. On assuming the throne in 1740, he launched an attack on Austria to acquire the province of Silesia. He succeeded, but only after two long, exhausting wars that brought Prussia to the brink of disaster. As a realist Frederick focused on state power (both internal and external); as an idealist he felt obliged to promote the welfare of his subjects. He was well aware of the contradiction between these interests. Their competing obligations presented Frederick with an ethical dilemma that he could never resolve.[11]

The Prussian challenge compelled Maria Theresa to reorganize and centralize the government of the Habsburg Empire. In 1755, Kaunitz plotted what became known as "the diplomatic revolution." He effected an alliance of Austria, France, and Russia against Prussia, whose defeat was, by his "political algebra," certain even before the first shot was fired. But Prussia survived the Seven Years' War and kept Silesia. Kaunitz's algebra could not accommodate such incalculable factors as Frederick's generalship and the mortality and whims of Russian rulers. On the verge of defeat in 1762, Frederick was rescued by the death of Tsarina Elizabeth and the succession of Peter III, who idolized the Prussian "philosopher king" and withdrew Russia from the anti-Prussian alliance.[12]

The balance of power ended the quest for universal monarchy; and yet it induced wars at least as often as it prevented them. Furthermore, the balance functioned to bring about the peaceful dissolution of one of Europe's largest states. Huge in size but politically and militarily impotent, Poland was liquidated by Russia, Prussia, and Austria in three partitions (1772, 1793, and 1795). Each of the participating powers feared that one or both of its eventual partners might gain a significant advantage by acting alone; hence they agreed to act in concert. This use of the balance of power as an instrument for mutual aggression shocked the western world. To a contemporary German historian, Arnold Heeren, the partitions began the dismantlement of the European state system ultimately completed by Napoleon. "The potentates themselves began its subversion! . . . What dismemberment could be illegal, if this should be regarded as lawful?"[13] Thomas Jefferson judged the liquidation of Poland to be an event no less significant than the French Revolution.[14]

Philosophers of the Age of Reason had the problem of reconciling the actuality of war and conflict with the ideals of peace and harmony. Perhaps, they speculated, the former was but a necessary stage toward the latter; the advance of reason would create an era of "perpetual peace."[15] In Immanuel Kant's famous essay on this subject, realism and idealism are necessary to each other; the progress of reason in the species, driven by conflicts between opposing interests, must lead within states to republican governments and between states to a federation of peoples (*Völkerbund*). In each case the evolving rule of law would compel men and nations to curb their baser instincts. The "mechanism of nature" would lead mankind from the real to the ideal—or, put another way, the ideal is ever in the process of becoming real in accordance with "nature's hidden plan." This philosophy of history enabled Kant to reconcile the spheres of phenomenal experience and noumenal values that were the two pillars of his philosophical system.[16]

Even as Kant composed his "philosophical sketch" in 1795, Europe was involved in what became a war for and against universal monarchy in a new form, that of a universal empire based on revolutionary reform, popular patriotism, and military dictatorship. Napoleon's conquests liquidated many sovereignties great and small, and nearly swept away the balance of power system itself. And yet the statesmen who assembled at Vienna in 1814–1815 to draft the peace that ended this great war belonged to the same aristocratic elite of the age of classical diplomacy. Metternich, Castlereagh, Hardenberg, and Talleyrand were all born, educated, and experienced in the old tradition. They thought in terms of *raison d'état* and the balance of power. The treaty they drafted largely maintained the peace of Europe for 40 years—until the Crimean War and the wars for Italian and German national unity.[17] And yet the relative stability of the Vienna system was owed not only to the balance of power but also to the reestablished authority of a ruling elite, whose economic and social power base had not yet been eroded by the industrial revolution.

But there were differences. Their predecessors in the eighteenth century had believed that the balance of power was a natural mechanism governing the political process. The ease with which Napoleon exploited the divisions of Europe for the expansion of France's frontiers and sphere of influence had proven them wrong. The peacemakers at Vienna were faced with the task of creating a new and hence artificial balance of power through the reallocation of territories and spheres of influence in Germany and Italy to frustrate a future attack either by France in the west or by Russia in the east. This reallocation made a mockery of the doctrine of "legitimacy" introduced at the congress by Talleyrand and designed to prevent a punitive loss of territory to France, now ruled by a restored Bourbon dynasty.

Until its legitimacy was challenged by the French Revolution, Europe's traditional ruling class of the *ancien régime* had wielded power without the need for a defensive ideology (other than divine right); but now in the early stages of the romantic era and the religious revival that accompanied it, organic or historical law provided a new idealism with which to consolidate and perpetuate the Vienna settlement and the endangered social elite of the "classical school." Out of the Congress of Vienna came the reactionary "Holy Alliance" and, more substantially, an agreement by the peacemakers to hold future congresses for the suppression of revolutionary movements. Four congresses were held between 1818 and 1822, but Great Britain would not cooperate and the congress system collapsed.[18]

The congress system, although doomed by its reactionary purpose, did not disappear without a trace. The tradition lingered that Europe possessed a common states system, that the balance of power was its regulative principle, and that congresses and conferences for the settlement of differences were acceptable substitutes for war. As the nineteenth century progressed, that system was generally termed the "Concert of Europe."[19] On occasion, the concert took steps to mitigate the use of violence in settling international conflicts (at Paris in 1856 and at the Hague in 1899 and 1907). By the centennial of his death in 1804, Kant's confidence in the progress of reason—and the mechanism of its propulsion—appeared to have, at least, some justification. Here it suffices to note that the linkage between realism and idealism in Western thought about international relations is again confirmed.

BISMARCK, A "CLASSICAL DIPLOMATIST?"

In the 1950s Bismarck was regarded by important German historians as having been the last great master of the art of "cabinet diplomacy" as practiced by the classical school of the eighteenth century. Born in 1815, he came to power in 1862 in an age increasingly dominated by national passions and crusading ideologies. And yet one prominent German historian of the post-World War II era asserted that Bismarck was "the last great cabinet statesman in European history . . . a spiritual successor of Frederick the Great in a completely changed world." He had "nothing to do with the nationalism of the nineteenth and twentieth centuries and its blind fanaticism. One cannot possibly stress that fact sharply enough."[20] A second German historian of the same era was equally emphatic, maintaining that Bismarck "had nothing in common with the dictators of the nationalistic era" and was completely devoid of that *moderne Vaterländerei* typical of the new national patriotism.[21] And a third testified that "Bismarck was not at all a man of national or popular ideas"; instead he was "a man of state and the reason of state . . . a man of pure *raison d'état*."[22] If these statements be true, Bismarck was an anachronism, a practitioner of eighteenth century statecraft in the nineteenth century, untouched by the "age of ideology" in which he lived and acted.

The judgment of these historians is obviously suspect. They were scholars born and educated in imperial Germany, whose professorial careers dated from the era of the Weimar Republic and who were eager to establish after the defeat of the Nazi regime that Germany's recent catastrophe was owed to the triumph in 1933 of an unsavory band of adventurers who came to power under the republic and were not representative of the German social and political tradition of the imperial age. They wanted to protect Bismarck against the charge of having been a precursor of Hitler. What better way than to find in him a latter-day Frederick the Great? But let us examine their case on its own merits, quite apart from their motives. Was Bismarck a man of pure *raison d'état*? Was he a realist unaffected by idealism in the emerging "age of ideology?"

During the 1850s Bismarck, not yet forty years old, was appointed Prussian delegate to the Diet of the German Confederation in Frankfurt am Main, at that time the most important diplomatic post of the Prussian government. From that post he strove to change Prussian foreign policy, which since 1815 had concentrated on preserving the Holy Alliance with Austria and Russia as the bulwark of the conservative order in Europe. He was convinced of the need for Prussia to expand in Germany "within the geographical area made dependent upon us by nature,"[23] achieving at least a role of equality with Austria in the leadership of the Confederation. What Prussia required, he concluded, was a new source of power capable of forcing Austria and its allies among the German small states either to bend or buckle. To this end Prussia must "hold open every door and every turning."[24] Isolated within Germany, Berlin must seek alliances in Europe capable of threatening Austria's security and terrorizing the lesser states. "Fear and fear again—that is the only thing which has any effect in the palaces from Munich to Bückeburg."[25] Prussia's logical partner for this purpose was France, which in Bismarck's opinion was no longer a danger to the stability of Europe.

Although affected by the argument, King Friedrich Wilhelm IV of Prussia could not be brought to take any step that might lead to a breach with Austria.

The traditions of Austrian leadership in the German Confederation and solidarity with Austria and Russia in the Holy Alliance were too deeply embedded in the king's thinking. One of the king's close advisers, Leopold von Gerlach, was deeply shocked by the radical proposals of the man he had considered to be his "pupil" in political affairs. The two men exchanged a series of letters, which illustrate the differences between realistic and idealistic views on foreign policy in this era.[26] Basically the dispute was one of relatives, not absolutes. While the interest of state and the struggle against revolution were important to both men, Bismarck gave precedence to the former, Gerlach to the latter.

Gerlach opposed *rapprochement* with Napoleon III on the ground that the Napoleonic dynasty, having been founded on revolution, had no claim to legitimacy. It did not belong to the respectable family of European monarchs. Self-interest would compel Napoleon, he argued, to ally himself with the popular forces of liberal and national revolution. Using Bismarck's own words, he wrote that *this* was the "reality" that it was folly to "ignore."

Bismarck's interviews with Napoleon in 1855 and 1857 had convinced him that the emperor was of a far different caliber than the first Napoleon. Where Napoleon Bonaparte had been bold, aggressive, and calculating, his nephew was sly, limited, and sentimental. There was no danger of a resurgence of French imperialism on a revolutionary scale; the founder of the second empire had neither the instincts of a conqueror nor the talents of a field commander. Nor was he impelled by the necessity of propagating revolution. On the contrary, liberalism was as great a threat to his own power as to that of any other European monarch. His imperial ambitions were centered on Italy rather than on the Rhine, where French expansion would certainly recreate the coalition that had crushed the first Napoleon.

Bismarck also attacked Gerlach's concept of "legitimacy," which he dismissed as historically untenable. All of the so-called legitimate dynasties of Europe, including the Hohenzollern, had revolutionary origins. The Napoleonic regime had as good a claim to legitimacy as any other.[27] "As a romanticist I can shed a tear for his fate," he wrote of King Louis Philippe of France, deposed in the revolution of 1848. "As a diplomat I would be his servant, were I a Frenchman. Being what I am, however, I count France only as a piece and to be sure an unavoidable one in the chess game of politics, no matter who happens to be her ruler. In this game it is my business to serve only my king and my country."[28]

Gerlach was a deeply religious man whose theology was inseparable from his politics. By contrast, Bismarck reached adulthood without religious convictions. In 1846 he underwent a conversion under the influence of German pietists, and thereafter prayer and Bible reading became daily habits. Unlike his pietistic friends, however, he did not find in religion a doctrinal basis for his politics. He concluded that the usefulness of prayer lay in its implied "submission to a stronger power." What he received from God, he believed, was the obligation to follow the dictates of his reason and conscience. Religion gave to his natural self-confidence a moral underpinning, and added to the certitude with which he asserted his will in the political process. But it did not otherwise affect his political conduct. In short, Bismarck could not share Gerlach's belief in the "Christian state" and his conviction that religious faith must inform state policy.[29]

Bismarck was a royalist, as one would expect given his Junker origins. Hence he preferred the vocabulary of feudalism to that of the modern state: "subject" instead of "citizen," "royal servant" instead of "state servant." In later years he often referred to himself as the "vassal" of his "liege lord," the king. And yet that was mere rhetoric. He rejected the views of romantic conservatives like Gerlach, who argued for the restoration in Prussia of a modernized version of the medieval *Ständestaat*. With a frequency that carries conviction Bismarck maintained that the Hohenzollern dynasty reigned by divine right ("by the grace of God"). From this it cannot be assumed that he had any overriding reverence for the institution of monarchy as such.[30] Under the stress of war in 1866 he was capable of supporting ethnic rebellions against the Habsburg empire and of liquidating traditional sovereignties in Germany. That he favored monarchical alliances after 1871 and accordingly built and rebuilt the Three Emperors League (Germany-Austria-Russia) was more a matter of geopolitical expediency than of doctrine or principle. Had Russia deserted the alliance, he would have sought a replacement in Great Britain.[31]

Bismarck's attitude toward the state was pragmatic, not theological. What impressed him was not its divine, legal, idealistic, or cultural nature, but its power. During his political career he saw himself as "the man of state and the king," standing above the chaos of social and political life and seeking without fear or favor, prejudice or partisanship, the ideal line of conduct in a foreign and domestic policy dictated by *raison d'état*. "I am," he once said, "a disciplined statesman who subordinates himself to the total needs and requirements of the state in the interest of peace and the welfare of my country."[32]

BISMARCK: A NATIONALIST?

Because he unified Germany, Bismarck is often assumed to have been a German nationalist, an assumption that would seem to place him in the category of an idealist. As already has been shown, Bismarck's primary motivation was the expansion of Prussia and its equality of power and status with Austria within the German Confederation; what we call "German unification" came out of that effort. Furthermore, the word "nation" has had more than one definition, and it is necessary to identify what it meant to Bismarck. In his early years he used the terms "Prussian nation" and "Prussian nationality." During 1866–1867 he is said to have often remarked, "My highest ambition is to make the Germans into a nation." The "establishment of the German nationality" is how he sometimes described his life's work. By the "German nation," a term that Bismarck used after 1871, he clearly meant the German Reich, not the German-speaking people of Europe. For him nations had concrete existence only when united under a sovereign state. Clearly he thought in terms of the "state-nation," not the "nation-state."[33]

The distinction is important for our purpose here. The frontiers of the Reich of 1871 excluded millions of German-speaking peoples in central and eastern Europe. To the end of his life Bismarck insisted that the ethnic Germans of Austria and Russia should remain subjects of the Habsburg and Romanov dynasties. The German Reich had no *irredenta* to be recovered. To attempt the union of all German-speaking peoples under a single political roof would have destroyed the balance of power system as the regulative principle of European international politics. It is safe to say that Bismarck never entertained such a revolutionary thought.

In the eighteenth-century tradition, he looked upon the balance of power as a shelter for the protection and consolidation of what he had created in 1864–1871. Diplomatic finesse enabled him to isolate the battlefields of the wars he fought. The foes of Prussia-Germany fought against it without supporting intervention by any outside power. During his last two decades as chancellor, Bismarck's skill in keeping the German Reich "one of *three* on the European chess-board," shielded his "revolution from above" from the uncertainties of a major European war. "All politics," he declared in a statement reminiscent of Kaunitz, "reduces itself to this formula: to try to be one of three, so long as the world is governed by the unstable equilibrium of five Great Powers."[34] Despite grave crises in 1876–1878 and 1885–1887, his management of the equilibrium preserved the peace of Europe—because in Bismarck's judgment it was in the rational self-interest of Germany to do so. The same can be said of his resolute refusal to countenance a preventive war against France, an action repeatedly urged upon him by Prussian generals during diplomatic crises after 1871.[35]

Here we have positive support for the claim that Bismarck was a diplomatist of the classical school in the eighteenth century tradition, which believed that foreign and military policy must be dictated by the reasoned interest of state and pursued within the limits of the balance of power system. His success at this would seem to place him in Robert Jackson's category of a "situational ethicist."[36]

BISMARCK: AN ANACHRONISM?

If this were his entire story, we would have to conclude that Bismarck was indeed an anachronism, a nineteenth century statesman in the eighteenth century tradition, a committed realist in an age of increasing idealistic commitment.

A candid, long overlooked statement by Bismarck himself, buried in an address of 1869 to the Prussian parliament, reveals the fallacy in such a conclusion. "In Europe's present situation, in the present state of civilization, it is impossible to undertake great political and perhaps warlike actions for secret reasons of cabinet diplomacy that may be unraveled later by historians. Now one can only conduct war out of national motives, from motives that are national to the degree that their compelling nature is recognized by the great majority of the population."[37] As noted, Frederick the Great went to war against Austria in 1740 to expand Prussia, an act of *Realpolitik* that required no idealistic explanation. One hundred and twenty-six years later Bismarck repeated the deed, but felt compelled to explain and justify the act before the bar of public opinion.[38]

The three wars that Prussia fought under Bismarck's leadership show in themselves the progression from the old diplomacy to the new. The occasion for war against Denmark in 1864 was the Danish attempt to incorporate Schleswig, which was inhabited by Germans except for a few districts on its northern frontier, into the Danish state. The Schleswig cause was considered in Germany to be a national one, but Bismarck fought the war in alliance with Austria and in defiance of German public opinion. The conflict of 1866 was a civil war within the German Confederation: Austria was backed by many Confederate states; Prussia, by none. The war became popular in Prussia only as it progressed. Bismarck's effort to depict the conflict as a war for German national unity was greeted initially with scorn. Prussia's outright annexation of Schleswig-Holstein, Hannover, Hesse-Cassel, and Frankfurt was accepted only in combination with the establishment of a North German Confederation under a constitution with many liberal features, including a parliament chosen by universal and secret male suffrage.[39]

Only the war against France in 1870–1871 can be considered a truly national war of modern character. In the preceding four years Bismarck's hope for a voluntary and evolutionary union of northern and southern Germany under the Hohenzollern crown had been dashed. Nothing was more likely to regalvanize national sentiment than a war against Germany's traditional foe. For that matter the war was popular on both sides of the Rhine. Continued French resistance under popular leadership after the defeat and capture of Napoleon III at Sedan in September 1870 aroused Bismarck himself to private utterances of ferocity toward the French. To bring the war to an end he urged the generals to hasten the bombardment of Paris. And yet even under these circumstances he insisted, as he had in 1866, that the war be contained, that political objectives take precedence over military expediency. The peace imposed on Austria in 1866 cost the Habsburg Empire no territory, because Bismarck wished to hold open the possibility of future reconciliation. Yet in 1870–1871 he insisted on the annexation of Alsace and Lorraine from France. He had concluded that the French would neither forgive nor forget their humiliation at German hands; hence the gate to the Rhine valley, France's traditional route for the invasion of Germany, had to be closed. Bismarck's third and final war was fought as a war of peoples as well as governments.[40]

By word and deed Bismarck never ceased after 1866 to convey the impression that the new Germany was not just an extension of the Prussian *Machtstaat*, to which the citizenry owed mere formal obedience, but also an organic national state requiring their patriotic allegiance. He deliberately exploited German national patriotism for the expansion of Prussia's territory, population, and power.

The stress he placed on the national character of the German Reich helped to consolidate it by overcoming particularistic loyalties among Germans, but it also served to estrange further the ethnic minorities living within the Reich's borders. The ethnic conception that helped to reconcile Hanoverians, Saxons, Bavarians, Swabians, and other German *Stämme* to the rule of Berlin could only heighten the sense of alienation felt by the Reich's Polish, Danish, and French citizens, who demanded for themselves the same right of ethnic self-determination claimed by Germans. Bismarck's tactical use of German nationalism as a moral reinforcement for a Reich created by Prussian power politics blocked the political assimilation of the empire's ethnic minorities and thereby endangered the security of its frontiers. Bismarck concluded that the only practical escape from this dilemma was Germanization. Greater ethnic homogeneity, it seemed, was a precondition for the final consolidation of the German Reich. And yet the government's attacks on their cultural identity only served to estrange further the Reich's ethnic minorities and alarm their ethnic brethren residing beyond its frontiers.[41]

Furthermore, the tactic had an effect upon the German-speaking people of the Habsburg empire that went beyond Bismarck's intentions. In negotiating the Dual Alliance between Germany and Austria-Hungary in 1879, he reckoned that such an alliance would be popular with ethnic Germans in both countries. But the result exceeded his expectations—to the point of embarrassment.

In 1892, two years after his dismissal as Reichskanzler by Wilhelm II, Bismarck traveled through Prague to Vienna and back through Munich. He went to attend the marriage of his eldest son to an Austrian countess, and the trip, undertaken despite his continuing feud with the German Kaiser, turned into a triumphal journey such as would have pleased a Roman emperor. In both countries he was received by thousands on thousands of citizens, who gathered wherever he appeared in public—at hotels where he stopped, at railway stations where he arrived or departed, and even along the railway tracks where his train passed. In Austria he was hailed by pan-German demonstrators, singing *Die Wacht am Rhein* and other German patriotic tunes. Bismarck responded by insisting, as he did on all similar occasions from 1866 to the end of his life in 1898, that ethnic Germans residing in the Habsburg and Russian empires were subjects of their respective rulers and should not expect inclusion in a united Germany. On his trip to Vienna he sought to discourage pan-German demonstrations, but with little success. His deeds and charisma spoke louder than his cautionary words, and echoed on into the future.[42]

Bismarck was not out of step with his own time. He lived and acted in an age of transition from an older society in which landowning magnates of a traditional ruling class still had a major voice in public policy in central and eastern Europe. The balance of power system, as reestablished in 1815, was still the primary mechanism of international politics in a divided Europe. War was still an accepted instrument of state policy. The wars he initiated and fought remained within the limits of the balance of power system, despite the territorial rearrangements of 1864, 1866, and 1870–1871. But, as we have seen, he recognized that warfare could no longer be conducted "for secret reasons of cabinet diplomacy" but only out of "national motives . . . whose compelling nature is recognized by the great majority of the population." For the same reason he also recognized that in this age an internal "revolution from above" could only be executed and consolidated through the exploitation of national sentiment, and with the help of a national parliament based on universal suffrage.

CONCLUSION

This chapter suggests that there was a persistent linkage between the politics of realism and idealism in European affairs during the approximately four centuries discussed here. The linkage can even be found during the era of "classical politics" in the eighteenth century, when it is often presumed to have been absent, and likewise in the nineteenth century career of Bismarck, of whom the same presumption has been made. That the linkage existed in the Middle Ages is obvious (consider the Crusades). And it is equally apparent that the linkage has been a central feature of twentieth century international politics (consider the Cold War).

In conclusion, it may be rewarding to speculate briefly on some of the reasons for this phenomenon. The politics of realism has a two-fold character. On the one hand, it demands that the statesman have a cool, rational intellect, uncorrupted by ethical or ideological bias, and be capable of analyzing and understanding the characteristics of the power structure within which he or she functions. On the other hand, it requires that intellect to evaluate with the same detachment the tactics needed for success in executing those functions in view of the observed realities. These calculations require that the person weigh both the possibilities and limits of state power. What contingencies may develop as a consequence of any contemplated action? What reactions are likely to follow, and how are they to be coped with? The answers to these questions call for the exercise of judgment. In the crucible of judgment are many ingredients other than reason: hopes, fears, prejudices, presumptions, errors of fact and logic, and, yes, personal and societal values.

This explains the persistent linkage between the politics of realism and the politics of idealism; i.e., the existence of a spectrum ranging from the objective calculation of power and possibility to the subjective influence of personal emotions, predispositions, and value systems. Idealism, because of its focus on what ought to be, can skew a statesman's sense of the real, and realism, because of its concentration on the power of coercion, can neglect the power of moral idealism, of human sentiments and values. The normal relationship between realism and idealism, then, is more dialectical than polar. What ought logically to be irreconcilable opposites have historically been joined in an uneasy, indeed unavoidable embrace.

NOTES

1. The most recent major study of Machiavelli assesses him chiefly as a moralist and moral philosopher, the inventor of a "new moral reasoning." Sebastian de Grazia, *Machiavelli in Hell* (Princeton, NJ: Princeton University Press, 1989).

2. Garrett Mattingly, *Renaissance Diplomacy* (London: Cape, 1955).

3. William F. Church, *Richelieu and Reason of State* (Princeton, NJ: Princeton University Press, 1972), pp. 372–415.

4. John B. Wolf, *Toward a European Balance of Power, 1620–1715* (Chicago: Rand McNally, 1970) and *The Emergence of the Great Powers, 1685–1715* (New York: Harper and Row, 1951).

5. Maurice Keens-Soper, "The Practice of a States-System," in Michael J. Donelan, ed., *The Reason of States: a Study in International Political Theory* (London: Allen and Unwin, 1978), pp. 25–44; Edward V. Gulick, *Europe's Classical Balance of Power: A Case History of the Theory and Practice of One of the Great Concepts of European Statecraft* (New York: Norton, 1955), pp. 3–89; and Moorhead Wright, ed., *Theory and Practice of the Balance of Power, 1486–1914: Selected European Writings* (Totowa, NJ: Rowman and Littlefield, 1975).

6. Felix Gilbert, *To the Farewell Address: Ideas of Early American Foreign Policy* (Princeton, NJ: Princeton University Press, 1961), p. 65. See also Gulick, *Classical Balance of Power*, pp. 30–51, and Donelan, ed., *The Reason of States*.

7. Gilbert, *Farewell Address*, p. 61.

8. See François de Callières, *De la Manière de Negocier avec les Souverains* [first published in 1716; probably written two decades earlier], translated as H.M.A. Keens-Soper and Karl W. Schweizer, eds., *The Art of Diplomacy* (London: Leicester University Press, 1983). Harold Nicolson called Callières' work "the best manual of diplomatic method ever written." See his *The Evolution of Diplomatic Method* (New York: Macmillan, 1954), p. 62.

9. Peter R. Rohden, *Die klassische Diplomatie von Kaunitz bis Metternich* (Leipzig: Koehler and Amelang, 1939), p. 24.

10. "The balance-of-power theory . . . can be shown to be, at best, a theory of the general good, a theory of self-discipline, a theory of survival for the group, and a theory of moderation." Gulick, *Classical Balance of Power*, p. 45. See also Rohden, *klassische Diplomatie*, pp. 1–30, and Georges Livet, *L'équilibre européen de la fin du XVe à la fin du XVIIIe siècle* (Vendome: Presses Universitaire, 1976).

11. On Frederick the Great see the classic work by Friedrich Meinecke, *Die Idee der Staatsräson in der neueren Geschichte* (Munich and Berlin: Oldenbourg, 1924), pp. 340–424; also the biographies of Gerhard Ritter, *Friedrich der Grosse, Ein Historisches Profil* (3rd ed., Heidelberg: Quelle and Meyer, 1954), and Theodor Schieder, *Friedrich der Grosse: ein Königtum der Widersprüche* (Frankfurt a. M.: Propyläen, 1983); and "Die Idee des Gleichgewichts bei Friedrich dem Grossen," in Klaus Hildebrand and Reiner Pommerin, eds., *Deutsche Frage und europäisches Gleichgewicht* (Cologne: Böhlau, 1985), pp. 1–14.

12. Walter Dorn, *Competition for Empire, 1740–1763* (New York: Harper, 1940), pp. 292–386; Rohden, *Klassische Diplomatie*, pp. 16–30.

13. Quoted by Henry L. Roberts in the foreword to Herbert H. Kaplan, *The First Partition of Poland* (New York: Columbia University Press, 1962), p. ix.

14. Hajo Holborn, *The Political Collapse of Europe* (New York: Knopf, 1951), p. 16.

15. Gilbert, *Farewell Address*, pp. 60–66.

16. *Zum ewigen Frieden, Ein philosophischer Entwurf.* Akademie Ausgabe, *Kants Werke*, Vol. VIII (Berlin: W. de Gruyter, 1912); Lewis White Beck, ed., *Immanuel Kant: Perpetual Peace* (Indianapolis: Bobbs-Merrill, 1957), and *Immanuel Kant: On History* (Indianapolis: Bobbs-Merrill, 1963).

17. After World War II, the comparative durability of the equilibrium established among the great powers at Vienna attracted the attention of historians and political scientists, who wanted to know why it had succeeded so well in contrast to the Versailles settlement a century later. For example, Harold Nicolson, *The Congress of Vienna, A Study in Allied Unity: 1812–1822* (New York: Viking Press, 1946); and Henry Kissinger, *A World Restored: Metternich, Castlereagh and the Problems of Peace, 1812–1822* (Boston: Houghton Mifflin, 1957).

18. See Walter Alison Phillips, *The Confederation of Europe, A Study of the European Alliance 1813–1823 as an Experiment in the International Organization of Peace* (London: Longmans, 1914; 2nd ed., 1920).

19. Carsten Holbraad, *The Concert of Europe: A Study in German and British International Theory, 1815–1914* (New York: Barnes and Noble, 1971); and KeensSoper, "Practice of a States-System."

20. Gerhard Ritter, *Europa und die deutsche Frage* (Munich: Münchener Verlag, 1948), pp. 77–108, "Das Bismarckproblem," *Merkur*, Vol. IV (1950), p. 673, *Staatskunst und Kriegshandwerk, Das Problem des "Militarismus" in Deutschland* (Munich: Oldenbourg, 1954), Vol. I, pp. 302–29.

21. Franz Schnabel, "Bismarck und die Klassische Diplomatie," *Aussenpolitik*, Vol. III (1952), pp. 635–42, and "Das Problem Bismarck," *Hochland*, Vol. XLII (1949), pp. 8–9.

22. Wilhelm Schüssler, *Um das Geschichtsbild* (Gladbeck: Freizeiten, 1953), pp. 120–21. Hans Rothfels, another prominent historian of the time, took a similar position, denying that Bismarck's German Reich could validly be called a "national state" because of its eastern frontiers, which included a few million Poles and excluded millions of Germans in Austria and Russia. See his *Bismarck und der Osten* (Leipzig: Hinrichs, 1934), and "Bismarck und das neunzehnte Jahrhundert," in Walther Hubatsch, ed., *Schicksalswege deutscher Vergangenheit* (Düsseldorf: Droste, 1950), pp. 233–48.

23. Herman von Petersdorff and others, eds., *Bismarck: Die gesammelten Werke* Vol. I (fifteen vols., Berlin: Verlags-Gesellschaft, 1923–1933), p. 17. Hereafter cited as Bismarck, *Werke*. For a full discussion of Bismarck's philosophy of politics, aims, and tactical methods see Otto Pflanze, "Bismarck's 'Realpolitik,' " *The Review of Politics*, Vol. XX (October 1958), pp. 492–514, and *Bismarck and the Development of Germany* (3 vols.) (Princeton, NJ: Princeton University Press, 1990), Vol. I, pp. 80–99.

24. Bismarck, *Werke*, Vol. XIV, p. 473; see also Vol. II, pp. 150, 223.

25. Bismarck, *Werke*, Vol. XIV, p. 372.

26. For the entire exchange see *Briefwechsel des Generals Leopold von Gerlach mit dem Bundestagsgesandten Otto von Bismarck* (3rd ed., Berlin: W. Hertz, 1893); also Bismarck, *Werke*, Vol. XIV, pp. 460ff., Vol. XV, pp. 110ff.

27. Bismarck, *Werke*, Vol. II, pp. 226ff., and Vol. XIV, pp. 470ff.

28. Bismarck, *Werke*, Vol. XIV, p. 465.

29. On Bismarck's religious views see Pflanze, *Bismarck and the Development of Germany*, Vol. I, pp. 48–53 (the references in footnotes 48–55 are important for discus-

sion of the long controversy over the character, genuineness, and depth of Bismarck's conversion). See also Arnold Oskar Meyer, *Bismarcks Glaube nach neuen Quellen aus dem Familienarchiv* (Munich: Beck, 1936) and Hajo Holborn, "Bismarck's Realpolitik," *Journal of the History of Ideas*, Vol. XXI (1960), pp. 85–90.

30. For Bismarck's conception of the state and its relationship to civil society see Pflanze, *Bismarck and the Development of Germany*, Vol. I, pp. 53–62.

31. Pflanze, *Bismarck and the Development of Germany*, Vol. II, pp. 246–78, 415–41, 490–510, and Vol. III, pp. 78–97, 218–59, 443.

32. To the Prussian chamber of deputies, December 17, 1873. Horst Kohl, ed., *Die politischen Reden des Fürsten Bismarck* (Stuttgart: Cotta, 1892–1905), Vol. VI, p. 131. This was, of course, a political statement intended to counteract the blood and iron public image Bismarck had acquired in Europe during the events of 1862–1871. But it can also be accepted, I believe, as Bismarck's image of himself.

33. For Bismarck's views on the nation and nationalism see Pflanze, *Bismarck and the Development of Germany*, Vol. I, pp. 66–70, also "Bismarck and German Nationalism," *American Historical Review*, Vol. LX (1955), pp. 548–66.

34. To Alexandrovitch Saburov, January 20, 1880. J.Y. Simpson, ed., *The Saburov Memoirs, or Bismarck and Russia* (New York: Macmillan, 1929), p. 111.

35. Gerhard Ritter, *Staatskunst and Kriegshandwerk* (Munich: Oldenbourg, 1954), Vol. I, pp. 238–329; Gordon A. Craig, *The Politics of the Prussian Army, 1640–1945* (Oxford: Clarendon, 1955), pp. 255, 268–70.

36. This volume, see pp. 21–36.

37. To the Reichstag of the North German Confederation, April 22, 1869. Bismarck, *Werke*, Vol. XI, p. 50.

38. A German liberal publicist is credited with inventing the term *Realpolitik*. See August Ludwig von Rochau, *Grundsätze der Realpolitik, angewendet auf die staatlichen Zustände Deutschlands* (Stuttgart: Cotta, 1853). Rochau believed that their idealism itself had been responsible for the failure of liberal-nationalists to unite Germany in 1848, and he urged a more realistic approach in the future—striking evidence of the linkage between idealism and realism in German political attitudes during this era.

39. At the time Bismarck was regarded by liberal nationalists as a black reactionary because of his quarrel, called the "constitutional conflict," with the Prussian Landtag. His hidden agenda in the Schleswig-Holstein affair was to annex the duchies to Prussia; nationalist opinion in Germany called for an independent principality under the rule of Prince Friedrich of Augustenburg. See Pflanze, *Bismarck and the Development of Germany*, Vol. I, pp. 257–316.

40. Pflanze, *Bismarck and the Development of Germany*, Vol. I, pp. 392–409, 470–506.

41. Pflanze, *Bismarck and the Development of Germany*, Vol. II, pp. 93–126, 247–51, Vol. III, pp. 198–209, 234–39, 434–36.

42. See Pflanze, *Bismarck and the Development of Germany*, Vol. III, pp. 395–99, 444–57.

CHAPTER 10

Konrad Adenauer, Arms, and the Redemption of Germany

Carl C. Hodge

Among other evils which being unarmed brings you, it causes you to be despised.

Niccolò Machiavelli, The Prince

The rearmament of Germany, whose armies had only recently lost the most ambitious and destructive campaign of conquest in history, represented the greatest controversy of West European politics after 1945. From the time of national unification in 1871, the German officer corps had constituted a reactionary state-unto-itself. Under Hitler, the *Wehrmacht* became the principal weapon of the Third Reich's war against the geopolitical status quo and modern civilization itself. Defeated Germany was despised because of its arms rather than in spite of them. "After the experience of 1914, of the interwar years and of 1939," asked a British weekly in November 1949, "can there be salvation in any course save that of seeing the Germans have no army at all, large or small?[1] Yet Konrad Adenauer, the first Chancellor of the Federal Republic, judged the arming of Germany's second democracy to be critical to its very survival. Rearmament was in part the product of changing international circumstance and the conviction in Washington that the containment of Soviet power in Europe would require a multilateral diplomatic, economic, and military effort in which defeated Germany had a important role to play. But equally, the terms of German military revival bore the stamp of Adenauer's personal commitment to

I am grateful for helpful commentary on an earlier draft of this essay by Cathal J. Nolan, Joel Rosenthal, Stephen Garrett, Robert H. Jackson, and Martin Kitchen.

democratic government and the redemption of Germany's claim to a place among civilized state. At the core of Adenauer's campaign for German rearmament lay the apparent contradiction that a man with no promilitary sentiment, who needed only to survey Germany's urban landscape to appreciate the price of its martial tradition, should pursue aggressively the constitution of a new German army. It becomes less surprising when one recalls the choices confronting Adenauer between 1949 and 1955, along with the specific political and diplomatic ends that rearmament was to serve.

For some time into the history of the Bonn Republic its first Chancellor had few assets, apart from his own reading of the fears and ambitions of Germany's wartime enemies and future allies, to mobilize on behalf of the Federal Republic's interests. His diplomacy depended preponderantly on acquired political instincts and a fairly coherent interpretation of his country's past. Adenauer believed that from 1871 to 1945 Germany had been consistently remiss in a task considered by Bismarck to be critical to successful foreign relations over the long-term, the establishment of friendship with other states. The maxim of nineteenth century *Realpolitik*, that between nations there could be no friendship but only a convergence or divergence of interests, was an intellectual fashion of its time the realism of which was profoundly overrated by its practitioners. Its impact on Germany had been devastating. Since Bismarck, the Reich had all too often relied on clever diplomacy at the expense of a more sober calculation of national interest. It had made itself powerful yet isolated. Only through membership in and commitment to an international political community, Adenauer reasoned, could Germany have escaped isolation, gained greater insight into the motivations of other nations, recognized good faith when it was on offer, and avoided the disastrous miscalculations that hubris brought in its train.[2] Adenauer also believed that the experience of the Third Reich had a more immediate relevance to postwar Europe. During the 1930s the appeasement of Germany by the major Western powers had itself fed the appetite of Nazi geopolitical ambitions. A similar failure to make a determined and multilateral stand against the gambits of Moscow's diplomacy would produce much the same result. Like the Third Reich, the Soviet state recognized no law beyond the application of power—its own power for the extension of Soviet influence or the power of its opponents to thwart the same.[3] A policy of strength and resolve alone would impress Moscow. If Germans, exhausted and demoralized by war, could be brought to recognize that sufficient strength was possible only in concert with the Western democracies, they could in time be shown that a higher *Realpolitik* incorporated amity and trust among like-minded governments into the diplomatic equation.

The notion of a political community was itself related to Adenauer's conviction that economic and technological change in the first half of the twentieth century had made it impossible to administer the domestic affairs of any state without constant reference to factors beyond its borders. As mayor of Cologne during the early Weimar Republic, he had had to acquire foreign credit for a debt-ridden city. It was in part the damage done to the local economy by the crises of international diplomacy and shocks to the world economy that made him an early advocate of some form of European economic integration. In this he thought that Europe should take instruction from the United States, whose integrated continental market had provided the solid economic foundations of its political constitution.[4] Along with leaders such as Robert Schuman and Jean Monnet in France and Alcide de Gasperi in Italy, Adenauer represents a founding father both of European Christian Democracy and of the European Community. The Christian Democratic Union (CDU), the party Adenauer built into the dynamic electoral force of postwar German politics, was an offspring of the Weimar-era Catholic Center Party remodeled into a broad-based nonconfessional force of the center-right.[5] In August 1949 the CDU ran on a platform of federalism, a socially responsible market economy, European unity, and militant anticommunism that elected Adenauer to the head of a three-party coalition government.

Adenauer approached democratic governance as a call to political trusteeship. Fortified by a Weberian ethic of responsibility, he assumed a mandate to interpret for himself the best interests of the German people and to seek public approval at the end of his term for the consequences rather than the intentions of his actions.[6] Adenauer's personal definition of politics spoke of "the art of realizing that which is recognized as ethically responsible." This required above all courage, consistency and determination to resist the ever-present temptation of convenient duplicity. "Don't lie, even in politics," he once told a junior colleague, "a politician cannot always speak openly, but when he does he should be sincere."[7] For Adenauer, sound political engagement was based on principles that one could defend in the best and worst of times. Consequences of lasting significance came only from a sense of the continuity of ultimate purpose without which even well-intentioned statesmanship all too easily went awry under the conflicting pressures of public affairs.

And yet Adenauer understood like few European democrats of his generation that success in the public arena often depended on a measure of opportunism, the ability to pounce at any chance to further a worthwhile policy. To Chancellor Adenauer, a worthwhile policy for the Federal Republic, indeed its very *raison d'être*, was to change the whole course of German history. Given the trajectory of that history from 1914 to 1945, it was a task daunting enough to require from its architect a good deal of opportunism and noble enough to excuse one or two outright falsehoods in the realization.

THE HIGHER REALISM OF A WESTERN ALLIANCE

For five years after World War II, the question of reestablishing Germany's armed forces was taboo in official debate concerning the future of Western Europe. Yet even with the establishment of the Brussels Pact in March 1948, and the North Atlantic Treaty Organization (NATO) in April 1949, plans for the defense of Western Europe against potential Soviet aggression were woefully inadequate. When in November 1949 American Secretary of State Dean Acheson informed British and French officials that the Truman administration considered West Germany an ally, he formalized the Washington position on what additional strength should be tapped.[8]

Adenauer was personally unenthused at the prospect of a new German army, but he came to regard rearmament as a military necessity in itself, as well as a political issue instrumental to the acquisition of diplomatic influence. The government of a provisional state such as the Federal Republic had to take into the account both the threat of Soviet military aggression and the implications of indirect political pressure for domestic stability. Rearmament also held out the promise that the Bonn Republic's status under the Potsdam Agreement could be revised through the investment in national sovereignty and self-determination that the establishment of an armed service symbolized. For Adenauer security and sovereignty were very much coincident, since a credible military barrier to Soviet expansion in Europe seemed critical to the chance of West German democratic consolidation.[9]

The collateral benefits were possibly even greater, especially if a German contribution to military security were to be associated with the larger project of West European integration. In such a connection Adenauer saw the chance to make a clean break with discredited tradition. In the past Germany had insisted on too many diplomatic options in Europe. From Bismarck's alliance strategies to the Treaty of Rapallo in 1922 and the 1939 Molotov-Rippentrop Pact, this insistence had resulted in a tendency to play off Russia against France, East against West. While *Schaukelpolitik* (see-saw policy) won foreign recognition of the Reich's power, at its core was a tendency toward equivocation and artifice that undermined any sense of German integrity in those Western capitals where it was needed most: Paris, London, and Washington.[10]

By virtue of culture alone, Adenauer the Rhinelander instinctively looked to France as Germany's natural partner for European reconstruction, but the preference also had a political utility. A German democracy firmly committed to Franco-German partnership within a Western alliance would ensure its neighbors against the spectre of recidivism, and simultaneously give them a stake in German economic revival. From this perspective, the polarities of the Cold War produced a unique opportunity, in so far as they forced the Federal Republic to choose between two fundamentally different political and economic systems and their concomitant strategic alignments.[11]

Because Adenauer could not rely on a liberal democratic tradition among his countrymen to make the choice easy, he was doubly concerned to establish a credible Western security regime. Germans who could not love the Bonn Republic for its democratic constitution could still be brought to appreciate the advantages of protection from Russian revanchism and Soviet communism. A December 1949 interview with the American daily, *The Cleveland Plain Dealer*, gave the Chancellor the opportunity for some calculated newsmaking with this concern in mind. In it Adenauer asserted that the Allied powers who had defeated and disarmed Germany had an obvious moral obligation to provide for its defense; that such provisions that existed were unimpressive; and that the addition of German forces under European command might help to improve the situation.

Controversy triggered by the interview on both sides of the Atlantic prompted Adenauer to temper his remarks almost immediately. But the cat was out of the bag. Adenauer's remarks caught Washington's foreign policy thinking at a point where it tended in the direction of a much more assertive stance toward Moscow. He prodded American insecurities, encouraged the new Cold War militancy of the Truman administration, and looked to enhance the benefits for the Federal Republic of the new resolve in the Truman administration. Soviet restraint could be had only through respect for Western arms. Equally, a German contribution to West European defense would win the respect of Western allies, upon whom the recovery of national sovereignty depended.[12]

Undeniably, the outbreak of the Korean conflict improved the Bonn government's bargaining position on the latter issue. But Adenauer also worried that where Korea encouraged policy-makers in the United States to view the contest with communism in *global* terms, it could also undermine the American commitment to Europe as the *primary* theater of struggle. Moreover, Adenauer considered the communist menace in Western Europe to be real and imminent. He was never among that coterie of European politicians who thought the invocation of Cold War themes a convenient device for turning Washington's head. His sincerity in this matter came through in correspondence with Dannie Heineman, a longtime friend and Director of the Sofina Konzern in Brussels, wherein the Chancellor maintained that every feature of the Soviet presence in Eastern Europe attested to Moscow's ambition to establish an imperial status over the entire continent.

A Soviet ideological invasion of the West was already underway in the form of strong communist parties in France and Italy whose potential Washington did not, in Adenauer's view, appreciate fully. In Germany, Soviet power confronted a demoralized populace loath to accept that it might yet have to make military sacrifices for its own freedom, and skeptical that the United States, Britain, or France would defend the Bonn Republic. Worse still, many Germans of the occupied Federal Republic did not consider themselves free in any sovereign sense. Popular defeatism could be overcome only by a dramatic improvement of the West's military strength and a fundamental change in the official status of the West German state.[13] Adenauer's biographer interprets the Heineman letter as a *cri du coeur* to a personal confidant to do what he could on behalf of a Chancellor afraid for the viability of the Federal Republic. Heineman forwarded Adenauer's concerns verbatim to the desk of General Eisenhower, then Supreme Allied Commander for Europe (SACEUR). By December 1950 copies had been passed on to U.S. Secretary of Defense George Marshall, and every other upper echelon official responsible for American policy in Europe.[14]

Into the newly-intensified debate on European security the French government tossed the Pleven Plan for a European Defense Community (EDC). The plan was a makeshift alternative to France's nightmare, the establishment of a West German national army and an independent general staff, and was designed to spin out rather than speed up official discussion of the security problem. But in retrospect this too had its advantages. Because the EDC idea resonated so well with the theme of West European integration, it was hard to oppose in principle. For Adenauer, the lengthy debate over the EDC turned out to be an important phase in the effort first to formulate, and then to legitimate, his foreign policy at home and abroad.

The EDC had a good many enemies in Germany. The venerable German Social Democratic Party (SPD) campaigned against it with considerable success in local and state elections in 1950–1951, and drew support from the Protestant church, most notably from the popular neutralist pastor, Martin Niemöller. The SPD leader, Kurt Schumacher, argued that the Federal Republic's membership in a security arrangement directed against the Soviet Union would scupper indefinitely the chances for what was surely the supreme ambition of any Bonn government, the reunification of West Germany with the eastern zone of occupation. He charged further that the EDC proposal would impose too many obligations on the Federal Republic in exchange for too few commitments from the Western powers for the defense of German soil, in effect that it would make West Germany the battlefield in the defense of other countries. Adenauer countered that the Federal Republic was at this juncture in no position to make demands of the Western allies. And though he would never admit it publicly, national reunification was not at all uppermost among the Chancellor's priorities. Any arrangement for a reunified Germany acceptable to Moscow, he believed, would lead to *de facto* neutrality and save *Schaukelpolitik* from the grave.[15]

Especially galling were pacifist claims to the moral high ground of the rearmament debate. In the face of Soviet policy and military might, West German pacifism seemed to Adenauer either the child of breathtaking credulity or a philosophical veneer for appeasement. He labeled Niemöller, an enemy of the West German state and accepted the resignation of Gustav Heinemann, a cabinet minister openly sympathetic to Niemöller, with undisguised contempt for the minister's views. In protest the Chancellor's most devoted critics named him "The Hammer" and wove the Heinemann episode into the folklore of the pacifist cause. For years they never tired of citing it as proof of his cold, authoritarian character.[16]

But Adenauer also had outspoken allies of considerable prestige. Korea, proclaimed Charles de Gaulle, made German rearmament inevitable, and Winston Churchill proposed to the European Council in Strasbourg the immediate creation of an integrated European army. Cardinal Frings of Cologne invoked the traditional Catholic notion of just war and denounced neutrality as moral abdication.[17] Sensing that there existed in Germany no popular majority for rearmament on any blueprint, Adenauer rejected a referendum on the issue and instead channeled his energies toward securing the kind of American defense commitment to Europe that might eventually turn the domestic debate in his favor.

His memorandum to U.S. High Commissioner John McCloy in June 1951, in which he touched upon the principal aspects of Germany's current position on the continent and its meaning to other European states, is a case in point. Adenauer played down any immediate danger of war but stressed the strategic importance of Europe to American policy with his own variation on domino theory. "For if Soviet Russia gains control of the manpower and resources of the Federal Republic," he warned, "its war-making potential and economic power will increase enormously. France, Italy and the Benelux states will then fall quickly to communism."[18] Adenauer then turned to the Federal Republic's occupied status and argued that Germans needed to see a political dividend in voluntary self-defense—in other words, that there could be no defense of Europe without Germany, and no meaningful German commitment without sovereignty. "In my opinion," he wrote, "the German people have, despite the experience of past decades, more than any other European people the qualities required to build a dike against the Soviet Union."[19] The words themselves were not especially forceful, but their logic was potent indeed. They told McCloy that the United States had a good deal to lose in Europe and that, like it or not, Germany was the key to American success there. In informal exchanges with the German press corps, Adenauer intimated that he thought stealth and discretion utterly essential to Bonn's diplomacy, but he also employed the term *Grossmacht* (great power) in characterizing the sovereignty he sought for the Federal Republic relative to Britain and France.[20] The Chancellor thought his government should drive a hard bargain with whatever it had to offer, and he was prepared to conjure for any ally, including the United States, the image of a demoralized German populace embracing neutrality if it were denied full recognition in a Western alliance.[21]

In mid-July of 1950 McCloy confided to Secretary of State Acheson that the price of denying Germans the right to fight in a military emergency, even if that were to mean inducting Germans into the U.S. army, would be "that we should probably lose Germany politically as well as militarily without hope of regain."[22] Expressed so dramatically, concerns such as these were critical in bringing Washington around to a European formula for German rearmament, despite its complications, in the hope that it would expedite the task of establishing a credible defense for Western Europe by removing French resistance to some form of German contribution.

Adenauer meanwhile assigned a panel of former *Wehrmacht* generals the task of drafting Bonn's own proposals for West European security. The resulting Himmeroder Memorandum envisaged the inclusion of a German force of 250,000 men in twelve armored and mobile divisions, supported by an air force of 825 planes and a navy of some 200 ships. It also called for a forward Defense of Western Europe such as would make the Elbe River, rather than the Rhine, the front line of conflict with Soviet forces. The plan was more ambitious than any security package then under serious consideration in Paris, London, or Washington, or anything Adenauer himself was willing to acknowledge publicly in Germany. It bore the signature of the *Wehrmacht*'s experience in Russia, and its vision of a "forward" defense of the Federal Republic flew in the face of the original NATO concept of placing the bulk of Western forces well to the west of the East German frontier.[23]

At the Petersberg talks of January 1951, during which the American, British, and French Deputy High Commissioners heard German ideas for rearmament, Adenauer's military advisors used the Himmeroder document as the basis for a set of very comprehensive proposals. It was an impressive presentation that complemented Adenauer's dialogue with McCloy by connecting the administrative aspects of defense to German sovereignty. At its core was the technical argument that military practicality required nationally-homogeneous German armored divisions under German command. To this the German delegation added a proposal for the creation of a German Ministry of Defense, arguing that the democratic constitution of the Federal Republic perforce required that its military be answerable to the Bonn parliament.[24] Finally, they pointed out that their recommendations on the overall organization of Western forces were based on experience acquired in four years of war against the Soviet Union and were entirely compatible with American military doctrine recorded in the *U.S. Army Field Manual*. Obviously taken aback by the thoroughness of the German presentation, U.S. representative General George Hayes wired Washington for advice "as to the position to be taken" regarding alternative forms of organization within the Brussels formula.[25]

In 1950–1951, Adenauer doubted that Washington could be relied upon to maintain a large U.S. military presence in Europe over the long-term. If the possibility of such a presence depended on Bonn's official endorsement of a supranational European force—because of Washington's concerns about burden-sharing and its desire to placate France—then he was determined to demonstrate Bonn's good intentions on European security *above all to the United States*. The content of the Himmeroder Memorandum report demonstrates that he nonetheless never accepted that the substance of a European force would have to conform to the Pleven Plan. One had to board the train first, then change its destination. The Chancellor understood and identified with the American concept of double-containment in Europe: containing Soviet influence within its present frontiers and containing German revival within a Western political constellation. Whereas Washington wanted to transform Germany into a West European democracy, Adenauer wanted to make the United States a West European power.[26]

With this in mind, he listed a number of outstanding grievances against France that collectively, he argued, could only benefit the nationalist rhetoric of the SPD in the Federal Republic. From McCloy he asked that Washington be reminded that only when sufficient American pressure was brought to bear on

Paris would French policy toward Germany be compatible with the larger goals of U.S. diplomacy in Europe.[27] When McCloy pushed the case with Paris for German sovereignty and rearmament, the American press ventured that McCloy was in the Chancellor's pocket. But the best evidence is that Adenauer and McCloy collaborated closely on rearmament above all because their personal views of the security problem genuinely converged. Reporting on an interview with Adenauer in March 1951, McCloy noted how the Chancellor went out of his way to express his distrust of British and French intentions relative to American policy. He then observed that German officials were "not above sowing a little dissension between Allies" and that it might therefore be wise to take the Chancellor's praise of the United States "with a grain of salt."[28]

Inevitably, the EDC was the target of Soviet gambits in sabotage. In March 1952, Stalin's note to the Western powers on the issue of a German peace treaty held out the prospect of German reunification, with a mind to driving a wedge between Bonn and its allies.[29] But by 1952 West Germany had turned its foreign trade deficit into a modest surplus, aided in part by a global demand for investment goods fueled by the Korean War. The benefits in jobs and wages increased popular support for Adenauer's policy of West European integration and a German military contribution to a European army. Stalin's *démarche* was too late. The economic boom strengthened structural ties between the Federal Republic and Western markets, and gave its populace reason to consider with skepticism the alleged alternatives to Adenauer's Cold War diplomacy.[30]

On May 26, 1952, German sovereignty came a step closer. On that date Bonn signed with Britain, France, and the United States a Convention on Relations with the Federal Republic of Germany, which terminated the Occupation Statute in return for Bonn's commitment to raise German forces as prescribed under the Contractual Agreement of the EDC.[31] Of course, none of this meant that the EDC was home and free. Its implementation awaited ratification in the national parliaments. The newly elected Eisenhower administration supported with increasing vigor German rearmament through the EDC as a credible collective security regime for Europe, not least of all because Eisenhower's military expertise recognized the need for a German defense contribution, while his experience as SACEUR told him that the Bonn Republic was a reliable ally while in Adenauer's hands.[32]

THE FEDERAL REPUBLIC, SOVEREIGN AND ATLANTICIST

Eisenhower launched an immediate diplomatic offensive on the EDC's behalf, with a view to speeding up ratification in France and Germany. His Secretary of State, John Foster Dulles, in fact applied considerable pressure on both Paris and Bonn throughout 1953, with repeated warnings that Washington was losing its patience.[33] For Adenauer, these cautions included a strong recommendation that his government reach agreement with Paris on the status of the Saar region, before 1939 a German province but considered by France a semiautonomous region since 1945. Faced with a general election in September 1953, Adenauer needed to accommodate Paris to an extent that would convince Washington of German reasonableness, while avoiding concessions that could weaken his position with a German electorate poised to pass judgment on his first term as Chancellor.[34]

When France declared in January 1953 that its ratification of the EDC would depend upon a resolution of the Saar dispute, Adenauer committed his government somewhat vaguely to the "continued organic development" of the treaty. When Paris announced the following May a Franco-Saar convention that would give the Saar government the right to make international agreements, he again refused to be drawn. After a formal protest of the convention, he temporized on counterinitiatives and allowed the Saar issue to drift until after the elections. He then assured Secretary Dulles that "Germany would make a serious attempt to solve the Saar problem" and blamed the delays on changes in the French government.[35] The Chancellor was aware of Eisenhower's growing annoyance at French linkage diplomacy, and saw some advantages in France's growing self-isolation over the EDC. It was a regrettable but possibly necessary price for real progress on a security arrangement acceptable to Bonn. Simple geography meant that there would be another time and opportunity to collaborate with Paris on the work of the New Europe. France could play at obstructionism, but French isolationism was not a serious option over the long haul.

Precisely how the maneuvers of 1953 were read by the West German voters is guesswork, but the electoral dividend was considerable. In the September election, the CDU popular vote jumped from 31 percent in 1949 to 45.2 percent, while that of the SPD atrophied to 28.8 percent. Adenauer entered a new term in a vastly strengthened domestic position. The victory left Adenauer's governing coalition in possession of two-thirds of the seats in the upper and lower houses of the Bonn parliament, and in a position to amend the Federal Republic's constitution, if necessary, in order to permit the Federal Republic to undertake whatever was required to fulfill its obligations under the EDC blueprint. As Adenauer saw it, this approach had two important virtues: it would deliver to Washington proof of German readiness to contribute to Western security, and it would make French efforts to add further amendments to the EDC more difficult.[36]

On the second calculation he was wrong. The French government of Pierre Mendès-France piled on new preconditions for French ratification, before the French parliament voted down the EDC outright in August 1954.[37] The disappointment was the bitterest of Adenauer's chancellorship. Yet, as depressed as he was that four years of painstaking statesmanship were now apparently wreckage, he had no difficulty in almost immediately adapting the priorities of his government to a new situation. Similarly, the Eisenhower administration switched rather smoothly to the NATO alternative for German rearmament. Two things helped to make the United States an enthusiast of this solution: the consistency of Adenauer's diplomacy over the preceding four years, now capped by Bonn's EDC ratification against France's veto, and the personal trust Adenauer had earned in Washington.

The first consequence of the EDC's demise was to make Adenauer into the most important man in Europe, in so far as the Chancellor's reaction "suddenly became the most immediate and critical factor in the European security situation."[38] Fully cognizant of the stronger position in which France had unintentionally placed him, Adenauer's initial gesture was to stress that proposed alternatives to the EDC would have to deliver full sovereignty to the Federal Republic. He was also concerned to make the most of Germany's image abroad, when he lamented publicly how France had isolated itself from Europe and the United States, and then he emphasized that Bonn's diplomacy would nonetheless continue to stress reconciliation and cooperation with Paris.[39]

The substantive initiative now shifted to London and Washington, and it was to fresh Anglo-American overtures that the newly-empowered Adenauer had to find the appropriate response. British Foreign Minister Anthony Eden made the first move, with Dulles' consent and advice, by touring continental capitals to win support for a security conference in London. Meanwhile, Dulles asked the other Western allies to surrender most of their powers of occupation in Germany and accept the Federal Republic as a member of NATO under the Brussels Treaty. In the autumn of 1954 the U.S. Secretary of State pressed the agenda on German admission to NATO, discreetly but firmly, buttressed by a resolute belief in the imperative of a West German security contribution and firm in his faith in Adenauer's integrity.

In London, Adenauer made the most of the pressure Washington was applying to its European allies for a successful resolution to the security crisis. The conference's turning point arrived with Adenauer's assurance that the Federal Republic would forswear the production of atomic, biological or chemical weapons. Because Mendès-France could make no such commitment on behalf of France, Adenauer was effectively saying that the Federal Republic would in principle agree to French military superiority. He accepted in addition the principle that German troops would come fully under NATO command, along with other qualifications of sovereignty that for the time being would make the Federal Republic less than a perfectly equal partner. At the moment in the four-year security debate when Germany's position was at its strongest, in other words, Adenauer calmly removed any intellectually respectable rationale for a French veto of German membership in NATO. Dulles hailed Adenauer's concession as an act of great statesmanship made by "a true European who made real sacrifices to European principles."[40] The Chancellor's commitments also prompted Mendès-France to drop the demand that a definitive solution to the Saar issue precede French acquiescence. Thus, the London conference essentially ended the first and fundamental stage of the debate on West Germany's role in Western Europe. According to the Paris agreements of October 1954, the Federal Republic was freed from the authority of the Allied High Commission, and was to have its own national armed forces, enrolled simultaneously in NATO and the Western European Union (WEU). At the same time, Bonn's allies recognized the Federal Republic as the only state legitimately constituted to speak for the German people.

Ever conscious of the havoc wrought by nationalism in Germany's history, Adenauer never openly admitted that for him democracy in part of a divided Germany was a greater good than reunification for the whole. As Chancellor, he would not defer to the attachments of countryfolk whose political judgment had been refuted by history; but neither would he abdicate in what he saw as his deeper obligation to them. The drawn out nature of the EDC debate itself enabled Adenauer to bring sufficient numbers of Germans to view postwar Europe from his perspective, and to accept that Western assurances on reunification were "the only reliable guarantee that the two parts of Germany would ever be rejoined."[41]

The double talk periodically employed in defending his policies to German voters was largely absent from Adenauer's dialogue with Bonn's Western allies, especially the United States. Indeed, the Chancellor's remarkable courage in standing up for what he considered the just claims of the Bonn government on behalf of its citizens was complemented by a frank revelation of his very real concern at the prospects of European security and democracy. His ever-present willingness to color Washington's view of Cold War Europe arose above all from a genuine fear of Soviet intentions, and equally honest doubts that Washington grasped the gravity of the situation. However often he argued Bonn's cause to a point that tested the patience of the American superpower, he nonetheless strengthened the Federal Republic's weak diplomatic position with the example of his personal reliability.

This point qualifies for special emphasis. For all its guile, Adenauer's diplomacy was hardly Florentine in inspiration or intent. The great irony is that someone of his background and disposition understood so well that rearming a nation infamous for its misadventures in war should be vital to the respect the Bonn Republic needed from its friends and foes. Adenauer used the rearmament issue to break with the past and reconstitute German diplomacy with a set of principles that eventually earned the Federal Republic a place of leadership in the European Community. In a reunified German state whose options are no longer subject to the polarities of Cold War, the foundations he laid are now being tested as never before. If, in the end, the Federal Republic is not equal to the burden of European leadership, scholars might yet look for some flaw in Adenauer's design. But they cannot charge him with moral irresponsibility. At a time when the Bonn Republic was not yet ten years old, the American historian Gordon Craig observed that "the nation whose unity was first forged by Bismarck, he [Adenauer] wished to submerge in a greater unity. Even failure should not be allowed to dim the grandeur of the attempt."[42]

NOTES

1. *The Economist* (November 26, 1949), p. 1.

2. Anneliese Poppinga, *Konrad Adenauer: Geschichtsverständnis, Weltanschauung und politische Praxis* (Stuttgart: Deutsche Verlags-Anstalt, 1975), pp. 119–214, 47–48. See also Hans-Peter Schwarz, *Adenauer*, 2 vols. (Stuttgart: Deutsche Verlags-Anstalt, 1986).

3. Poppinga, *Adenauer*, p. 46.

4. Ibid., pp. 58–61; Schwarz, *Adenauer*, I, pp. 301–4; Werner Weidenfeld, *Konrad Adenauer und Europa* (Bonn: Europa Union Verlag, 1976).

5. Rudolf Morsey, "Der politische Aufstieg Konrad Adenauers, 1945–1949," in Rudolf Morsey and Konrad Repgen, eds., *Adenauer Studien I* (Mainz: Matthias-Grünewald-Verlag, 1971), pp. 20–57; on Christian Democracy see: Michael Fogarty, *Christian Democracy in Western Europe, 1820–1953* (London: Routledge and Kegan Paul, 1957), pp. 27–40; Arnold J. Heidenheimer, *Adenauer and the CDU* (The Hague: Martinus Nijhoff, 1960); Dorothee Buchhaas, *Die Volkspartei* (Düsseldorf: Droste, 1981).

6. See Robert H. Jackson, "The Situational Ethics of Statecraft," in this volume; Max Weber, "Politics as a Vocation," in H.H. Gerth and C. Wright Mills, eds., *From Max Weber: Essays in Sociology* (New York: Oxford University Press, 1958), pp. 120–28; Raymond Aron, "Max Weber and Modern Social Science," in Franciszek Draus, ed., *History, Truth, Liberty: Selected Writings of Raymond Aron* (Chicago: University of Chicago Press, 1985), pp. 348–50.

7. Quoted in Poppinga, op. cit., p. 27.

8. Dean Acheson, *Present at the Creation* (New York: W.W. Norton, 1969), pp. 435–37; Christian Greiner, "The Defense of Western Europe and the Rearmament of Western Germany," in Olav Riste, ed., *Western Security: The Formative Years* (Oslo: Norwegian University Press, 1985), pp. 150–57; Theo Sommer, "Wiederbewaffnung und Verteidigungspolitik," in Hans-Peter Schwarz and Richard Löwenthal, eds., *Die zweite Republik: 25 Jahre Bundesrepublik Deutschland, Eine Bilanz* (Stuttgart: Seewald, 1974), pp. 580–81.

9. Schwarz, *Adenauer*, I, pp. 763–65.

10. Hans-Peter Schwarz, "Das aussenpolitische Konzept Konrad Adenauers," in Rudolf Morsey and Konrad Repgen, eds., *Adenauer Studien I* (Mainz: Matthias-Grünewald-Verlag, 1971), pp. 83–85; Michael Stürmer, *Die Grenzen der Macht* (Berlin: Siedler, 1990), pp. 106–7.

11. Wolfram F. Hanrieder, *Germany, America, Europe: Forty Years of German Foreign Policy* (New Haven: Yale University Press, 1989), pp. 148–49; Werner Link, "Die aussenpolitische Staatsräson der Bundesrepublik Deutschland," in Manfred Funke et al., eds., *Demokratie und Diktatur: Geist und Gestalt Politischer Herrschaft in Deutschland und Europa* (Düsseldorf: Droste, 1987), pp. 400–16; Edwina S. Campbell, *Germany's Past and Europe's Future: The Challenges of West German Foreign Policy* (Washington: Pergamon-Brassey's, 1989), pp. 15–16.

12. Konrad Adenauer, *Erinnerungen, 1945–53* (Stuttgart: Deutsche Verlags-Anstalt, 1965), pp. 245–46; Schwarz, *Adenauer*, 1, pp. 735–36; Thomas Allen Schwartz, *America's Germany: John J. McCloy and the Federal Republic of Germany* (Cambridge, MA: Harvard University Press, 1991), pp. 116–18; R.G. Foerster, "Innenpolitische Aspekte

der Sicherheit Westdeutschlands, 1947–1950," in R.G. Foerster et al., *Anfänge west-deutscher Sicherheitspolitik, 1945–1956*, 2 vols. (Munich: R. Oldenbourg, 1982), I, pp. 451–52.

13. Nr. 348, November 15, 1950 (Bonn): An Dannie Heineman, in Peter Mensing, ed., *Adenauer Briefe, 1949–1951* (Berlin: Siedler, 1985), pp. 305–8.

14. Schwarz, *Adenauer*, I, pp. 837–38. Heineman also wrote to John McCloy, U.S. High Commissioner to the Federal Republic, with a character sketch of Adenauer. He drew attention both to the Chancellor's periodic "dictatorial tendencies" and his moral courage, and he speculated that Adenauer probably failed to appreciate how strong was Western skepticism about Germany's good intentions no matter what kind of government was in power.

15. F. Roy Willis, *France, Germany and the New Europe, 1945–1967* (New York: Oxford University Press, 1969), pp. 151–53; G.D. Drummond, *The German Social Democrats in Opposition, 1949–1960: The Case Against Rearmament* (Norman: University of Oklahoma Press, 1982), pp. 34–37; Karl Barr, ed., *Deutsche Verteidigungspolitik, 1947–1967: Dokumente and Kommentare* (Boppard am Rhein: Harald Boldt, 1968), p. 80; Hanrieder, op. cit., pp. 155–56; Kurt Sontheimer, *Die Adenauer-Ära: Grundlegung der Bundesrepublik* (Munich: DTV, 1991), p. 43.

16. Johanna Vogel, *Kirche und Wiederbewaffnung* (Göttingen: Vandenhoeck und Ruprecht, 1978) pp. 130–40; Schwarz, *Adenauer*, I, pp. 771–74.

17. A. Doering-Manteuffel, *Katholizismus und Wiederbewaffnung* (Mainz: Grünewald, 1981), p. 85.

18. Nr. 44, June 7, 1951 (Bonn): An den Hohen Kommissar der Vereinigten Staaten von Amerika, John J. McCloy, Frankfurt/Main, *Adenauer Briefe, 1951–1953*, p. 67.

19. Ibid., pp. 69–70.

20. Nr. 15, June 1, 1951, in Hans Jürgen Küsters, ed., *Adenauer Teegespräche, 1950–1954* (Berlin: Siedler, 1984), p. 93.

21. Nr. 17, July 13, 1951, *Adenauer Teegespräche, 1950–1954*, pp. 101–3. See also Anne Deighton, "Arming the Key Battleground: German Rearmament, 1950–1955," *Diplomacy and Statecraft*, Vol. 3, No. 2 (July 1992), p. 351.

22. Quoted in Schwarz, op. cit., p. 128; Acheson, op. cit., p. 436.

23. Schwarz, *Die Ära Adenauer*, p. 137.

24. Gerhard Wettig, *Entmilitarisierung und Wiederbewaffnung in Deutschland, 1943–1955* (Munich: Oldenbourg, 1967), pp. 407–8; U.S. Department of State, *Foreign Relations of the United States* (hereafter: *FRUS*), 1951, Vol. III, p. 995; Schwartz, op. cit., pp. 211–13.

25. *FRUS*, 1951, Vol. III, pp. 998–99, 1001.

26. Hans-Jürgen Schröder, "Kanzler der Alliierten? Die Bedeutung der USA für die Außenpolitik Adenauers," in Joseph Foschepoth, ed., *Adenauer und die deutsche Frage* (Göttingen: Vandenhoeck und Ruprecht, 1988), pp. 118–45; Hanrieder, op. cit., pp. 6–11, 156–57.

27. Nr. 44, June 7, 1951 (Bonn): An den Hohen Kommissar der Vereinigten Staaten von Amerika, John J. McCloy, Frankfurt/Main, *Adenauer Briefe, 1951–1953*, p. 65.

28. Schwarz, *Adenauer*, I, p. 840; *FRUS*, 1951, III, pp. 1026–27; Irwin Wall, *The United States and the Making of Postwar France, 1945–1954* (New York: Cambridge University Press, 1991), p. 192; John Gillingham, *Coal, Steel and the Rebirth of Europe, 1945–1955* (New York: Cambridge University Press, 1991), pp. 260–62.

29. Nr. 26, April 2, 1952, *Adenauer Teegespräche, 1950–1954*, pp. 231–33; Han-

rieder, op. cit., pp. 153–54, 155–58; Rolf Steininger, *Eine vertane Chance: Die Stalin-Note vom 10. März 1952* (Bonn: Dietz, 1985); Hermann Graml, "Die Legende von der verpassten Gelegenheit," *Vierteljahreshefte für Zeitgeschichte*, Vol. 29 (1981), pp. 307–41; Joseph Foschepoth, "Wesintegration statt Wiedervereinigung: Adenauers Deutschlandpolitik 1949–1965," in Foschepoth, op. cit., pp. 29–60.

30. Wilfried Loth, "The Korean War and the Reorganization of the European Security System, 1948–1955," R. Ahmann, A.M. Birke, and M. Howard, eds., *The Quest for Stability: Problems of West European Security, 1918–1957* (London: Oxford University Press, 1993), pp. 481–84; F. H. Tenbruck, "Alltagsnormen und Lebensgefühl in der Bundesrepublik," in Schwarz and Löwenthal, op. cit., pp. 289–310.

31. The agreement provided for a West German ground force of 500,000 men, a tactical air force, and a coastal defense. In other words, it moved significantly in the direction of the Himmeroder proposals and was bound to be displeasing to France. Willis, op. cit., p. 138.

32. Dwight D. Eisenhower, *The White House Years, 1953–1956: Mandate for Change* (Garden City: Doubleday, 1963), pp. 396–99.

33. The Eisenhower administration simultaneously undertook to forward the case for a restoration of German sovereignty on the grounds of the proven political maturity of the Adenauer government. A special effort was made to coordinate U.S. and British policy and to indicate to Bonn that, in the event of a French veto of the EDC, the United States and Britain were prepared to admit the Federal Republic to NATO even over France's protests. Wettig, op. cit., pp. 566–67; Frederick W. Marks III, *Power and Peace: The Diplomacy of John Foster Dulles* (Westport: Praeger, 1993), pp. 55–58; B.R. Duchin, "The 'Agonizing Reappraisal': Eisenhower, Dulles and the EDC," *Diplomatic History*, Vol. 19, No. 2 (1992), pp. 201–21.

34. James G. Hershberg, " 'Explosion in the Offing': German Rearmament and American Diplomacy," *Diplomatic History*, Vol. 16, No. 4 (1992), p. 541. On the background to France's claims on the Saar see F. Roy Willis, *The French in Germany, 1945–1949* (Stanford, CA: Stanford University Press, 1962), pp. 15–16, 34–35, 141–43.

35. Willis, *France, Germany and the New Europe*, p. 201; Schwarz, *Adenauer*, II, p. 59; *FRUS*, 1952–1954, Vol. VII, p. 431.

36. Wettig, op. cit., pp. 599–60, 546.

37. Raymond Aron and Daniel Lerner, *France Defeats the EDC* (New York: Praeger, 1957); Paul Noack, *Das Scheitern der Europäischen Verteidigungs-gemeinschaft: Entscheidungsprozesse vor und nach dem 30. August 1954* (Düsseldorf: Droste, 1977).

38. Edward Fursdon, *The European Defense Community: A History* (London: Macmillan, 1980), p. 309.

39. Ibid., pp. 309–10; Konrad Adenauer, *Erinnerungen, 1953–1955*, Vol. II, pp. 302–4.

40. Schwarz, *Adenauer*, I, pp. 153–57; Marks, op. cit., pp. 57–60; Hans-Jürgen Grabbe, "Konrad Adenauer, John Foster Dulles, and West German-American Relations," in R.H. Immerman, ed., *John Foster Dulles and the Diplomacy of the Cold War* (Princeton, NJ: Princeton University Press, 1990), pp. 114–20; Rolf Steininger, "Das Scheitern der EVG und der Beitritt der Bundesrepublik zur NATO," *Aus Politik und Zeitgeschichte*, B 17/85 (1985), pp. 3–18; G. Ziebura, *Die deutsch-französischen Beziehungen seit 1945* (Stuttgart: Neske, 1970), pp. 65–81.

41. A. James McAdams, *Germany Divided: From the Wall to Reunification* (Princeton, NJ: Princeton University Press, 1993), p. 20; Hanrieder, op. cit., pp. 157–58; Hans-

Peter Schwarz, "Die Politik der Westbindung oder die Staatsraison der Bundesrepublik Deutschland," *Zeitschrift für Politik*, Vol. 22, No. 4 (1975), pp. 307–37.

42. Gordon Craig, *From Bismarck to Adenauer: Aspects of German Statecraft* (Baltimore: Johns Hopkins University Press, 1958), p. 148.

CHAPTER 11

Eduard Shevardnadze and the End of the Soviet System: Necessity and Choice

Paul Marantz

> We have to face up to the issue of politics and morality, of morality in
> politics, of bringing the ideals of society in line with its practice.[1]
>
> —Shevardnadze (1988)

> "Chernobyl Day" tore the blindfold from our eyes and persuaded us that
> politics and morals could not diverge. We had to gauge our politics con-
> stantly by moral criteria. Lest I be thought too sanctimonious, I shall say
> that moral politics is the credo of the pragmatist, a person whom life has
> taught that immoral politics go nowhere.[2]
>
> —Shevardnadze (1991)

Communist *apparatchiks*, the officials who spend their careers toiling away
within the Party bureaucracy, are not usually thought of as individuals with
strong principles and well-developed moral codes. For the most part, they have
proven to be opportunists, careerists, or worse. Yet Eduard Shevardnadze may
well be a striking exception. Even though his ambitions and well-developed
political skills brought him to the highest levels of the Communist Party and
government of the Soviet Union, it appears that he somehow retained a strong
sense of personal morality and a belief that principles must play an important
role in guiding policy. As Soviet Foreign Minister from July 1985 to early 1991,
he was able to put some of his beliefs into practice. He played a crucial role in
transforming Soviet foreign policy, accommodating the Soviet Union to its declining position in world affairs, and bringing about an unexpectedly rapid and
peaceful end to decades of Cold War and confrontation.

Shevardnadze was a very unlikely choice for the post of Foreign Minister.
He spent most of his career far from Moscow in his native republic of Georgia.

Unlike his immediate predecessor, Andrei Gromyko, who had labored for almost two decades in the diplomatic service and had been an ambassador to the United States and Great Britain as well as Permanent Representative to the United Nations prior to being selected as Foreign Minister, Shevardnadze had virtually no background in foreign policy. His only vaguely related experience was the various brief trips he had made abroad as a Party official, a short period of service as a member of the Soviet Committee for Solidarity with Asian and African countries, and his participation in Politburo meetings as a Candidate Member from 1978 to 1985.[3]

The son of a school teacher, Shevardnadze was born in 1928 in a small village in Georgia. At the age of 20, he joined the Communist Party. Like so many other aspiring politicians of his generation, Shevardnadze advanced his career by moving up through the ranks of the *Komsomol* (Communist Youth League). By 1957, he had become First Secretary of the Georgian *Komsomol*. In 1965, after holding various other *Komsomol* and Party posts, he became head of the Georgian Ministry for the Maintenance of Public Order, a position he occupied for the next seven years. As the top police official in the republic, he was responsible for combatting crime and corruption as well as dissent. In 1972, he was promoted to the most powerful post in the republic, the First Secretary of the Georgian Communist Party. He occupied this position until he was selected by Gorbachev in 1985 to come to Moscow to become Foreign Minister. During Brezhnev's domination of Soviet politics, which lasted from 1964 until 1982, only an astute, hard-headed, determined, and flexible politician could have survived in these demanding positions.[4]

Although Shevardnadze's career followed the path of a typical successful official at the republic level, he was not an ordinary Party hack. He was highly intelligent, hard-working, energetic in his fight against corruption, modest, and approachable.[5] Despite the conservatism of the Brezhnev period, he was able to take some modest initiatives to promote market-oriented reform in agriculture and industry, to defend the Georgian language and culture, to encourage greater openness, and to give more attention to public opinion.[6] At the same time, he was politically astute and willing to make the compromises that the system required of all ambitious politicians. In 1976, for example, he was not above pandering to the Party leadership in Moscow by proclaiming at a meeting that "for us Georgians the sun rises not in the east but in the north, in Russia."[7]

Shevardnadze owed his appointment as Foreign Minister to his long-standing friendship with Mikhail Gorbachev. By 1985, they had known each other for some twenty-five years. Their careers had followed a similar trajectory. Like Shevardnadze, Gorbachev was also a *Komsomol* official in the 1950s and early 1960s, serving in a nearby region of southern Russia. Both were promoted to the position of Candidate Member of the Politburo of the Communist Party of the Soviet Union in the late 1970s. They met often, became good friends, and frequently vacationed together. Gradually, they came to trust one another and to be ever franker in their conversations about the Soviet Union's many problems. According to Shevardnadze, by the late 1970s, "we no longer held any-thing back."[8] In the winter of 1984–1985, a few months before Gorbachev became General Secretary, Shevardnadze was especially frank in his indictment of the Soviet system. He evidently told Gorbachev: "Everything is rotten. It has to be changed."[9]

Shevardnadze's appointment as Foreign Minister came as a great surprise to Shevardnadze himself and to most observers in the Soviet Union and the West. In a moment of angry candor, Anatoly Dobrynin, the long-time Soviet Ambas-sador to the United States, who evidently hoped that he would become Foreign Minister, remarked to the American Secretary of State George Shultz: "Our foreign policy is going down the drain. They have named an agricultural type."[10]

Shevardnadze initially tried to decline the appointment, citing his lack of experience, but Gorbachev insisted that he wanted his good friend in this key position. Western observers took the appointment of the inexperienced Shev-ardnadze as a sign that Gorbachev would take personal charge of Soviet foreign policy. There was some truth in this, and Gorbachev remained heavily involved in the formulation and conduct of Soviet foreign policy throughout his term in office. But it was a mistake to underestimate Shevardnadze. He threw himself into his job with great energy, working brutally long hours until he completely mastered his portfolio. Shevardnadze became a key player in the transformation of Soviet foreign policy, changing Moscow's adversarial relationship with the capitalist world to one of active cooperation and partnership.

Shevardnadze embodies an unusual combination of traits. He is a man of conviction who also values moderation and pragmatic compromise.[11] Though he was a beneficiary of the Communist system, having risen from humble origins to a position of great power and privilege, he was acutely aware of the system's failures and was willing to change them. He was a very skilled politician and policy-maker, but was modest about his attainments, frank about his shortcom-ings, and genuinely interested in encouraging his subordinates to be candid in their criticism of the Foreign Ministry's actions.

When Gorbachev's policies veered away from reform in the autumn of 1990, Shevardnadze felt that he could no longer support his long-time friend. On a number of previous occasions he had warned that he would resign rather than compromise strongly held positions.[12] This time he followed through on his threat.

On December 20, 1990, he stunned the Soviet people and heightened anxiety throughout the world by unexpectedly announcing his resignation as Foreign Minister. He complained that his foreign policy of conciliation with the West had been unfairly attacked and warned that the danger of dictatorship loomed before the Soviet Union.[13] His resignation speech was a protest against the trend toward authoritarianism and an attempt to get the reformers to stop their frat-ricidal bickering with one another and unite against the old guard. When Shev-ardnadze's prophecy of approaching dictatorship came to pass with the attempted coup of August 1991, he quickly joined the crowds outside Boris

Yeltsin's headquarters and courageously helped to rally the opposition to the seizure of power.

With the disintegration of the Soviet Union in December 1991, Shevardnadze's career took a new turn. At age 64, he could have chosen a comfortable retirement. Ensconced in a Moscow foreign policy think tank that he had helped found, he could have assumed the role of elder statesman, lecturing to appreciative Western audiences, writing his memoirs, and enjoying a comfortable standard of living based upon hard currency earnings from lecture fees and royalties.

Instead, in early 1992 he returned to strife-torn Georgia as the newly elected head of the government to take up the daunting task of trying to unify this newly independent country, which was being ripped apart by secessionist movements, by a smoldering civil war waged by the supporters of his ousted predecessor, Zviad Gamsakhurdia, by the rise of various armed militias, by the breakdown of law and order, and by economic collapse. His life has been repeatedly threatened, and on several occasions he has narrowly escaped assassination attempts.[14]

Shevardnadze's personal odyssey has not ended. In November 1992, he revealed that he had abandoned atheism and had been baptized in the Georgian Orthodox Church. His journey has been a long one. As he put it, "I have an icon in my office now, though there was a time when I had Stalin's portrait on the wall."[15]

During his five and one-half years as Foreign Minister, Shevardnadze presided over a remarkable transformation of Soviet foreign policy. It is true, of course, that a string of failures—which included the costly stalemate in Afghanistan, the crushing burden of the arms race, the fall of the Berlin Wall, and the collapse of communism in Eastern Europe—compelled the Soviet leadership to reconsider past policies. But the particular response they made to these setbacks, and the fact that the Soviet Union accommodated itself to its sharply reduced international status so quickly and with so little violence, is in significant measure a result of the creative leadership of Shevardnadze.

Shevardnadze was certainly not alone in articulating the basic principles of what came to be called the "new political thinking." Gorbachev was very active in espousing these principles, and many scholars and policy advisers played a pivotal role in persuading the leadership of the need for a new approach to foreign policy.[16] Nonetheless, Shevardnadze was especially important in advocating and implementing these new principles because of his key roles as Foreign Minister, member of the Politburo, and close associate of Gorbachev.

Moreover, unlike many veterans of the Soviet foreign policy establishment, for him the new thinking was not just another political line that had to be mouthed because it was decreed by the leadership. He spoke with apparent conviction and evident passion on behalf of a major reversal of past policy. While some of the principles he espoused (such as establishing mutual trust) might seem to be no more than empty clichés or meaningless platitudes, in the context of traditional Soviet policy—which was often based upon confrontation, mistrust of the "class enemy," and a short-sighted view of what the Soviet national interest was—these principles were nothing less than revolutionary.

Three main themes recur again and again in Shevardnadze's speeches and writings. These concern the need for the Soviet Union to overcome its isolation from the international community by showing other nations that it could be trusted, the necessity of forging a new conception of Soviet national security, and the vital importance of bringing greater openness to the formulation and debate of Soviet foreign policy. In an attempt to convey the unusual combination of pragmatism and moral force that Shevardnadze brought to the analysis of Soviet foreign policy, his statements are quoted at some length in the discussion here.

Throughout much of Russian history, there has been a sharp conflict between two different outlooks, that of the Westernizers and that of the Slavophiles. The Westernizers have argued that Russia could best overcome its lamentable backwardness by emulating the more advanced West, by borrowing from it, and by associating with it as closely as possible. In contrast, the Slavophiles have stressed Russia's distinctiveness, its need to find its own path, and the necessity of rejecting the corrupt and alien ways of the West.[17]

Paradoxically, the official Soviet ideology of Marxism-Leninism had a great deal in common with the Slavophile rejection of the West, despite the lip service that was paid to Marx and his supposedly universal model of social development. Soviet ideology and foreign policy were built on the premise that there existed two separate and deeply antagonistic worlds—the capitalist world and the socialist world—which were totally incompatible. Scorn was heaped upon "bourgeois" institutions, conceptions of human rights, and foreign policy.

Despite Shevardnadze's unimpeachable credentials as a member of the Communist establishment, he is a fervent Westernizer. He believed that the Soviet Union had erred in counterpoising its system and its values to those of the West, that the Soviet Union needed to heal its breach with the outside world. For him, there were not two mutually opposed worlds—the socialist and the capitalist—but one international community from which the Soviet Union had foolishly estranged itself, thereby doing grievous harm to its economy, its political institutions, and its fundamental moral health. The advanced nations of the West were not the class enemy but "the civilized world," which the Soviet Union urgently needed to join.

In the memoirs that he published in 1991, Shevardnadze was scathing in his criticism of past Soviet behavior:

People did not trust us. How many times before had various statements been made by the political leadership, a certain line of action proclaimed, while everything remained unchanged? . . . [A]greements with the "bourgeoisie" or with the "imperialists" were always regarded in our country as a necessary evil at best, but more often as a means to gain time, a tactical maneuver. . . . An ideological struggle was on, and any means were fair. The main thing was to protect our goalposts. . . . The image of the Soviet Union in the eyes of the world was of little real concern.[18]

In a major statement on Soviet foreign policy, which he delivered on July 25, 1988, at a high-level conference organized by the Ministry of Foreign Affairs, Shevardnadze set out his views at some length, lecturing his more cynical colleagues:

Here I want to talk about a problem which, as far as I know, is extremely rarely addressed by researchers. The point at issue is the image of a country as an important aspect of its existence in the international community, in the modern civilized world. . . . We should not pretend, Comrades, that norms and notions of what is proper, of what is called civilized conduct in the world community do not concern us. If you want to be accepted in it you must observe them.[19]

In reply to his critics, he stated:

Sometimes one hears the view that we pay too much attention to what the outside world will say about us. In this connection I would like the stress the following. . . . [W]e cannot exhibit indifference to what others are saying and thinking about us. For our self-respect, our well-being, our position in the world hinge largely on the attitude of others towards us as well.[20]

This unorthodox conception of Soviet relations with the outside world was forcefully expressed in Shevardnadze's discussion of Soviet foreign policy before the Soviet legislature on October 23, 1989. He stated:

The notion that we can ignore the world around us and disregard other people's interests has cost our people and socialism dearly in the past. . . . If we want to be part of a civilized world, we must consider how our actions and words are perceived. The diplomatic service can and should provide supreme organs of power with more prompt and precise information about those instances when our positions, approaches, and actions conflict with prevailing international opinions, legal norms, and moral and ethical standards.[21]

In condemning the harm done to Soviet foreign policy by the invasion of Afghanistan, Shevardnadze stated:

When more than 100 UN members kept condemning our action for a number of years, did we need anything else to make us realize: We had placed ourselves in opposition to the world community, had violated norms of behavior and gone against common human interests.[22]

For Shevardnadze, it was vitally important that the Soviet Union become a full member of "the civilized world." This could only be done by admitting past errors, putting new policies in place, winning the trust of other nations, and restoring—as he put it—"the good name of the country."[23]

Another major theme that recurs in Shevardnadze's speeches and writings concerns the need for the Soviet Union to be guided by a new conception of what constitutes its national security. In his view, a redefinition of Soviet security interests was necessary to get rid of the past preoccupation with unlimited military might. He argued that the Soviet arms buildup had done great harm to the country's fundamental interests by causing other nations to be fearful of Soviet intentions, by undermining the domestic economy, and by lowering the people's standard of living.

Shevardnadze strongly attacked the neglect of the people's well-being, which he blamed on a fundamental misunderstanding of what constitutes security and strength in the modern world.

[T]he category of the power and security of the state under modern conditions is something entirely different from what it was during the thirties when we sang: "The Red Army is stronger than all." Can a state be strong and secure when its economy fails, fundamental sciences are in a state of stagnation, agriculture can in no way get on its feet, and the citizens are suffering from a shortage of literally everything?[24]

In his memoirs, Shevardnadze further elaborated on this view:

We became a superpower largely because of our military might. But the bloated size and unrestrained escalation of this military might was reducing us to the level of a third-rate country, unleashing processes that pushed us to the brink of catastrophe. Our military expenditures as a percentage of gross national product were two and a half times greater that those of the United States. . . . We have captured first place in the world weapons trade (28 percent of the entire sales total), and have made the Kalashnikov submachine gun the hallmark of our advanced technology. But we occupy about sixtieth place in standard of living, thirty-second place in average life expectancy, and fiftieth in infant mortality. What kind of national security is this? It is not just immoral but politically dangerous to equate national security with tanks and warheads, while leaving out such "trivia" as human life and welfare.[25]

In short, he argued that "a country of socially and politically humiliated people cannot gain security."[26]

In opposition to the past preoccupation with military strength, Shevardnadze advanced a few simple propositions: the country should recognize that it possessed limited resources and there were certain things in the foreign sphere which it could not afford; foreign policy should be tailored to domestic priorities rather than vice versa; and in view of the low Soviet standard of living, resources should be found to increase the people's well-being. All of this sounds like self-evident common sense, the kind of elementary considerations that any policymaker would be sure to take into account. But in the closed world of Soviet politics, where a handful of privileged leaders imposed their own narrow con-

ceptions of what was good for the country on a long-suffering and largely pow-
erless population, this represented a frontal challenge to traditional practices.

As Shevardnadze noted during an interview with a Soviet newspaper in the
spring of 1989:

In the times before restructuring "counting kopecks" when making decisions in the political area (I include defense issues here) was regarded as almost disgraceful. Foreign
policy was like a thing unto itself. . . . Actually the "residual principle" was in effect with
respect to the entire national economy. The domestic civilian economy got what was left
over after the foreign economic and defense measures were taken care of. We directly
ignored the fact that in the international and defense spheres there could be things which
our country simply could not afford.[27]

In an address in June 1987 to a meeting of members of the Soviet foreign
policy establishment, Shevardnadze was brutally frank:

Beyond the borders of the Soviet Union you and I represent a great country which in
the last 15 years has been steadily losing its position as one of the leading industrially
developed countries. . . . If we are finally honest, we frequently encouraged and at times
even induced enormous material investments in hopeless foreign policy projects and
tacitly promoted actions which both in the direct and the indirect sense have cost the
people dearly even to this day. . . . The fact that the foreign policy service—one of the
most important and most sensitive links in the system of state management—carried out
its obligation out of touch with the country's fundamental vital interest is on our conscience.[28]

While in the past, domestic needs were subordinated to foreign policy considerations, Shevardnadze argued that now the reverse was vitally necessary.
Far-reaching internal reform was absolutely essential, and the key task of Soviet
foreign policy was to do everything possible to facilitate and promote domestic
development: "[T]he most important function of our foreign policy is to create
the optimal conditions for the economic and social development of our country."[29]

Shevardnadze made one of his most important contributions to the reform of
Soviet domestic and foreign policy by fighting against the obsessive secrecy that
characterized Soviet policy making. He was a leading champion of greater openness and played an important role in securing the release of the anti-Stalin film
Repentance in late 1986.[30] This powerful film created a sensation and helped
unleash an ever-growing stream of historical revelations that provided a powerful impetus to further reform.

By mid-1987, the discussion of Soviet domestic affairs was becoming increasingly open. Day by day and month by month, the bounds of permissible
discussion were widened. However, foreign policy questions were almost totally
insulated from this process. Scholars and journalists were not allowed to en-
croach on this sensitive domain.

Shevardnadze took the lead in bringing *glasnost* to the discussion of Soviet foreign policy. He rejected the traditional pretence of infallibility and was remarkably candid about the errors and shortcomings of Soviet foreign policy. He ensured that his speeches were openly published so that they would stimulate discussion and fresh thinking. He attacked the walling off of foreign policy from critical scrutiny. In a speech on October 27, 1987, he stated:

Bold, interesting, and controversial articles have appeared on many basic questions of domestic life in all its manifestations, party and state construction, the economy, culture, art, and science. But there is nothing like it in the field of foreign policy. Is it really because everything is correct with us and variants other than those which are being implemented do not exist?[31]

Shevardnadze backed up his words with decisive action. In early 1988, the editor of the journal *Mezhdunarodnaya Zhizn'* (published in English as *International Affairs*) was replaced. The new editor was Boris Pyadyshev, an associate of Shevardnadze at the Ministry of Foreign Affairs. His mandate was to transform the journal so that it would provide a forum for the discussion of previously restricted questions. Up until that time, *Mezhdunarodnaya Zhizn'* had been the tame house organ of the Ministry of Foreign Affairs. In wooden language that was heavily laden with ideological rhetoric, it unimaginatively toed the official line, avoiding even the slightest hint of controversy or originality. Under Pyadyshev's editorship, *Mezhdunarodnaya Zhizn'* quickly advanced to the front ranks of the battle for greater openness, and one by one many of the taboos that prevented the open discussion of Soviet foreign policy fell.[32]

Shevardnadze supported greater openness on both principled and pragmatic grounds. If greater democracy was to be promoted and if the Soviet parliament, which for the first time was gaining genuine powers of oversight, was to be able to carry out its new responsibilities, then the public discussion of foreign policy matters had to be elevated to a higher level. Moreover, one of the most effective ways to break the grip that the military and the Party bureaucracies had on the formulation of Soviet foreign policy was by highlighting the failure of past policies and by supporting demands for greater openness about the true cost of military spending and foreign aid. Frank discussion in the press and open hearings in the Soviet legislature would strengthen Shevardnadze's hand as he did battle with those resisting change.

When Gorbachev, Shevardnadze, and other members of the Soviet leadership first began articulating the principles of the "new thinking" in 1986 and 1987, their statements were greeted with skepticism in the West. Many Western analysts saw this as little more than a propagandistic exercise aimed at improving the Soviet Union's image without changing the substance of Soviet foreign policy. The "new thinking" was dismissed as consisting of vacuous clichés and empty slogans. Tough-minded analysts argued that what really counted were deeds, not words.[33]

Even when Soviet policy began to change quite substantially, and Moscow agreed to withdraw its troops from Afghanistan, accepted the "zero option" for the elimination of intermediate-range nuclear forces, and announced sharp cuts in its conventional forces, some Western analysts remained highly skeptical about the Soviet embrace of "new thinking." They saw the Soviet talk of a "world community," of a new role for the United Nations, and of "comprehensive security" and "universal human interests" as a smoke screen that was being used to hide a Soviet defeat behind the verbiage of high principle.[34] According to this argument, Soviet power was in sharp decline, and Soviet foreign power was in retreat. Rather than frankly acknowledge these unpleasant facts, Soviet spokesmen attempted to claim that the Soviet Union was in the forefront of the struggle to elevate international politics to a higher level and to ensure that the enlightened principles of cooperative security rather than narrow considerations of unilateral advantage prevailed. The Soviets were simply attempting to disguise defeat as victory by portraying the changes that were taking place as the triumph of principles that the Soviet Union had long championed.

Some analysts further argued that the key explanatory variable accounting for the alteration in Soviet policy was not changes in the belief system or values of the Soviet leadership but irresistible economic, social, and political forces which were largely beyond their control. The Soviet leadership was compelled by circumstances to modify their policies. Individual preferences and values mattered little. New realities left the Soviet leadership little choice but to bend to the powerful forces reshaping the world.[35]

The thesis of this paper is very different. It argues that for Shevardnadze, who played such a critical role in Soviet foreign policy, support for "new thinking" was much more than a propaganda ploy or the forced and grudging acceptance of declining Soviet power. In his case, it represented nothing less than a paradigm shift, a fundamental change in how the world was understood. Shevardnadze was breaking with decades of confrontation and class warfare. He moved away from class perspectives that emphasized division and antagonism between "the two camps" to a more complex perspective that stressed the common concerns and interests that all nations shared regardless of ideological divisions.

In July 1988, Shevardnadze made a deceptively simple statement. He declared that "the rivalry between the two systems can no longer be viewed as the leading tendency of the modern age."[36] This statement signified a fundamental break with the outlook that had previously animated Soviet foreign policy. It did not come easy to lifelong Communist Party officials. As Shevardnadze remarked in an earlier interview with Don Oberdorfer of the *Washington Post*: "Our basic, fundamental position was the position of class and class values and this is how we were brought up—all of us."[37] Shevardnadze noted that the shift to new principles of Soviet foreign policy beginning in 1986 "gave rise to a very stormy reaction" in the Foreign Ministry and elsewhere.[38] Similarly, Marshall Sergei Akhromeev, Chief of the General Staff, remarked: "For me personally, to rethink all these things and to view the situation from a different angle was very painful. ... Most of my life I've thought in a different manner."[39] Indeed, for Akhromeev, the change was so painful that when the attempted coup of August 1991 failed, signifying the end of a powerful and cohesive Soviet Union, he committed suicide.

Shevardnadze's statement set off a sharp debate within the Soviet leadership. Yegor Ligachev, the most powerful conservative voice within the Politburo, quickly responded to Shevardnadze. In a speech given on August 5, 1988, Ligachev stated: "We proceed from the class nature of international relations. Any other formulation of the issue only introduces confusion into the thinking of Soviet people and our friends abroad."[40] However, Shevardnadze enjoyed the support of Gorbachev, and his position prevailed. The traditional dichotomous and confrontational view of the world was scrapped. Forms of cooperation with the capitalist world that had previously been unthinkable now became possible.

The question remains, however, whether this change in outlook was compelled by circumstances. Was the Soviet leadership forced to act as they did by domestic economic crisis and the deterioration of Moscow's international position? Did they lack any real room for choice?

By their very nature, questions such as these, which involve speculation about alternative futures, are very difficult to answer. Historians and political scientists lack the intellectual tools to decide conclusively the "iffy" questions of history. However, several observations are in order.

It should be recalled that the very changes in Soviet policy that some observers now see as having been inevitable were viewed during the Cold War as being just about impossible. By the early 1980s, many Western observers recognized that the Soviet system was performing poorly and was beset by a number of serious domestic and foreign problems. But the general consensus was that these problems could be managed for the foreseeable future. The Soviet leadership was seen as being firmly in control and as having both the will and the ability to avoid fundamental change. The Soviet Union had survived many past crises (e.g., collectivization in the 1920s, the purges in the 1930s, World War II in the 1940s, and the transition to a new leadership and partial de-Stalinization in the 1950s), and almost all observers expected that it would successfully weather its current difficulties. To portray the opening up of the Soviet Union in the late 1980s and the disintegration of Communist Party rule in 1991 as having been inevitable betrays a failure of imagination and an unwillingness to recognize that what happened was not mandated by irresistible economic and social forces but was the outcome of conscious choices made between a number of different policy options. Economic problems and foreign policy setbacks framed and influenced the choices that were made, but they did not determine them.

When the Politburo met in March 1985 to chose a successor to Konstantin Chernenko, its members apparently did not believe the country was in crisis. They chose Gorbachev as the new General Secretary, not because they wanted him to transform the Soviet system, but because they expected him to make it work better. Whatever reformist objectives Gorbachev may have had in 1985 he kept well hidden. His main strength was that his Politburo colleagues saw him as a much needed change from the tired and ill old men who had preceded him as General Secretary. Gorbachev's vast energy, capacity for hard work, intelligence, and apparent political skill helped solidify his support among the members of the Politburo, who had buried three General Secretaries in the past two and one-half years and recognized that the country needed more energetic leadership.

The cautious conservatives who dominated the Soviet leadership thought that Gorbachev was a safe choice. He had demonstrated his ability and reliability during his five years on the Politburo, and he had displayed no overt signs of radicalism. In his speech to the March 11, 1985, crucial meeting of the Politburo, which chose him as General Secretary, he neither sought nor received a mandate for radical change. Gorbachev stated: "Our economy needs more dynamism. This dynamism is needed for the development of our foreign policy."[41] But he also reassuringly said:

We do not need to change policy. It is correct and it is true. It is genuine Leninist politics. We need, however, to speed up, to move forward, to disclose shortcomings and overcome them and realize our shining future. . . . I assure you I will do everything to justify the trust of the Party.[42]

By the time Boris Yeltsin wrote his memoirs in 1990, he was locked in a bitter power struggle with Gorbachev, and he had few good words to say about his former colleague, who had presided over his expulsion from the Soviet leadership in late 1987. Yet even he acknowledged the critical role that Gorbachev played in initiating reform:

The chief problem in his launching of *perestroika* was that he was practically alone, surrounded by the authors and impresarios of Brezhnev's "era of stagnation," who were determined to ensure the indestructibility of the old order of things.[43]

Yeltsin also said of Gorbachev:

He could have gone on just as Brezhnev and Chernenko did before him. I estimate that the country's natural resources and the people's patience would have outlasted his lifetime, long enough for him to have lived the well-fed and happy life of the leader of a totalitarian state.[44]

The year 1989 was a pivotal period for the Soviet Union. It was then that the leadership lost its control over events. In 1986–1988, Gorbachev presided over a revolution from above. The leadership directed the pace of change and could have reimposed tight controls at any time. However, by mid-1989, this was no longer so. In 1989, the economy began to decline sharply after several years of modest growth, fueling popular discontent.[45] Long suppressed national grievances burst forth, and the republics began to assert themselves. The revelations produced by glasnost robbed the Communist Party of its remaining claims to legitimacy. From 1989 on, the Politburo became the prisoner of events rather than their master.

However, in large measure this new situation was a direct result of the course followed in 1988: the misconceived economic reforms, the toleration of greater openness in the media, and the attempt to open up the political system in a controlled fashion by reinvigorating the Supreme Soviet. In March 1988, Yegor Ligachev, who was the number two man in the Politburo, attacked Gorbachev's reformist policies. Ligachev's challenge was repulsed only after a stormy two-day meeting of the Politburo at which Gorbachev used all the power and authority that his position as General Secretary conferred upon him.[46] Gorbachev's victory was by no means preordained. It owed more to his political skill and power than to the merits of his program. Whereas he could count on the support of the two committed reformers in the Politburo, Shevardnadze and Aleksandr Yakovlev, the political loyalties of the other members were much less certain. Had Ligachev prevailed at this critical juncture, the whole course of Soviet development might have turned out very differently.[47]

By the mid-1980s, it was becoming increasingly clear that the rigid and inefficient Soviet economy was unable to match the dynamism and innovativeness of the free market economies of the West. Economic weakness was bound to undermine its international power. But if a Soviet decline was in some sense inevitable, there was nothing inevitable about its timing or the form it would take. The veteran Sovietologist Myron Rush provides the following characterization of the situation that existed in 1985 when Gorbachev came to power:

The Soviet Union, while manifestly in trouble as many observed, was not posed for a collapse, nor was it even in acute crisis. The Soviet Union was viable and probably could have lasted another decade or two, with good fortune a good bit longer; but deeply flawed, it was vulnerable to adverse chance events.[48]

An economist, Vladimir Kontorovich, shares this perspective. He points out that the Soviet economy did not decline significantly in the immediate pre-Gorbachev period of 1979–1984, and that it may have even grown at the rate of 1–2 percent per year.[49] There also appear to have been alternatives to the destabilizing reforms undertaken by Gorbachev. The economy could have been accelerated by making some quick cuts in military spending, by embracing detente so that the arms race would have been curbed, thus yielding more substantial reductions in the military budget, and by soliciting Western technical assistance and financial aid to develop the Soviet Union's abundant oil and natural gas reserves. This would have created modest economic growth that would have enhanced stability and allowed the Soviet system to muddle along for some time. It would not have enabled the Soviet Union to catch up with the West, and it would not have reversed the Soviet Union's long-term decline, but it would have significantly delayed it.[50]

Paul Kennedy's much acclaimed work *The Rise and Fall of the Great Powers* called attention to the Soviet Union's economic difficulties and the implications they had for Moscow's international standing. He warned, "[T]here is nothing in the character or tradition of the Russian state to suggest that it could ever accept imperial decline gracefully."[51] A number of other analysts argued either that Soviet foreign policy was incapable of change, for the regime needed the image of a powerful enemy to rationalize its domestic power, or that a declining and pessimistic Soviet leadership might be even more dangerous than an optimistic one because this might lead to risky foreign policy adventures aimed at salvaging Soviet power.[52] The fact that contrary to these expectations Soviet foreign policy did accommodate itself so "gracefully" and with so little violence to a very painful series of defeats, ranging from Afghanistan and the loss of its East European empire to the reunification of Germany and the disintegration of the Soviet Union itself, suggests that individual choice in response to highly dangerous circumstances did make a difference.

Decades of unrelenting striving for power, of ruthless imperial rule, and of amoral geopolitical maneuvering had cost the Soviet Union dearly. The Soviet Union was saddled with a military budget it could not afford, its population was alienated and dispirited, the country was widely feared, it had few genuine friends, and its rigid economy languished in isolation from the stimulating influences of a competitive world economy.

The policies that Shevardnadze supported went right to the heart of the problem. He argued that the Soviet Union needed to be trusted rather than feared, that it had to guide its policies by "universal human values," that it had to respect international human rights agreements, that it should lower military expenditures and look upon the people's well-being as a crucial element of national power, that it should respect "freedom of choice" in Afghanistan and Eastern Europe, and that it should rejoin "the civilized world."

Needless to say, the rethinking of Soviet foreign policy did not happen in a vacuum. An uncompetitive economy and a collapsing empire compelled a reexamination of past policy. In response to these problems, "new thinking" was embraced by Gorbachev and promoted by Soviet scholars and policy-makers. Shevardnadze was not an isolated figure. But at a crucial time in world affairs, he helped the Soviet Union navigate through a very dangerous passage and achieve a safe landing under very difficult circumstances.

Despite the greater openness of Soviet political discourse in the late 1980s, there is much that we still don't know. The memoirs of Shevardnadze and other top Soviet officials are not especially revealing about the leaders' private thoughts or how key decisions were reached. How far did Shevardnadze go in his questioning of the basic features of the Soviet political system? What was he trying to change and what was he trying to save? How much of his seeming moral conviction was genuine and how much was skillful political packaging aimed at selling needed changes to resistant Communist officials at home and skeptical policy-makers abroad? Perhaps in the future, if our very limited access to Soviet archives covering the Gorbachev years improves, we may be able to answer some of these questions. For now, we can simply reflect on how skillfully Shevardnadze used the language of moral conviction to reorient Soviet foreign policy away from traditional patterns of behavior and to create the basis for a new relationship between the Soviet Union and the West.

Shevardnadze was very fortunate in that he became Soviet Foreign Minister at a time when a more principled foreign policy was very much in the country's interest. The dictates of morality and self-interest coincided to an unusual extent. But it is to his credit that he very ably made the most of this opportunity. Even though he was unable to preserve the Soviet Union, he has secured a place in history by helping to bring about a remarkably peaceful end to one of the most intractable and dangerous confrontations the world has witnessed.

NOTES

1. Eduard Shevardnadze, Report to the Ministry of Foreign Affairs Conference, July 25, 1988, in *International Affairs*, No. 10 (1988), p. 23.

2. Eduard Shevardnadze, *The Future Belongs to Freedom* (London: Sinclair-Stevenson, 1991), pp. 175–76.

3. The careers of Gromyko and Shevardnadze are detailed in Alexander G. Rahr, ed., *A Biographic Directory of 100 Leading Soviet Officials*, 3rd. ed. (Munich: Radio Liberty Research, 1986), pp. 80–82, 186–88.

4. Shevardnadze's praise of Brezhnev and his support for the decision to send Soviet troops into Afghanistan are cited in Yegor Ligachev, *Inside Gorbachev's Kremlin* (New York: Pantheon Books, 1993), pp. 168–69.

5. Carolyn McGiffert Ekedahl and Melvin A. Goodman, *The Wars of Eduard Shevardnadze* (University Park: Pennsylvania State University Press, 1997), pp. 7–28; Elizabeth Fuller, "A Portrait of Eduard Shevardnadze," *Radio Liberty Research Bulletin*, RL 219/85 (July 3, 1985), pp. 1–11.

6. Don Oberdorfer, *The Turn from the Cold War to a New Era: The United States and the Soviet Union, 1983–1990* (New York: Poseidon Press, 1991), pp. 118–20.

7. Fuller, "A Portrait of Eduard Shevardnadze," p. 10. Also see Yegor Ligachev, *Inside Gorbachev's Kremlin* (New York: Pantheon, 1993), pp. 168–69.

8. Shevardnadze, *The Future Belongs to Freedom*, p. 23.

9. Ibid., p. 37. Gorbachev gave a similar version in a speech to cultural leaders on November 28, 1990. Gorbachev's remarks were published in *Pravda* on December 1, 1990, and are translated in Foreign Broadcast Information Service, *Daily Report: Soviet Union*, December 5, 1990, p. 44. (Hereafter cited as FBIS.)

10. George P. Shultz, *Turmoil and Triumph: My Years As Secretary of State* (New York: Charles Scribner's Sons, 1993), p. 572. In his memoirs, Dobrynin was much more diplomatic. Anatoly Dobrynin, *In Confidence* (New York: Random House, 1995), pp. 575–77.

11. The American Secretaries of State George P. Shultz and James A. Baker were

able to establish a very constructive working relationship with Shevardnadze, and they praised his openness, honesty, pragmatism, and flexibility in hammering out solutions to difficult problems. Shultz, *Turmoil and Triumph*, p. 886; Michael R. Beschloss and Strobe Talbott, *At the Highest Levels: The Inside Story of the End of the Cold War* (Boston: Little, Brown, 1993), pp. 96, 121, 179–82.

12. *Pravda*, October 24, 1989, as translated in FBIS, October 24, 1989, p. 45; Oberdorfer, *The Turn*, p. 409.

13. The text of his resignation speech is reprinted in Shevardnadze, *The Future Belongs to Freedom*, pp. 201–4; Pavel Palazchenko, *My Years with Gorbachev and Shevardnadze* (University Park: Pennsylvania State University Press, 1997), pp. 238–43.

14. Georgie Anne Geyer, "Conversations with Eduard Shevardnadze," *The Washington Quarterly*, Vol. 23, No. 2 (Spring 2000), pp. 55, 61, 63.

15. *The Globe and Mail* (Toronto), November 24, 1992, p. A1.

16. Allen Lynch, *Gorbachev's International Outlook: Intellectual Origins and Political Consequences* (New York: Institute for East-West Security Studies, 1989); Jeff Checkel, "Ideas, Institutions, and the Gorbachev Foreign Policy Revolution," *World Politics*, Vol. 45, No. 2 (January 1993), pp. 271–73.

17. Tibor Szamuely, *The Russian Tradition* (London: Fontana Press, 1988), pp. 251–59.

18. Shevardnadze, *The Future Belongs to Freedom*, p. 87.

19. *International Affairs*, No. 10 (October 1988), p. 23.

20. Ibid., p. 24.

21. *Pravda*, October 24, 1989, as translated in FBIS, October 24, 1989, p. 43.

22. Ibid., p. 45.

23. Ibid., p. 24; Shevardnadze, *The Future Belongs to Freedom*, p. 87.

24. *Argumenty i Fakty*, May 6–12, 1989, as translated in FBIS, May 15, 1989, p. 92.

25. Shevardnadze, *The Future Belongs to Freedom*, p. 54.

26. Ibid., p. 55.

27. *Argumenty i Fakty*, May 6–12, 1989, as translated in FBIS, May 15, 1989, p. 93.

28. *Vestnik Ministerstva Inostrannykh Del SSSR*, No. 2 (1987), as translated in FBIS, October 27, 1989, p. 52.

29. *Vestnik Ministerstva Inostrannykh Del SSSR*, No. 3 (September 1987), as translated in FBIS, November 3, 1987, p. 91.

30. David Remnick, *Lenin's Tomb: The Last Days of the Soviet Empire* (New York: Random House, 1993), pp. 42–46.

31. *Vestnik Ministerstva Inostrannykh Del SSSR*, No. 2 (1987), as translated in FBIS, October 27, 1987, p. 54.

32. For example, see Alexei Izyumov and Andrei Kortunov, "The USSR in a Changing World," *International Affairs*, No. 8 (1988), pp. 46–56. Also see John Van Oudenaren, *The Role of Shevardnadze and the Ministry of Foreign Affairs in the Making of Soviet Defense and Arms Control Policy*, Rand Report R-3898-USDP (July 1990), p. 18.

33. Harry Gelman, "Gorbachev's Dilemmas and His Conflicting Foreign-Policy Goals," *Orbis*, Vol. 30, No. 2 (Summer 1986), pp. 231–47; Thane Gustafson, "Will Soviet Foreign Policy Change under Gorbachev?" *The Washington Quarterly*, Vol. 9, No. 4 (Autumn 1986); Dimitri K. Simes, "Gorbachev: A New Foreign Policy?" *Foreign Affairs*, Vol. 65, No. 3 (1987), pp. 477–500; Abraham Becker et al., *The 27th Congress of the Communist Party of the Soviet Union: A Report from the Airlie House Conference* (Santa Monica: Rand, 1986).

34. Stephen Sestanovich, "Gorbachev's Foreign Policy: A Diplomacy of Decline," *Problems of Communism*, Vol. 37, No. 1 (January–February 1988), pp. 1–15.

35. Daniel Deudney and G. John Ikenberry, "Soviet Reform and the End of the Cold War: Explaining Large-Scale Historical Change," *Review of International Studies*, Vol. 17, No. 3 (July 1991), pp. 225–50.

36. *International Affairs*, No. 10 (October 1988), p. 20; Jack F. Matlock, Jr., *Autopsy on an Empire* (New York: Random House, 1995), pp. 143–48.

37. Oberdorfer, *The Turn from the Cold War to a New Era*, p. 161.

38. Ibid.

39. Ibid.

40. *Pravda*, August 6, 1988, as translated in FBIS, August 8, 1988, p. 39.

41. Remnick, *Lenin's Tomb: The Last Days of the Soviet Empire*, p. 520.

42. Ibid.

43. Boris Yeltsin, *Against the Grain: An Autobiography* (New York: Summit Books, 1990), p. 140.

44. Ibid., p. 139.

45. Vladimir Kontorovich, "The Economic Fallacy," *The National Interest*, No. 31 (Spring 1993), pp. 38–41; Peter Rutland, "Sovietology: Notes for a Post-Mortem," ibid., p. 121.

46. Remnick, *Lenin's Tomb: The Last Days of the Soviet Empire*, p. 84; Yegor Ligachev, *Inside Gorbachev's Kremlin: The Memoirs of Yegor Ligachev* (New York: Pantheon Books, 1993), pp. 304–11.

47. Christopher Young, "The Strategy of Political Liberalization: A Comparative View of Gorbachev's Reforms," *World Politics*, Vol. 45, No. 1 (October 1992), pp. 57–64.

48. Myron Rush, "Fate and Fortune," *The National Interest*, No. 31 (Spring 1993), p. 19. Also see the excellent discussion in Alexander Dallin, "Causes of the Collapse of the USSR," *Post-Soviet Affairs*, Vol. 8, No. 4 (October–December 1992), pp. 279–302.

49. Kontorovich, "The Economic Fallacy," p. 35.

50. Ibid., p. 44.

51. Paul Kennedy, *The Rise and Fall of the Great Powers* (London: Fontana Press, 1989), p. 664. Also see John Lewis Gaddis, *The Long Peace* (New York: Oxford University Press, 1987), p. 244.

52. Colin S. Gray, "The Most Dangerous Decade: Historic Mission, Legitimacy, and Dynamics of the Soviet Empire in the 1980s," *Orbis*, Vol. 25, No. 1 (Spring 1981), pp. 13–28; Edward N. Luttwak, *The Grand Strategy of the Soviet Union* (New York: St. Martin's Press, 1983); Richard Pipes, *Survival Is Not Enough* (New York: Simon & Schuster, 1984).

Select Bibliography

JOURNALS

Daedalus, Vol. 112, No. 4 (Fall 1983). Theme issue on human rights. Also see selected articles.
Ethics, Vol. 95 (April 1985). Special issue on deterrence. Also see selected articles.
Ethics and International Affairs.
Ethics, Religion, and Politics: Collected Philosophical Papers. University of Minnesota Press, 1981.
Human Rights Quarterly.
International Journal: Ethics in World Politics, Vol. 43, No. 2 (Spring 1988). Theme issue.
Journal of Philosophy. Selected issues and articles.
Nomos, Vol. 24.
Paradigms: Kent Journal of International Relations, Vol. 8, No. 1. Special issue on international ethics.
Philosophy and Public Affairs. Selected issues and articles.
Soundings (Summer 1984). Special issue.

OTHER NOTABLE ARTICLES/BOOK CHAPTERS

Beitz, Charles. "Bounded Morality: Justice and the State in World Politics," *International Organization*, Vol. 33 (1979).
Bennett, Edward M. "Ethics and Foreign Policy," *Phi Kappa Phi Journal*, Vol. 45 (1965).
Berlin, Isaiah. "Realism in Politics," *Spectator*, December 17, 1954.
Best, Geoffrey. "World War II and the Law of War," *Review of International Studies*, Vol. 7 (1981).
Bull, Hedley. "Recovering the Just War for Political Theory," *World Politics*, Vol. 31 (1979).

Butterfield, Herbert. "The Scientific vs. the Moralistic Approach in International Affairs," *International Affairs*, Vol. 27 (1951).

Carr, E.H. "The Moral Foundations for World Order," in Ernest Llewellyn, ed. *Foundations for World Order*. Macmillan, 1950.

Catholic Bishops, United States National Conference of. *The Challenge of Peace*. Pastoral Letter on War and Peace. Washington, 1983.

Clinton, W. David. "The National Interest: Normative Foundations," *Review of Politics*, Vol. 48 (1986).

Cutler, A. Claire. "The 'Grotian Tradition' in International Relations," *Review of International Studies*, 1991.

Cutler, Lloyd. "The Right to Intervene," *Foreign Affairs*, Vol. 64 (1985).

Donelan, Michael. "Reason in War," *Review of International Studies*, Vol. 8 (1982).

Doyle, Michael. "Liberal Institutions and International Ethics," *American Political Science Review*, Vol. 80.

———, "Liberal Internationalism," in Cathal J. Nolan and Carl C. Hodge, eds. *Shepherd of Democracy? America and Germany in the Twentieth Century*. Greenwood Press, 1992.

Dunne, John C. "*Realpolitik* in the Decline of the West," *Review of Politics*, Vol. 25 (1959).

Forsyth, Murray. "Thomas Hobbes and the External Relations of States," *British Journal of International Studies*, Vol. 5 (1979).

Gooch, G.P. "Bismarck's Legacy," *Foreign Affairs*, Vol. 30 (1952).

Hartigan, R.S. "Non-combatant Immunity: Reflections on its Origins and Present Status," *Review of Politics*, Vol. 29 (1967).

Jackson, Robert H. "Dialectical Justice in the Gulf War," *Review of International Studies*, Vol. 18 (1992).

Kennan, George F. "Morality and Foreign Policy," *Foreign Affairs*, Vol. 64 (Winter 1985–1986).

McKenna, Joseph C. "Ethics and War: A Catholic View," *American Political Science Review*, Vol. 54.

Morgenthau, Hans J. "The Evil of Politics and the Ethics of Evil," *Ethics*, Vol. 56 (1945).

———. "National Interest and Moral Principles in Foreign Policy," *American Scholar*, Vol. 18 (1949).

———. "The Moral Dilemma in Foreign Policy," *Yearbook of World Affairs* (1951).

———. "The Dilemmas of Freedom," *American Political Science Review*, Vol. 51 (1957).

———. "To Intervene or Not to Intervene." *Foreign Affairs*, Vol. 45 (1967).

Pangle, Thomas. "The Moral Basis of National Security: Four Historical Perspectives," in Klaus Knorr, ed. *National Security Problems*. University Press of Kansas, 1976.

Rosenthal, Joel H. "Rethinking Morality and Foreign Policy," in Charles W. Kegley, Jr., ed. *Realism and the Neoliberal Challenge*. Forthcoming, 1995.

Slater, Jerome, and Terry Nardin. "Nonintervention and Human Rights," *Journal of Politics*, Vol. 48 (1986).

Tilchin, William N. "Morality and Presidency of Theodore Roosevelt," *The Long Term View*, Vol. 3 (Fall 1996).

Vincent, R.J. "Human Rights and Global Politics," Paper #24 in *Global Politics*. Open University, 1989.

Walker, J. Samuel. "The Decision to Use the Bomb," *Diplomatic History*, Vol. 14 (1990).
Wolfers, Arnold. "Statesmanship and Moral Choice," *World Politics*, Vol. 1 (1945).

MONOGRAPHS, COLLECTED ESSAYS, EDITED VOLUMES

Acton, John (Lord). *Essays in the Liberal Interpretation of History*. University of Chicago Press, 1967.
———. *The History of Freedom and Other Essays*. Books for Libraries Press, 1907; 1967.
Angell, Norman. *The Great Illusion*. Penguin Books, 1908; 1939.
Aron, Raymond. *Peace and War*. Doubleday, 1966.
———. *Politics and History*. Free Press, 1978.
———. *History, Truth, Liberty: Selected Writings*. University of Chicago Press, 1985.
Bailey, Sydney. *Prohibitions and Restraints in War*. Oxford University Press, 1972.
Beitz, Charles R. *Political Theory and International Relations*. Princeton University Press, 1979.
———, et al., eds. *International Ethics*. Princeton University Press, 1985.
Bell, Coral. *President Carter and Foreign Policy: The Costs of Virtue?* Australian National University, 1980.
Berki, R.N. *On Political Realism*. Dent, 1981.
Berlin, Isaiah. *Four Essays on Liberty*. Oxford University Press, 1969.
Best, Geoffrey. *Humanity in Warfare: The Modern History of the International Law of Armed Conflicts*. George Weidenfeld & Nicolson, 1980.
Brown, Chris, ed. *Political Restructuring in Europe: Ethical Perspectives*. Routledge, 1994.
Brown, Seyom. *International Relations in a Changing Global System*. Westview Press, 1992.
Bull, Hedley. *The Anarchical Society*. Macmillan, 1977.
———. *Justice in International Relations*. Hagey Lectures, University of Waterloo, 1983.
———, ed. *Intervention in World Politics*. Oxford University Press, 1984.
Butterfield, Herbert. *Christianity and History*. Charles Scribner's Sons, 1950.
———. *Christianity, Diplomacy and War*. Epworth Press, 1953.
———. *International Conflict in the 20th Century: A Christian View*. Harper & Brothers, 1960.
Butterfield, Herbert, and Martin Wight, eds. *Diplomatic Investigations*. Allen & Unwin, 1966.
Buzan, Barry. *People, States, and Fear*. University of North Carolina Press, 1983.
Canham, Erwin D. *The Ethics of United States Foreign Relations*. Fourth series, Paul Anthony Brick Lectures. University of Missouri Press, 1964.
Carr, E.H. *The Twenty Years' Crisis: 1919–1939*. Harper & Row, 1939; 1946.
Church, William. *Richelieu and Reason of State*. Princeton University Press, 1972.
Cingranelli, David L. *Ethics, American Foreign Policy, and the Third World*. St. Martin's Press, 1993.
Clark, Ian. *Reform and Resistance in International Order*. Cambridge University Press, 1980.
Claude, Inis. *Power and International Relations*. Random House, 1962.

————. *Swords Into Ploughshares*. Fourth edition. Random House, 1984.

Cohen, Marshall, et al., eds. *International Ethics*. Princeton University Press, 1985.

————, eds. *War and Moral Responsibility*. Princeton University Press, 1974.

Crabb, Cecil V. *American Diplomacy and the Pragmatic Tradition*. Louisiana State University Press, 1990.

Cranston, Maurice. *What Are Human Rights?* Basic Books, 1962; 1973.

Decosse, David, ed. *But Was it Just? Reflections on the Morality of the Persian Gulf War*. Doubleday, 1992.

Donelan, Michael, ed. *The Reason of States*. Allen & Unwin, 1978.

Donnelly, Jack. *The Concept of Human Rights*. St. Martin's Press, 1985.

————. *Universal Human Rights in Theory and Practice*. Cornell University Press, 1989.

Dougherty, James E., et al. *Ethics, Deterrence and National Security*. Pergammon-Brassey's, 1985.

Ekirch, Arthur. *Ideas, Ideals and American Diplomacy*. Appleton, Century & Crofts, 1966.

Elfstrom, G. and N. Fotion. *Military Ethics*. Routledge and Kegan Paul, 1986.

Ellis, Anthony, ed. *Ethics and International Affairs*. Manchester University Press, 1986.

Elshtain, Jean, ed. *Just War Theory*. New York University Press, 1992.

Falk, Richard. *The Vietnam War and International Law*. Princeton University Press, 1971.

————, ed. *Human Rights and State Sovereignty*. Holmes and Meier, 1981.

Falk, Richard, et al., eds. *Toward a Just World Order*. Westview Press, 1982.

Farer, Tom. *Toward a Humanitarian Diplomacy: A Primer for Policy*. New York University Press, 1980.

Fawcett, James. *Law and Power in International Relations*. Faber and Faber, 1982.

Ferguson, J. *War and Peace in the World's Religions*. Sheldon Press, 1973.

Figgis, John N. *Studies of Political Thought from Gerson to Grotius*. Cambridge University Press, 1956.

Finnis, John, et al. *Nuclear Deterrence, Morality, and Realism*. Clarendon Press, 1987.

Fishkin, James. *The Limits of Obligation*. Yale University Press, 1982.

Forsythe, David. *Human Rights and World Politics*. University of Nebraska Press, 1983.

————. *Human Rights and U.S. Foreign Policy*. University of Florida Press, 1988.

————. *The Internationalization of Human Rights*. Lexington Books, 1991.

Fossedal, Gregory. *The Democratic Imperative*. Basic Books, 1989.

Frost, Mervyn. *Towards a Normative Theory of International Relations*. Cambridge University Press, 1985.

————. *Ethics in International Relations: A Constitutive Theory*. Cambridge University Press, 1996.

Gallie, W.B. *Philosophers of War and Peace*. Cambridge University Press, 1978.

Garrett, Stephen A. *Ethics and Airpower in World War II*. St. Martin's Press, 1993.

Gong, Gerrit. *The Standard of "Civilization" in International Society*. Clarendon Press, 1984.

Goodwin, Geoffrey, ed. *Ethics and Nuclear Deterrence*. Croom Held, 1982.

Gould, Lewis L. *The Presidency of Theodore Roosevelt*. University Press of Kansas, 1991.

Grotius, Hugo. *De Jure Belli ac Pacis Libri Tres*. Translated by F.W. Kelsey. Oceana, 1964.

Gulick, Edward. *Europe's Classical Balance of Power*. W.W. Norton, 1955.

Halle, Louis J. *Civilization and Foreign Policy*. 1955.

———. *Foreign Policy and the Democratic Process*. University Press of America, 1978.

———. *History, Philosophy and Foreign Relations*. University Press of America, 1987.

Halle, Louis J., and Theodore Hesburgh, eds. *Foreign Policy and Morality*, 1979.

Halperin, Morton, et al. *Self-Determination in the New World Order*. Carnegie Endowment for International Peace, 1992.

Hardin, Russell, et al., eds. *Nuclear Deterrence: Ethics and Strategy*. University of Chicago Press, 1985.

Hare, J. and Carey B. Joynt. *Ethics and International Affairs*. St. Martin's Press, 1982.

Hart, H.A.L. *The Concept of Law*. Oxford University Press, 1972.

Henkin, Louis. *How Nations Behave: Law and Foreign Policy*. Council on Foreign Relations, 1968; 1979.

———. *The Age of Rights*. Columbia University Press, 1990.

Henkin, Louis, et al. *Right vs. Might: International Law and the Use of Force*. Council on Foreign Relations, 1989; 1991.

Herz, John. *Political Realism and Political Idealism*. University of Chicago Press, 1951.

Hinsley, F.H. *Power and the Pursuit Of Peace*. Cambridge University Press, 1963.

Hoffmann, Stanley. *The State of War*. Praeger Publishers, 1965.

———. *Duties Beyond Borders: On the Limits and Possibilities of Ethical International Politics*. Syracuse University Press, 1981.

———. *Janus and Minerva: Essays on the Theory and Practice of International Relations*. Westview Press, 1987.

———. *The Political Ethics of International Relations*. Carnegie Council on Ethics and International Affairs, 1988.

Howard, Michael. *War and the Liberal Conscience*. Rutgers University Press, 1978.

———, ed. *Restraints on War*. Oxford University Press, 1979.

Howard, Rhoda. *Human Rights and the Search for Community*. Westview Press, 1995.

Hunt, Michael H. *Ideology and U.S. Foreign Policy*. Yale University Press, 1987.

Huntington, Samuel P. *The Dilemma Of American Ideals and Institutions in Foreign Policy*. American Enterprise Institute, 1981.

Jackson, Robert H. *Quasi States: Sovereignty, International Relations and the Third World*. Cambridge University Press, 1990.

———. *The Global Covenant: Human Conduct in a World of States*. Oxford University Press, 2000.

Jackson, Robert H., and Alan James, eds. *States in a Changing World*. Oxford University Press, 1993.

Jensen, Kenneth and Elizabeth Faulkner, eds. *Morality and Foreign Policy: Realpolitik Revisited*. United States Institute for Peace, 1991.

Johansen, Robert C. *The National Interest and the Human Interest*. Princeton University Press, 1980.

Johnson, James Turner. *Ideology, Reason, and the Limitation of War: Religious and Secular Concepts, 1200–1740*. Princeton University Press, 1975.

———. *Just War Tradition and the Restraint of War*. Princeton University Press, 1981.

———. *Can Modern War be Just?* Yale University Press, 1984.

———. *The Quest for Peace*. Princeton University Press, 1987.

———. *Morality and Contemporary Warfare*. Yale University Press, 1999.

Johnson, James Turner, and John Kelsey, eds. *Cross, Crescent and Sword*. Greenwood Press, 1990.

Johnson, James Turner, and George Weigel. *Just War and the Gulf War*. Ethics and Public Policy Center, 1991.

Jones, Dorothy. *Code of Peace: Ethics and Security in the World of the Warlord States*. University of Chicago Press, 1991.

Kaplan, M. and Paul Ramsey, eds. *Strategic Thinking and its Moral Implications*. University of Chicago Center for Policy Study, 1973.

Kavka, Gregory. *Moral Paradoxes of Nuclear Deterrence*. Cambridge University Press, 1987.

Kegley, Charles W. and Kenneth L. Schwab, eds. *After the Cold War: Questioning the Morality of Nuclear Deterrence*. Westview Press, 1991.

Kennan, George F. *American Diplomacy: 1900–1950*. University of Chicago Press, 1951.

Kenny, Anthony. *The Logic of Deterrence*. University of Chicago Press, 1985.

Kipuis, Kenneth and Diana T. Meyers, eds. *Political Realism and International Morality*. Westview Press, 1987.

Kirkpatrick, Jeanne. *Dictatorships and Double Standards: Rationalism and Reason in Politics*. Simon & Schuster, 1982.

Kissinger, Henry. *A World Restored*. Houghton Mifflin, 1957.

———. *Diplomacy*. Simon and Schuster, 1994.

Korey, William. *The Promises We Keep: Human Rights, the Helsinki Process, and American Foreign Policy*. St. Martin's Press, 1993.

Kratochwil, Friedrich. *Rules, Norms, and Decisions*. Cambridge University Press, 1989.

Ku, Charlotte, and Paul F. Diehl, eds. *International Law*. Lynne Rienner, 1998.

Kubalkova, V. and A.A. Cruickshank. *Marxism-Leninism and the Theory of International Relations*. Routledge & Kegan Paul, 1980.

———. *Marxism and International Relations*. Clarendon Press, 1985.

Lackey, Douglas. *Moral Principles and Nuclear Weapons*. Rowman & Allanheld, 1984.

Lacroix, W.L. *War and International Ethics*. University Press of America, 1987.

Lang, Anthony F., Albert C. Pierce, and Joel H. Rosenthal, eds. *Ethics and the Future of Conflict: Lessons from the 1990s*. Pearson/Prentice Hall, 2004.

Lee, Steven P. *Morality, Prudence, and Nuclear Weapons*. Cambridge University Press, 1993.

Lefever, Ernest. *Ethics and United States Foreign Policy*. Meridian, 1957.

———, ed. *Ethics and World Politics*. Johns Hopkins University Press, 1972.

———. *Morality and Foreign Policy*. Georgetown University Ethics and Public Policy Center, 1977.

———. *The Apocalyptic Premise*. Georgetown University Ethics and Public Policy Center, 1982.

Levi, Werner. *Contemporary International Law*. Westview Press, 1991.

Lifton, Robert J. and Richard Falk. *Indefensible Weapons*. Basic Books, 1982.

Lillich, Richard B. *Humanitarian Intervention and the United Nations*. University Press of Virginia, 1973.

Lopez, George A. and Drew Christiansen, *Morals and Might: Ethics and the Use of Force in Modern International Relations*. Westview Press, 1995.

Luard, Evan. *War in International Society*. Yale University Press, 1986.

Luper-Foy, Steven, ed. *Problems of International Justice*. Westview Press, 1988.

MacIntyre, Alasdair. *A Short History of Ethics*. Routledge & Kegan Paul, 1967.

Marks, Frederick W., III. *Velvet on Iron: The Diplomacy of Theodore Roosevelt*. University of Nebraska Press, 1979.

Mastny, Vojtech, ed. *Helsinki, Human Rights, and European Security*. Duke University Press, 1986.

———. *The Helsinki Process and the Reintegration of Europe, 1986–1991*. New York University Press, 1992.

Maxwell, Mary. *Morality Among Nations: An Evolutionary View*. SUNY Press, 1990.

Mayall, J., ed. *The Community of States*. Allen & Unwin, 1978.

Mayers, David. *George Kennan and the Dilemmas of U.S. Foreign Policy*. Oxford University Press, 1988.

McCleary, Rachel. *Seeking Justice: Ethics and International Affairs*. Westview Press, 1992.

McDougal, Myres S., and Florentino P. Feliciano. *Law and Minimum World Public Order*. Yale University Press, 1961.

McElroy, Robert W. *Morality and American Foreign Policy*. Princeton University Press, 1992.

Mearsheimer, John J. *The Tragedy of Great Power Politics*. W.W. Norton, 2001.

Meinecke, Friedrich. *Machiavellianism: The Doctrine of Raison D'État and its Place in Modern History*. Yale University Press, 1952; Westview Press, 1984.

Midgley, E.B.F. *The Natural Law Tradition and the Theory of International Relations*. Harper & Row, 1976.

Miller, Linda B. and Michael J. Smith, eds. *Ideas & Ideals*. Westview Press, 1993.

Miller, Richard B. *Interpretations of Conflict: Ethics, Pacifism, and the Just War Tradition*. University of Chicago Press, 1991.

Minear, Larry and Thomas G. Weiss. *Mercy Under Fire: War and the Global Humanitarian Community*. Westview Press, 1995.

Minear, Richard. *Victor's Justice: The Tokyo War Crimes Trials*. Princeton University Press, 1971.

Morgenthau, Hans J. *Scientific Man vs. Power Politics*. University of Chicago Press, 1946.

———. *Truth and Power*. Praeger Publishers, 1970.

———. *Human Rights and Foreign Policy*. Council on Religion and International Affairs, 1979.

———. *Politics Among Nations*. 6th edition, edited and revised by Kenneth W. Thompson. Alfred A. Knopf, 1985.

Mueller, John. *Retreat From Doomsday: The Obsolescence of Major War*. Basic Books, 1988.

Muravchik, Joshua. *Uncertain Crusade: Jimmy Carter and the Dilemmas of Human Rights Policy*. Hamilton Press, 1986.

Nagle, W. *Morality and Modern Warfare*. Helicon, 1960.

Nardin, Terry. *Law, Morality, and the Relations of States*. Princeton University Press, 1983.

Nardin, Terry, and David R. Mapel, eds. *Traditions of International Ethics*. Cambridge University Press, 1992.

Neibuhr, Reinhold. *Moral Man and Immoral Society: A Study in Ethics and Politics*. Charles Scribner's Sons, 1932.

———. *Christianity and Power Politics*. Charles Scribner's Sons, 1940.

———. *The Children of Light and the Children of Darkness*. Charles Scribner's Sons, 1944.

———. *Reinhold Neibuhr on Politics: His Political Philosophy and its Application to*

Our Age As Expressed in His Writings. H.R. Davis and Robert C. Good, eds. Charles Scribner's Sons, 1960.

Newsom, David, ed. *The Diplomacy Of Human Rights.* University Press of America, 1986.

Nichols, Bruce and G. Loescher, eds. *Moral Nation.* Notre Dame University Press, 1989.

Nolan, Cathal J. *Principled Diplomacy: Security and Rights in U.S. Foreign Policy.* Greenwood Press, 1993.

Novak, Michael. *Moral Clarity in the Nuclear Age.* Thomas Nelson, 1983.

Nye, Joseph S. *Nuclear Ethics.* Free Press, 1986.

O'Brian, William Vincent. *Nuclear War, Deterrence and Morality.* Newman Press, 1967.

————. *War and/or Survival.* Doubleday, 1969.

————. *The Conduct of a Just and Limited War.* Praeger Publishers, 1981.

Osgood, Robert E. *Ideals and Self-Interest in America's Foreign Relations.* University of Chicago Press, 1953.

Osgood, Robert E., and Robert W. Tucker. *Force, Order and Justice.* Johns Hopkins University Press, 1967.

Pettmann, Ralph, ed. *Moral Claims in World Affairs.* St. Martin's Press, 1979.

Phillips, Robert L. *War and Justice.* University of Oklahoma Press, 1984.

Pipes, Daniel and A. Garfinkle. *Friendly Tyrants.* St. Martin's Press, 1990.

Potter, Ralph B. *War and Moral Discourse.* John Knox Press, 1969.

Ramsey, Paul. *War and the Christian Conscience.* Duke University Press, 1961.

————. *The Just War: Force and Political Responsibility.* Charles Scribner's Sons, 1968.

Rappoport, David and Y. Alexander. *The Morality of Terrorism: Religious and Secular Justifications.* Pergamon Press, 1982.

Robin, Ron. *The Making of the Cold War Enemy: Culture and Politics in the Military-Intellectual Complex.* Princeton University Press, 2001.

Rosenthal, Joel H. *Righteous Realists: Political Realism, Responsible Power, and American Culture in the Nuclear Age.* Louisiana State University Press, 1991.

————, ed. *Ethics and International Affairs: A Reader.* Georgetown University Press, 1995.

Rothstein, Robert L., ed. *The Evolution of Theory in International Relations.* University of South Carolina Press, 1992.

Rubin, Alfred P. *Ethics and Authority in International Law.* Cambridge University Press, 1997.

Russell, Greg. *Hans J. Morgenthau and the Ethics of American Statecraft.* Louisiana State University Press, 1990.

Seckinelgin, Hakan, and Hideaki Shinoda, eds. *Ethics and International Relations.* Palgrave, 2001.

Shue, Henry and Peter Brown, eds. *Boundaries: National Autonomy and its Limits.* Rowman & Littlefield, 1981.

Sims, Nicholas A. *Explorations in Ethics and International Relations.* Croom Helm, 1981.

Singer, Peter. *Practical Ethics.* Cambridge University Press, 1980.

Smith, Gaddis. *Morality, Reason, and Power.* Hill & Wang, 1986.

Smith, Michael J. *Realist Thought from Weber to Kissinger.* Louisiana State University Press, 1986.

Sterling, Richard. *Ethics in a World of Power.* Princeton University Press, 1958.

Stoessinger, John G. *Crusaders and Pragmatists.* W.W. Norton, 1985.

Teichman, J. *Pacifism and the Just War*. Basil Blackwell, 1986.

Thompson, Kenneth W. *The Moral Issue in Statecraft: Twentieth Century Approaches and Problems*. Louisiana State University Press, 1966.

———. *Ethics, Functionalism and Power in International Relations*. Louisiana State University Press, 1979.

———. *Morality and Foreign Policy*. Louisiana State University Press, 1980.

———. *The Moral Imperatives of Human Rights*. University Press of America, 1980.

———, ed. *Moral Dimensions of American Foreign Policy*. Transaction Books, 1984.

———, ed. *Ethics and International Relations*. Transaction Books, 1985.

———. *Moralism and Morality in Politics and Diplomacy*. University Press of America, 1985.

———. *Moral and Political Discourse: Theory and Practice in International Relations*. University Press of America, 1987.

———. *Traditions and Values in Politics and Diplomacy*. Louisiana State University Press, 1992.

Thompson, W. Scott and Kenneth M. Jensen. *Approaches to Peace: An Intellectual Map*. United States Institute of Peace, 1991.

Tilchin, William N. *Theodore Roosevelt and the British Empire: A Study in Presidential Statecraft*. St. Martin's Press, 1997.

Tucker, Robert W. *The Just War*. Johns Hopkins University Press, 1960.

———. *Just War and Vatican Council II: A Critique*. Council on Religion and International Affairs, 1966.

———. *The Inequality of Nations*. Basic Books, 1977.

Tucker, Robert W., and David C. Hendrickson. *The Imperial Temptation: The New World Order and America's Purpose*. Council on Foreign Relations, 1992.

Valls, Andrew, ed. *Ethics in International Affairs: Theories and Cases*. Rowman & Littlefield Publishers, 2000.

Van Dyke, Vernon. *Human Rights, the U.S. and World Community*. Oxford University Press, 1970.

Vann, Gerald. *Morality and War*. London, 1939.

Vasquez, John. *The Power of Power Politics: A Critique*. Rutgers University Press, 1983.

Vaux, Kenneth L. *Ethics and the Gulf War: Religion, Rhetoric, and Righteousness*. Westview Press, 1992.

Vincent, R.J. *Nonintervention and International Order*. Princeton University Press, 1974.

———. *Human Rights and International Relations*. Cambridge University Press, 1986.

Waltz, Kenneth. *Man, the State, and War*. Columbia University Press, 1959.

Waltzer, Michael. *Just and Unjust Wars: A Moral Argument with Historical Illustrations*. Basic Books, 1977; 1992.

———. *Spheres of Justice*. Basic Books, 1983.

Wasserstrom, Richard A., ed. *War and Morality*. Wadsworth, 1970.

Weisband, Edward. *The Ideology of American Foreign Policy: A Paradigm of Lockean Liberalism*. Sage, 1973.

Welsh, David. *Justice and the Genesis of War*. Cambridge University Press, 1993.

Wight, Martin. *Power Politics*. Hedley Bull and Carsten Holbraad, eds. Penguin, 1977.

———. *Systems of States*. Hedley Bull, ed. Leicester University Press, 1977.

Woods, Martin T. *The Morality of Peace and War*. 1974.

Index

Franco-Prussian War (1870–1871), 6, 159, 160
Frederick the Great, 5, 152, 155, 159
Free French, 18, 69
free will, xvi
freedom. *See* liberty
French Revolution, xvi
Friedrich Wilhelm IV, 155–156
Fulbright, William, 81, 89–90

Gaddis, John, xvi–xvii, xxi
Geneva Accords (1954), 77, 79, 91 *n.* 9
Geneva Conference (1954), 76
Geneva Conventions, 23
Georgia, 182–195
Gerlach, Leopold von, 156–157
German Confederation, 155–156, 159
Germany, xxiii, 2, 6, 8, 122–123, 127–130, 149–161, 165, 166; Nazi period, 6–7, 35–57, 85, 100, 165, 166; under Adenauer, xxiii, 165–180; under Bismarck, 6, 149–161, 166. *See also* Austria; Frederick the Great; Hitler, Adolf; Holy Roman Empire; Moroccan Crisis; Nazism; Nazi-Soviet Pact; Paris Peace Conference (1919–1920); Prussia; Roosevelt, Franklin Delano; Roosevelt, Theodore; Versailles, Treaty of (1919); Weimar Republic; Wilson, Woodrow; World War I; World War II
glasnost, 186–189
Gorbachev, Mikhail, 10–11, 181–195
governing norms of international society, 12. *See also* international moral norms
Great Britain, 40–43, 97–115, 121–132, 137–140; and Germany, 168–176. *See also* Allies, in World War I; Allies, in World War II; Churchill, Winston; Cold War; Lend-Lease; Lloyd George, David; World War I; World War II
Great White Fleet, 106–107, 115
Gromyko, Andrei, 182
Gulf War (1990–1991), 22, 23
Gustavus Adolphus, 150

Habsburgs, 122, 150–151, 158, 160
Hague Conferences (1899, 1907), 154
Hague Draft Rules (1923), 60–61

Hague Tribunal, 112, 113
Hamburg, bombing of (1943), 61
Hammarskjöld, Dag, 3, 8–9, 133–146; background experience of, 134–137; civility and, 135; Lebanon crisis and, 9; temporal perspective of, 9; unique institutional position of, 9, 134, 138–139. *See also* Unden, Osten; United Nations Charter
Hapsburg dynasty. *See* Habsburgs
Hardenberg, Karl August Fürst von, 153–154
Harding, Warren G., 110, 121
Harris, Arthur, 70, 72. *See also* Bomber Command; Churchill, Winston; city bombing
Hay, John, 102, 104, 106
Hay-Bunau-Varilla Treaty (1903), 104–105
Hayes, George, 172
Hay-Pauncefote Treaty (1901), 108
Heineman, Dannie, 169–170, 178 *n.* 14
Heinemann, Gustav, 170
Hertzstein, Robert, 42
Hilsman, Roger, 85–86
Himmeroder Memorandum, 171, 172, 179 *n.* 31
Hiroshima, atomic bombing of, 24–25
history, xiii, xv, xvi, 1, 5, 12, 123, 166–167; tyranny of, 123
Hitler, Adolf, 7, 40, 41, 43–57, 61, 85, 165
Ho Chi Minh, 76
Ho Chi Minh Trail, 80
Hobbes, Thomas, 11, 13 *n.* 1
Hohenzollern dynasty, 158, 159
Holmes, Oliver Wendell, 106
Holocaust, xv, 39, 40, 56 *n.* 39
Holy Alliance, 155, 156
Holy Roman Empire, 151
Hopkins, Harry, 44–45
human agency, xi–xiii, xvii, xxi, 1–2, 5
human rights, xv, xix, 194
humanism, as an approach to foreign policy, xi–xiii, 21–22, 89–90
humanitarian intervention, xxii, 25, 78
Hussein, Saddam, 27
hypocrisy, 8, 71–72

About the Editor and Contributors

DAVID ARMSTRONG is Professor of International Relations and Director of the Centre for International Studies at the University of Exeter. He previously held professorships at the Universities of Birmingham and Durham. His first degree was from the London School of Economics, while he received his Ph.D. from the Australian National University. He specializes in the international relations of East Asia and of revolutionary states. Among his major works are *Revolutionary Diplomacy* (1987), *The End of the Cold War* (1990), *Revolution and World Order* (1993), and *From Versailles to Maastricht* (1996). He is the editor of the *Review of International Studies*.

STEPHEN A. GARRETT is Professor of International Studies in the International Policy Studies Division, Monterey Institute of International Studies. His books include *Bangkok Journal: A Fullbright Year in Thailand* (1986), *From Potsdam to Poland: American Policy Toward Eastern Europe* (1986), and *Ethics and Airpower in WWII* (1993).

CARL C. HODGE is Professor of Political Science at Okanagan University College in British Columbia, Canada. He is widely published in journals of history, comparative politics, and international relations in Europe and the United States. His books include *Shepherd of Democracy? America and Germany in the Twentieth Century* (1992), *The Trammels of Tradition: Social Democracy in Britain, France, and Germany* (1994), *All of the People, All of the Time: American Government at the End of the Century* (1998), *Redefining European Security* (1999), *NATO for a New Century* (2002), *North American Politics* (2003), and *Atlanticism for a New Century* (2004). His current research interests include U.S. foreign policy and the history of imperialism.

ROBERT H. JACKSON is Professor of International Relations at Boston University. He is the author of *The Global Covenant: Human Conduct in a World of States* (2000) and *Quasi-States: Sovereignty, International Relations and the Third World* (1990). He is currently working on two books: *From Anarchy to Cosmopolis: Classical and Modern International Thought* and *Sovereignty: Evolution of an Idea*. His research focuses on international relations as seen through the lenses of the history of ideas, political thought, and jurisprudence.

DOROTHY V. JONES is a scholar-in-residence at the Newberry Library, Chicago, and an associate in the history department of Northwestern University. She received her Ph.D. in diplomatic history from the University of Chicago where she studied with Akira Iriye. Among her books are *Splendid Encounters: The Thought and Conduct of Diplomacy*, *Code of Peace: Ethics and Security in the World of the Warlord States* (winner of the Lionel Gelber award), and *Toward a Just World: The Critical Years in the Search for International Justice*. She is currently working on a project to examine the connections between military tactics and weaponry, and restraints on the use of force.

ARTHUR S. LINK (deceased) was the George Henry Davis 1986 Professor of American History, Emeritus, Princeton University, and Director and Editor-in-Chief of the authoritative, sixty-nine volume document collection, *The Papers of Woodrow Wilson* (1966–1993). He was the author and/or editor of numerous other books about Wilson and his times, including *Wilson* (1947–1965, 5 vols.), *Woodrow Wilson: Revolution, War, and Peace* (1979), and *The Deliberations of the Council of Four* (1992).

PAUL MARANTZ is Professor of Political Science at the University of British Columbia and has served as the Chair of its International Relations Program. He is the author of *From Lenin to Gorbachev: Changing Soviet Perspectives on East/West Relations* (1988) and is co-editor of *The Decline of the Soviet Union and the Transformation of the Middle East* (1994).

CATHAL J. NOLAN is Associate Professor of History and Executive Director of the International History Institute at Boston University. His books include *Shepherd of Democracy? America and Germany in the Twentieth Century* (1992, co-editor); *Principled Diplomacy: Security and Rights in U.S. Foreign Policy* (1993); *The Longman Guide to World Affairs* (1995); *Notable U.S. Ambassadors Since 1775* (1997, editor), a *Choice* "Outstanding Academic Book" in 1998; and the *Greenwood Encyclopedia of International Relations* (2002, 4 vols.), a *Choice* "Outstanding Reference Work" in 2002. He is currently writing an eight-volume history of modern war, from 1400. He edits the Praeger series "Humanistic Perspectives on International Relations," and co-edits the Praeger series "International History."

OTTO PFLANZE is a former editor of *The American Historical Review* and Emeritus Professor of History, Indiana University and Bard College. He is widely regarded as the foremost contemporary writer on Bismarck. He has written several landmark works, culminating in his magnum opus, *Bismarck and the Development of Germany* (1990, 3 vols.). Other topics in his works include the characteristics of nationalism, the tactics of *Realpolitik*, German/American relations and the philosophy of history.

JOEL H. ROSENTHAL is President of the Carnegie Council on Ethics and International Affairs. He is also editor of the journal *Ethics and International Affairs*. He is the author of *Righteous Realists: Political Realism, Responsible Power, and American Culture in the Nuclear Age* (1991) and editor of *Ethics and International Affairs: A Reader* (1995). Among his most recent publications is "Rethinking Morality and Foreign Policy," to appear in Charles W. Keagley, Jr., ed., *Realism and the Neoliberal Challenge* (1995).

WILLIAM N. TILCHIN is Associate Professor of Social Science in the College of General Studies at Boston University. He received a Ph.D. in History from Brown University, and he is the author of *Theodore Roosevelt and the British Empire: A Study in Presidential Statecraft* (1997). Currently he is working on two books (both of which will be published by Praeger): a volume on the enduring importance of Theodore Roosevelt's statecraft and a co-edited (with Charles Neu) collection of essays on the foreign policies of Theodore Roosevelt and Woodrow Wilson.